THE KING OF ALMAYNE

THE KING OF ALMAYNE

T. W. E. ROCHE

JOHN MURRAY

Printed in Great Britain for
John Murray, Albemarle Street, London
by Cox & Wyman Ltd, London,
Fakenham and Reading

TO YETTA

FOREWORD

IN THE PRESENT CLIMATE of this country's awakening interest in closer ties with Europe the efforts of a thirteenth-century Englishman to become Holy Roman Emperor remind us that this has happened before. The figure of Richard of Cornwall is scarcely known either in his native land or in his adopted country of Germany; but had his success been greater the whole history of Central Europe might have been changed and the Habsburg dynasty might never have existed.

The author has produced a work of art which points to horizons never yet trodden, and he has knitted together facts which will be of great advantage to the student of the thirteenth century. When I met him I delved into his knowledge of the period and know it to be the result of intense research not only in the libraries of Oxford and Cambridge but in the steps of Richard himself from Cornwall to the Palatinate and from the Cotswolds to Provence.

When I first began reading the book I was afraid it might be purely a dull work of scholarship, but as I read I found the interest carried me along and as I turned the last page I gave a sigh of regret.

AGNES DE STOECKL

Coppins Cottage
Iver

CONTENTS

Author's Note xv

Introduction 1

PART ONE: THE EARL OF CORNWALL AND ISABELLA MARSHAL (1209–1240)

Chapter 1 Lackland and Jezebel 11
2 The Marshal and his daughter 19
3 Gascony and Cornwall 25
4 Marriage and Montfort 34
5 Family Problems 45
6 The victim of jaundice 57

PART TWO: THE KING OF THE ROMANS AND SANCHIA OF PROVENCE (1240–1261)

Chapter 1 An eventful French journey 63
2 The Crusader 72
3 To parley with Saint Louis 84
4 Marriage to Sanchia 94
5 Financier of the realm 100
6 Power politics 112
7 A fateful family party 121
8 The long road to Aachen 129
9 Lord of the Rhineland 139
10 An urgent summons home 146
11 To Rome or not? 155
12 The Queen of Almayne 163

Contents

PART THREE: THE PRISONER OF MONTFORT AND BEATRIX VON FALKENBURG (1261–1272)

Chapter 1 The uncrossed Alps 171
2 The King in the windmill 175
3 The prisoner of Simon de Montfort 185
4 The aftermath of Evesham 193
5 The pearl of womanhood 201
6 Murder at Viterbo 209
7 Brief twilight 214

Appendices 219

Genealogical Tables: 1 Richard of Cornwall 2 Isabella Marshal 3 Sanchia de Provence 4 Beatrix von Falkenburg 226

Bibliography 230

Notes 236

Index 249

ILLUSTRATIONS

facing page

The King of Almayne, Richard in his imperial crown, from the roof boss at Beaulieu. *Reproduced by kind permission of Lord Montagu of Beaulieu* 16

Richard of Cornwall's father, King John, from the effigy in Worcester Cathedral. *Reproduced by courtesy of the British Travel Association* 17

Isabella of Angoulême, Richard's mother, from the effigy in the Abbey Church of Fontevrault. *Reproduced by courtesy of Monsieur l'Abbé Pohu, curé de Fontevrault, Maine-et-Loire* 17

William Marshal the Elder, father of Richard of Cornwall's first wife, from the effigy in the Temple Church, London. *Reproduced by kind permission of the Master of the Temple* 32

The grave-slab of Isabella Marshal, now in the Lay Brothers' Refectory, Beaulieu Abbey. *Reproduced by kind permission of Lord Montagu of Beaulieu* 32

Henry III's tomb in Westminster Abbey. *Reproduced by kind permission of A. F. Kersting* 33

The Seal of Simon de Montfort. *Reproduced by courtesy of the Trustees of the British Museum* 33

Blanche de Castille, Louis IX's mother, from the effigy in the Abbey of Saint-Denis. *Reproduced by kind permission of Caisse Nationale des Monuments Historiques, Paris* 64

The Emperor Frederick II, Richard of Cornwall's brother-in-law, from the statue known as 'Der Reiter' at Bamberg Cathedral, Germany, erected *c.* 1230 and said to represent Frederick II. *Reproduced by kind permission of Bildarchiv Foto Universität Marburg* 64

Illustrations

facing page

Louis IX (Saint Louis), King of France, husband of Marguerite de Provence. *Photo: the late Chanoine Bretocq. Reproduced by kind permission of Editions Schaefer, 25 rue St. Sulpice, Paris VIe* 65

Marguerite de Provence, sister of Sanchia, Richard's second wife and wife of King Louis IX of France, from a statue in the Louvre modelled 150 years later by Jeanne de Bourbon. *Reproduced by courtesy of Caisse Nationale des Monuments Historiques, Paris* 65

The treaty between Richard and Nasir, from Matthew Paris's 'Chronica Majora', MS. 16. C.C.C.C. *Reproduced by courtesy of the Master and Fellows of Corpus Christi College, Cambridge* 80

The release by Richard of the French prisoners of the Sultan, from Matthew Paris's 'Chronica Majora', MS. 16. C.C.C.C. *Reproduced by courtesy of the Master and Fellows of Corpus Christi College, Cambridge* 81

Frederick II's state elephant sent to meet Richard of Cornwall in the streets of Cremona on his return from the Holy Land, from Matthew Paris's 'Chronica Majora'. *Reproduced by courtesy of the Courtauld Institute of Art, University of London* 81

Raymond Bérenger of Provence, Sanchia's father, from the effigy called 'le Chevalier à la Rose' in the Church of St. Jean de Malte in Aix-en-Provence. *Reproduced by kind permission of Editions de France and of M. le Curé de l'Eglise Saint Jean de Malte* 112

Beatrice de Savoie, Countess of Provence, wife of Raymond Berenger and mother of Richard's second wife, Sanchia, from the statue in the Church of St. Jean de Malte, Aix-en-Provence. *Photo: Henry Ely, Aix. Reproduced by courtesy of M. l'Abbé Destrieux* 113

Konrad von Hochstaden, Archbishop of Cologne, from the effigy in Cologne Cathedral. *Reproduced by courtesy of Herr Theo Felten* 113

Illustrations

facing page

Beatrix von Falkenburg, third wife of Richard of Cornwall. *Reproduced by courtesy of The Burrell Collection, Glasgow Art Gallery and Museum* 128

The cloisters, Hayles Abbey 129

The dorter range, entrance to the modern Chapel, Burnham Abbey, Buckinghamshire. *Reproduced by kind permission of the Reverend Mother Superior S.P.B.* 129

MAPS

Richard of Cornwall's campaigns and journeys in Europe 8/9

Richard of Cornwall's principal possessions in the West Country 31

The Holy Land at the time of Richard of Cornwall's crusade 81

AUTHOR'S NOTE

MY PARTICULAR THANKS are due to the Baroness de Stoeckl for reading this book and writing a foreword, especially at a time when she herself was busy on her book on Madame Du Barry; to Mrs. Patricia Ann Semler, for her continued interest and encouragement and for personally undertaking the considerable task of typing the original draft; to Mrs. Elizabeth Hollings-Bap, for suggesting sources and for reading and criticizing; to Madame Simone Noceti, for her unflagging energy in pursuing rare sources for me in Paris and Provence; to Dr. Richard Vaughan, of Corpus Christi College, Cambridge, for permitting me extensive use of the Library and of Matthew Paris's manuscripts, and to the Master and Fellows of the College for permitting me to reproduce five of Paris's illustrations; to the Reverend Mother Superior, the Sisters of the Precious Blood, Burnham Abbey, for the use of relevant documents and photographs; to Captain H. Widnell, of Beaulieu Abbey, for the loan of books and the use of photographs and for his advice and interest; and to Mr. D. Matthews, Librarian, Home Office, for the extensive loan of works of reference and for obtaining sources from libraries at home and abroad.

In Germany there has been a considerable reappraisal of Richard's importance, arising from studies instituted at the seven hundredth anniversary of the death of Archbishop Konrad von Hochstaden; these were initiated by the scholarship of Dr. Arnold Güttsches, of the Erzdiozesanisches Museum, Cologne, to whom I am very grateful for the loan of manuscripts and records of the period. I express my grateful thanks also to Herr Domvikar Erich Stephany of Aachen Cathedral; to Monsieur A. de Kerversan, Conservateur, Bibliothèque Méjane, Aix-en-Provence; and to

Monsieur F. Benoit, Directeur du Musée Archéologique, Château Borely, Marseilles – all for their advice regarding sources; also to Monsieur l'Abbé J. Pohu, of Fontevrault L'Abbaye, Maine-et-Loire; to Herr Theo Felten, of Cologne; to the Bildarchiv Foto Marburg, Marburg an der Lahn; and to the Receiver General, the Chapter Office, Westminster Abbey and to Mr. A. F. Kersting, all for permission to publish photographs. I also wish to thank Monsieur l'Abbé M. Desthieux, of the Church of Saint Jean-de-Malte, Aix-en-Provence, for permission to reproduce the photograph of the statue of Raymond Bérenger and for specially arranging to photograph the statue of Béatrice de Savoie so that it might be used as an illustration to this book.

I am also indebted to the Caisse Nationale des Monuments Historiques, Paris; to the Master of the Temple, London; to the Curator, the Burrell Art Collection, London; and to the British Travel Association for permission to publish other photographs.

Finally I am particularly indebted to my wife and family for their forbearance over a long period and for their willingness to accompany me in my quest round Europe.

T. W. E. ROCHE

Dorney, Bucks
October 1965

INTRODUCTION

ALMAYNE – Allemagne – an English King of Germany? The words have an unfamiliar ring. For though every schoolboy knows that a German Elector became King George I of England, how many adults know that an English Earl once did the opposite, and became King Richard of Germany? Judging by the paucity of literature about him, very few, either in his native or his adopted country.

In this respect I was fortunate. From my early childhood onwards I was constantly reminded of this remarkable man. The castles in my native West Country all seemed to have belonged to Richard of Cornwall. Whether we were clambering about the cliffs of Tintagel, negotiating the wall-walk of sylvan Restormel, staring up at high-piled Launceston or shivering a little at grim Lydford, his was the name which echoed down the years. Easter holidays spent at Lydford from the age of seven onwards taught me a great deal about Dartmoor, not least that it was Richard of Cornwall who had first laid down the boundaries of the Forest and Commons which in seven hundred years had changed hardly at all.

An Oxford friend and I meant to celebrate the 700th anniversary of Richard's Perambulation of Dartmoor in 1240 by doing it ourselves. Unfortunately in 1940 we were both otherwise engaged. At the University I read modern languages, and encountered references to Richard, albeit uncomplimentary ones, in the pages of Schiller and Grillparzer. As to the arid wastes of Old High and Middle High German, though I wondered at the time whether they were really worth negotiating, I have had cause to be very glad that I did when confronted with the study of medieval documents in Cologne.

I married a Rheinländerin with a French mother. Wherever we

went in either country there were constant reminders of Richard of Cornwall. The more we followed his journeys, the more amazed I was how, with all the attendant difficulties of medieval transport, he had contrived to cover vast distances of Europe which even today, with the facility of aircraft, car and train, represent quite an undertaking.

When in 1952 we came to live in Dorney, in Buckinghamshire, and found that the manor had once belonged to Richard, who had founded Burnham Abbey, barely a mile away, in 1266, I could resist it no longer. His little-known story cried out to be pieced together and written. Considering that he was the only Englishman ever to become 'King of the Romans', aspirant to the crown of the Holy Roman Empire, one would have expected a considerable literature about him to exist in both countries. In fact there is only one fairly recent English book and three very old German ones specifically on the subject. Elsewhere Richard comes in for only passing mention, the sole fairly comprehensive study being found in Sir Maurice Powicke's *King Henry III and the Lord Edward*.

It is therefore not surprising that an unsatisfactory picture of Richard is generally current, and the aim of this book is to evaluate him at his true worth as one of the most likeable and influential figures of thirteenth-century Europe. If I have concentrated rather more on the Continental than on the English aspects of his life, it is because the latter are the better documented of the two. But modern German scholarship, sparked off by the 700th anniversaries of the foundation of Cologne Cathedral and the death of Archbishop Konrad von Hochstaden, has recently awoken to the importance of the Anglo-Rhenish connection epitomized by Richard, and, indeed, to the whole question of the diplomatic relations between the Holy Roman Empire and England during the Middle Ages.

This does not aspire to be an historical textbook, but rather to present to the general reader a picture of Richard and to suggest the reasons for the election of an Englishman to the German crown – to the status of 'King of the Romans' as the aspirant to the Empire was called prior to achieving the full imperial dignity at the hands of the Pope. Three principal influences were at work, the profoundest being Konrad von Hochstaden. This far-sighted, able but disputatious churchman is familiar to later generations as the founder of the Gothic Cathedral of Cologne. His desire to see this protégé flourish made him welcome Richard's wealth; his political acumen saw in an Englishman the answer to the dangers of Italian and French influence; he realized through his local interests that the choice would give a great impetus to the trade of his diocese. With Richard he hoped to found a dynasty capable of replacing the fallen Hohenstaufen and at the same time acceptable to the Holy See.

Second only to Konrad's influence in securing the Englishman's kingship was that of Richard's second wife, Sanchía of Provence – the third of the four beautiful daughters of Raymond Bérenger, all of whom became queens. This fascinating family deservedly captured the imagination of contemporary chroniclers. A fateful family party in Paris in 1254 set the seal on Sanchia's ambitions to become a queen like her elder sisters, Marguerite and Eleanor, and encouraged her to exert continuous pressure on Richard to accept the German crown.

The third contributory factor to Richard's election was the interest of his erratic brother, Henry III, who saw in it a way to the realization of two of his dearest dreams – the recovery of the lost lands of Normandy by means of a pincer movement on the King of France, and the procurement of the crown of Sicily for his son, Edmund Crouchback.

Henry's character was indeed a profound drawback for Richard. Unrealistic, artistic, pious, unstatesmanlike, prone to violent rages, the King was continually in debt and continually in dispute with his barons. Years of conflict with them as to whether he was to be forced to rule with the restraint of their Council or not, reached a climax with the Provisions of Oxford in 1258. This coincided with Richard's first year in Germany, and the troubles between his brother and the baronage bedevilled the whole of the rest of his reign. Time and time again he was on the point of being summoned by the Pope to Rome for his imperial coronation – for his rival in the dual election, Alfonso of Castile, never troubled to visit Germany – when a crisis in England forced him to hurry home, partly to support his brother's tottering régime, partly to ensure the safety of his own vast estates on which the financial foundations of his German kingship rested.

Richard's very great achievements in Germany have been insufficiently appreciated. Threats of opposition melted away on his first arrival, and he was astonishingly successful in uniting at least the Rhineland and its immediate surroundings in acknowledgement of him. The power of his personality and presence is illustrated by the way in which, in 1268, after four years' absence and the degradation of imprisonment, he rallied all the princes and nobles to his side again and abolished the Rhine tolls which had cropped up like mushrooms and which, while throttling trade on the great river, lined the pockets of the nobility. Ever since Schiller, the arch-patriot, wrote of '*die kaiserlose, die schreckliche Zeit*' – the terrible, Emperorless time – it has been fashionable to regard Richard as a failure; but happily a truer appreciation of what he stood for and what he tried to do is now emerging in his adopted country.

His was a complex, fascinating and entirely human personality, utterly unlike that of his brother. To the common people he was a turncoat, 'ever trickard', because he changed from the baronial to the royalist cause in his younger years. To some of the barons he appeared hypocritical, amassing wealth while professing piety; to the more serious-minded he was the great statesman on whose wisdom and fairness they were ready to call. His ability as a mediator was almost legendary; preferring diplomacy to conflict, he secured throughout his life an impressive sequence of agreements between disputing parties.

His Crusade of 1240 was crowned with the success of able statesmanship. He was the last Christian prince really to exercise the supreme authority in the old Frankish kingdom of Jerusalem. Moreover, his release of the French prisoners captured in the disastrous campaign of Thibaut de Champagne was to stand him in very good stead two years later, when Henry and he found themselves *in extremis* at Taillebourg across the river from a much larger French army, above which flew the oriflamme – the signal of no quarter to the enemies of France. Then occurred one of the most colourful incidents in Richard's life, when he went alone, unarmed, in his pilgrim's smock to parley with King Louis.

Richard always had an eye for effect. Perhaps his lack of enthusiasm for knightly exercises caused his ego to seek another outlet for self-advertisement. He loved magnificence, splendid ceremonies and feasts, fine clothes and vivid colours, especially red and purple. The splendour of his secular occasions was more than matched by the magnificence of his religious foundations, epitomized by Hayles, where at the feast which followed the consecration he bemoaned to Matthew Paris that he had not spent all the money he had lavished on Wallingford Castle 'in so wise and salutary a manner'.

We are fortunate indeed that Matthew Paris, the chronicler of St. Albans, had direct access to Richard and obtained much of his information first-hand. Conversations between them are doubtless quoted verbatim. Matthew's great *Chronica Majora* covers forty-three years of Richard's life, and his doings figure largely therein. Paris was, of course, very prejudiced, and – as Dr. Vaughan points out in his book – very unfair to Henry III, who was one of his principal *bêtes noires*. 'Henry, according to Matthew,' writes Dr. Vaughan, 'was avaricious in the extreme, tyrannical, weak-minded . . . . On the whole, Matthew's picture of him is a vicious, spiteful caricature.' Indeed, it is suspected that Paris, in one of his sketches, deliberately drew the King with a drooping eyelid in order to mock him.

Richard comes off considerably better at Paris's hands, especially in his later years; but generally the monk of St. Albans was against authority in any form. Nevertheless, his colourful gossip provides a not unattractive review of contemporary events, however much distorted by strong prejudice and lack of depth. Indeed, his death in 1259 leaves a great gap, which the writings of Thomas Wykes of Oseney Abbey only partly fill. Among the Continental sources, which must be pieced together painstakingly, no single chronicler comes as close to portraying Richard as do these two English monks.

Richard's statesmanship caused him to be chosen Regent of England for several periods during Henry's illnesses or absences abroad. Only from 1264 to 1265 was he divorced from the direction of affairs. Incensed by baronial attacks on his personal property, he threw in his lot whole-heartedly with his nephew, the Lord Edward, in persuading Henry to teach the barons a lesson. In the event this misfired badly at Lewes, and Richard spent over a year as the prisoner of Simon de Montfort.

His relations with the Montfort family provide the great tragic element of his life. Richard had been instrumental in helping the penniless young French knight Simon to gain the earldom of Leicester in 1231; had protected him repeatedly from Henry III's unreasoning wrath; had stood co-godfather with him to the baby Prince Edward in 1239; had gone on Crusade with him in 1240; and three years later had taken his two young sons Guy and Simon into his house as pages along with his own boy Henry. From that period stemmed the animosity of the two young Montforts to Henry, later surnamed 'of Almayne' because he was knighted in Germany at his father's coronation. When in later years this dashing but untrustworthy young man deserted the baronial cause, the Montforts' hatred became unreasoning. Through some warped thought processes they came to regard him as responsible for their father's death at Evesham, at which battle he had not even been present. The final denouement came with their brutal murder of Henry in the church of San Lorenzo at Viterbo, a senseless crime which precipitated Richard's death.

He was fortunate to have at his side to the end the third of his three beautiful wives – the Englishwoman, the Frenchwoman and the German – who each had such a profound influence on his career. He always revelled in female company, and Isabella, Sanchia and Beatrix were respectively described by their contemporaries as 'a woman of wonderful beauty', 'of inestimable loveliness' and 'the pearl of womanhood'. While Isabella was alive Richard's interests naturally lay with those of her family, the sons of 'the flower and pattern of knighthood', William the Marshal; as Sanchia was the Queen's sister he then became more inclined to the royalist cause; while in Beatrix he finally identified himself with his German kingdom.

Such then was the man who stands against a background of the colourful thirteenth century. Conceptions of kingship, religious belief, the structure of society, and the arts, were all changing profoundly, and the year of his death can be said to mark the end of the High Middle Ages. Respected by those who mattered – Pope Gregory, the Emperor Frederick, King Louis, his own nephew the Lord Edward – Richard's epitaph could well be the Saracen soothsayer's description of him: 'He would carry through to the end whatever task he set himself.'

Richard's journeys in Gascony, Poitou, Brittany, France and the Empire
Harwich
LONDON
Gravesend
Canterbury
Dover
Portsmouth
Dartmouth
Wissant
St Omer
Boulogne
Dordrecht
R. Rhine
ARCHBISHOPRIC OF COLOGNE
FLANDERS
Ghent
DUCHY OF BRABANT
Neuss
Valkenburg
Cologne
Bonn
Linz
Aachen
Liège
R. Ahr
Sinzig
Andernach
Koblenz
ARCHBISHOPRIC OF TRIER
Boppard
Oberwesel
Mainz
Bingen
Trier
R. Moselle
Oppenheim
Arras
HAINAULT
Cambrai
Avesnes
R. Meuse
Donnersberg
Worms
Kaiserslauten
Speyer
Weissenburg
ALSACE
Hagenau
Strasbourg
Schlettstadt (Selestat)
R. Seine
St Denis
St Germain
PARIS
NORMANDY
Perros Guirec (Penros)
St Malo
Mont St Michel
St Mathieu
COMTÉ DE BRETAGNE
Dinan
St James de Bouvron
Douarnenez
Rennes

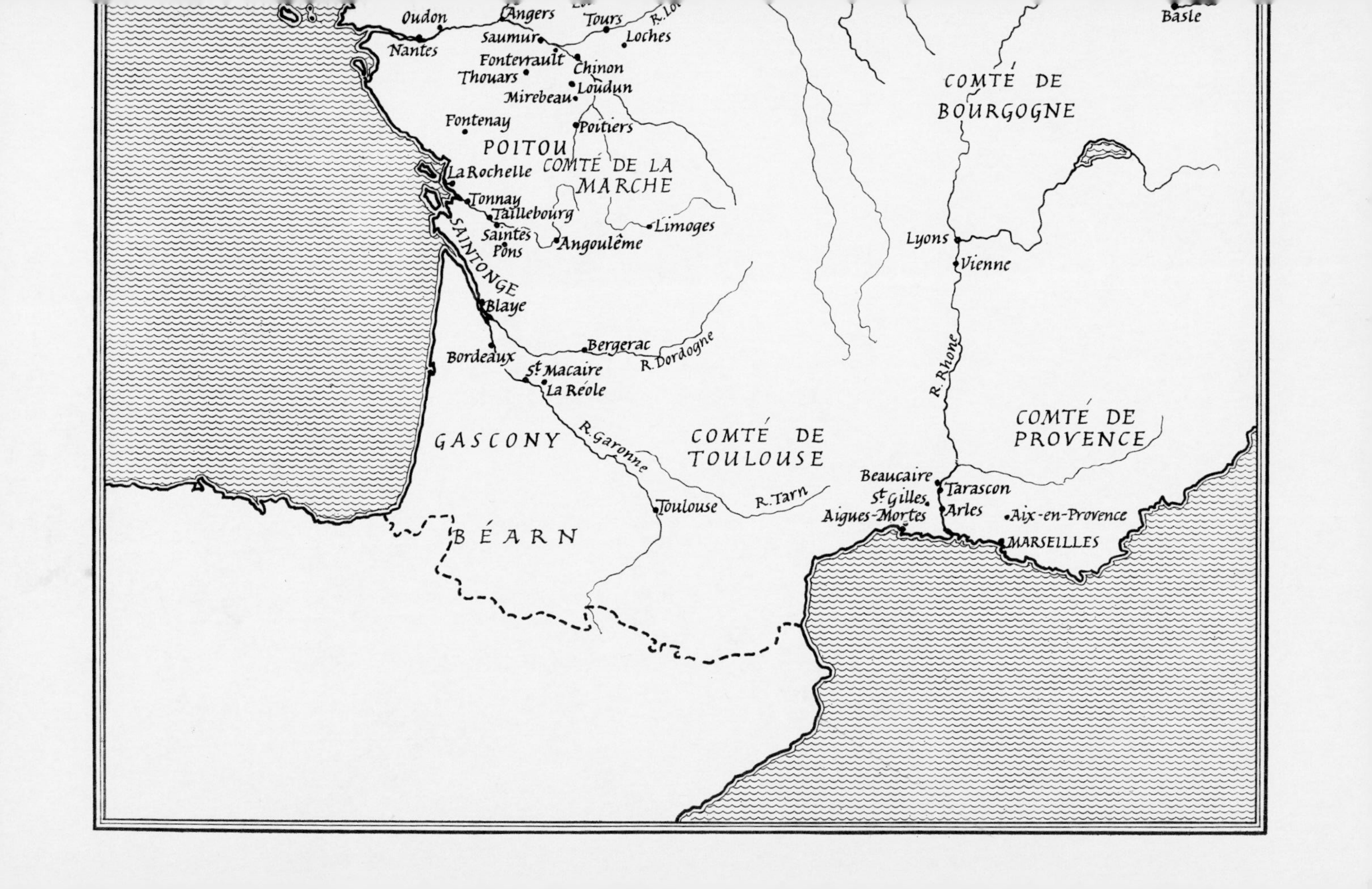
Oudon
Angers
Tours
Basle
Nantes
Saumur
Loches
Fontevrault
Chinon
Thouars
Loudun
Mirebeau
COMTÉ DE BOURGOGNE
Fontenay
Poitiers
POITOU
COMTÉ DE LA MARCHE
La Rochelle
Tonnay
Taillebourg
Saintes
Pons
Limoges
Angoulême
Lyons
Vienne
SAINTONGE
Blaye
Bergerac
R. Dordogne
Bordeaux
St Macaire
La Réole
R. Rhone
COMTÉ DE PROVENCE
GASCONY
R. Garonne
COMTÉ DE TOULOUSE
Beaucaire
Tarascon
St Gilles
Arles
Toulouse
R. Tarn
Aigues-Mortes
Aix-en-Provence
MARSEILLES
BÉARN

PART ONE

THE EARL OF CORNWALL AND ISABELLA MARSHAL

1209–1240

CHAPTER ONE

LACKLAND AND JEZEBEL

ON EPIPHANY EVE, 1209, Isabella of Angoulême bore King John his second son in Winchester Castle, where fifteen months before she had given birth to Henry. The inhospitable gloom of a winter's day was accentuated by the darkness and silence of the great Cathedral in the valley below. In common with all other English churches it was closed, and huge beams were nailed across its west door. The whole country lay under a Papal Interdict, imposed the preceding year because of the intransigence of the King.

Fortunately for the new royal infant, the Bishop of Winchester was a countryman of the Queen's and a loyal supporter of John. Alone of all the prelates he had remained in England, and the royal parents persuaded him to perform the ceremony of baptism in the chapel of their castle on the hill.

The circumstances surrounding the baby's birth could indeed hardly have been less propitious. He was the offspring of violent and passionate parents, with a violent lineage behind him, born into a country torn by discord and destined to remain so for most of his childhood. According to legend the royal family of England, the Angevins, were descended from a certain Melusine, a mythical enchantress, more properly a fiend than a fairy.[1] From her the trail of violence was unbroken. The baby's uncle, King Richard Cœur-de-Lion, and his father, King John, had warred against his grandfather, King Henry II. Even his parents' marriage had been barefaced robbery, for when Isabella of Angoulême was twelve years old, John had snatched her out of the hands of her betrothed, the Count Hugo de la Marche, a leading baron of Poitou. John had been motivated partly by her already evident beauty, but chiefly by political considerations: for the marriage would prevent Hugo becoming too powerful by uniting the lordship of Angoulême with his existing lands of Lusignan.[2] Having lost Normandy to Philip Augustus of France, 'Lackland' had to keep a firm hold on the territories which remained.

John and Isabella had been crowned together in Westminster Abbey on 8th October, 1200. As she grew and matured the Queen became one of the most desirable women of the age, and very free with her favours; because of this, John gave orders that any lover found in her bed was to be throttled on the spot. Even her own countrymen of Poitou dubbed her 'not Isabel, but most impious Jezebel'. She was a fitting match for John, with a temperament as volatile and vicious as his own.

In the eyes of Matthew Paris, the chronicler of St. Albans, John was indeed the incarnation of evil. Later centuries have, however, pieced together the complexities of his character and found him to be a much-hated but not entirely wicked man; he was spasmodically a good general, habitually an able administrator, personally fastidious, sadistically cruel and unpredictably contrary.

This same contrariness led John to call his eldest son after his father, against whom he had taken up arms, and to choose for the new baby born at Winchester the name Richard, to commemorate the brother of whom he had been so intensely jealous. Perhaps in his heart he harboured a sneaking hope that the child would emulate the dashing Lionheart: but in the event, ironically, he was to prove to be an administrator of even greater ability than his grandfather and far more of a diplomat than a soldier.

The early years of the young child's life were destined to be conditioned entirely by his father's erratic policies at home and abroad. His life was frequently in danger, and he was moved about the country hastily for safety. When he was only three his father left him and the Queen at Marlborough Castle while he went north to Chester to deal with a rebellion by Llewellyn of Wales. John had scarcely got there when a rumour reached him that Richard had been murdered and Isabella raped. He came scurrying back south, confirmed that the rumours were false, and attacked the castles of the barons suspected of putting them about. Young Henry meanwhile was placed in safe keeping and his custodian ordered to allow no one access without written authority. Not that it was really surprising that the barons deliberately circulated unsettling rumours. They had little cause to love John, who exhibited towards them both his unpredictability and his sadism. At the very time when he was excommunicated and isolated by the Interdict, one might have imagined that he could have done with loyal support at home; yet he did his best to alienate his staunchest friends, chief of whom was William the Marshal, the faithful vassal of his father and brother.

When Philip Augustus had driven John out of Normandy in 1204 many English barons found themselves with fiefs on both sides of the water and the agonizing choice of loyalty to two kings. The Marshal, not wishing to lose his Norman lands, solved the problem by making an accommodation with Philip, whereby he regarded him as his liege lord in France, and John in England. He was incapable of treacherous intent, but this is precisely what John's suspicious nature professed to see in his action. At the King's command he was accused before his peers, but they sided with him unanimously; thereafter the Marshal wisely retired with his wife and daughters to her castle of Kilkenny in her lands of Leinster in Ireland, leaving his sons hostages in John's hands.

The King did not even clothe them properly; but their fate was at least better than that meted out to Matilda de Briouze and her son because she had declined to surrender him as a hostage, saying: 'I will not deliver my sons up to King John, who has basely murdered his nephew Arthur.'[3] For her temerity she and her son were seized, cast into a dungeon at Windsor, and starved to death with a bale of corn and a flitch of bacon to tantalize them.[4]

While John was reducing his barons' castles, a prophesy spread like wildfire that he would not be King after Ascension Day. This had originated with Peter of Pomfret, an emaciated hermit and soothsayer, whom John seized and caused to be conveyed to his strong castle of Corfe to await the predicted date.[5] But although outwardly he mocked the old man's prophesy, John was nervous;

his friends were deserting him, and he transferred Richard from Marlborough Castle to the greater safety of Durham.

At this juncture a proffer of help came from the Marshal, which John gratefully accepted; and the old man, now nearly seventy, came back from Leinster to his castle of Striguil, or Chepstow, and placed himself entirely at his lord's disposal.

There was another quarter in which it was essential to secure peace, and in November, 1212, John dispatched envoys to Rome to proffer an olive branch to the Pope. Late the following February the Papal Legate Pandulf started for England; and on 15th May John himself went down to meet him at the Templars' Preceptory at Ewell near Dover, and, kneeling at the legate's feet, received absolution from excommunication. In return, in what Paris calls '*carta detestabilis*', he offered England and Ireland as fiefs of the Apostolic See.[6]

The soothsayer had been right. By this action John virtually parted with his crown and made himself a vassal of Innocent III; but Ascension Day had come and gone and he was still nominally on the throne. Neglecting no minor detail of revenge, John had Peter of Pomfret dragged on a hurdle from Corfe to Wareham and back, and then hanged before the castle gate.[7]

Archbishop Stephen Langton, in exile for the past five years, was readmitted to England to make formal arrangements for the lifting of the Interdict. This was done on 2nd July, 1213, after John had agreed to make substantial recompense to the Church for his seizure of her lands and persecution of her clergy. It was fortunate for England that to the Marshal's probity was now added Langton's wisdom, and to him more than to any other man is due the credit for the completion of Magna Carta. He made an initial attempt the year after his return, when the Marshal and he drew up a charter of liberties[8] which John refused to accept;[9] the King was feeling emboldened by a resounding English naval victory over the French fleet at Damme on the coast of Flanders, and considered he could dispense with compromise.

Indeed he felt so strong that he decided to embark for a campaign in Poitou which he had postponed because of troubles at home. Leaving Peter des Roches, the Bishop of Winchester, in charge as Justiciar, John sailed on 6th February, 1214, taking with him Isabella of Angoulême, the five-year-old Richard, the Demoiselle of Brittany (sister of the murdered Arthur) and his army. This consisted of only a few earls but of 'an infinite number of low-class soldiers of fortune, and an incalculable treasure of gold, silver and precious stones'.[10]

At the same time the victor of Damme, William Longespée, set sail for Flanders on a secret errand. Longespée, the bastard son of Henry II and Fair Rosamund, and thus John's half-brother, was one of the foremost soldiers of the age. His mission was to raise against Philip Augustus the Rhineland confederation on which John had been working clandestinely for years, and to advance with them from the north-east as John advanced from the south-west – a pincer movement calculated to bring the King of France to his knees, in retaliation for having thrown John out of Normandy in 1204.

At first all went well for the King in Poitou, but it was necessary to win over the powerful Count Hugo de la Marche. This was a difficult task, since John had robbed him of a bride, but the King did not flinch from such cold-blooded diplomacy. He offered Count Hugo his daughter Joan as a bride for the younger Hugo, his son. He then informed the Poitevin barons that Philip Augustus had deceitfully tried to oust the younger Hugo by getting Joan for his own son, the Dauphin Louis.[11] This was a complete fabrication, but the Poitevin nobles swallowed the bait, and witnessed the marriage contract between Hugo and Joan. John was well satisfied, but his wife had other ideas. The visit to La Marche had awakened old passions within her, but for the moment she bided her time.*

John now hustled about the province, feinting with the adroitness of a boxer. In an attack on Nantes he captured the Count of Brittany, cousin of the King of France. This gave him his chance to set up a pro-English lordship in Brittany, the very purpose for which he had brought with him the unfortunate Demoiselle, whom

* See p. 28.

he normally kept a prisoner in Corfe. But to achieve this end he had to reduce one more castle, La Roche-au-Moine near Angers, and its stubborn defence kept him at bay for a fortnight, long enough for Louis the Dauphin's forces to approach, and in that vital moment the Poitevin barons deserted John. From that time forward his carefully-laid plans began to miscarry.

Meanwhile William Longespée had made himself master of Flanders and was waiting for the Emperor Otto IV to join him. Otto was half English, the son of the Empress Matilda and thus the grandson of Henry I. He had originally been the Pope's protégé but had turned against his protector once he felt his throne in Germany was secure. The Pope had therefore to find a new champion, and papal money and mercenaries went pouring into France to the aid of Philip Augustus.

The French King marched towards Flanders, intending to cut the Anglo-German force off from the coast; but Longespée, sensing his intention, passed behind him to Valenciennes. Nothing daunted, Philip turned and attacked him near the village of Bouvines on 27th July, 1214. For three hours the fortunes of the battle ebbed and flowed. At first the Anglo-Imperial forces looked like winning, but eventually the French carried the day. The Emperor himself escaped on a borrowed horse, and the eagle lay on the field. Only William Longespée fought on till he was clubbed off his horse and taken prisoner.

The battle, called a 'medieval Austerlitz', completely changed the fortunes of Europe. The House of Capet was settled firmly on the French throne; Otto IV was hounded from his, to make room for Frederick Hohenstaufen; and John's pincer movement had utterly failed. Normandy was irrevocably lost, Poitou in grave danger. After concluding a hurried truce with Philip, John hastened back to England. With Isabella, Richard and the Demoiselle he came into Dartmouth in October, 1214, to find the barons seething with discontent, not least at the autocratic government of his viceroy, Peter des Roches.[12]

In this threatening situation the young Prince Richard must again be protected, so John had him sent to Corfe Castle under the

The King of Almayne, Richard in his imperial crown, from the roof boss at Beaulieu. Recently confirmed by the College of Arms as the head of Richard

Richard of Cornwall's father, King John, from the effigy in Worcester Cathedral

Isabella of Angoulême, Richard's mother, from the effigy in the Abbey Church of Fontevrault

custody of his trusted castellan, Peter de Mauley. The little boy rode up to the great frowning fortress, crowning its small hill between two massive shoulders of the Purbecks, accompanied by two trumpeters and a washerwoman, and under the guard of his newly-appointed tutor, Roger of Acaster.

The grim castle was enough to strike a chill into any child's heart. The grisly skeletonized remains of Peter of Pomfret, the unfortunate soothsayer, still hung from the gatehouse. Within, the Demoiselle was already back in prison, and with her the two Princesses of Scotland, daughters of William the Lion, held by John as hostages through trickery. Richard became the page of the three girls; but his principal training and education was in the hands of Acaster, who taught him English, a considerable accomplishment in a prince in the early thirteenth century.[13] In knightly exercises he was not so successful, and throughout his life he remained averse to fighting.

While Richard was feeling his feet at Corfe, events in the country at large were hastening to a climax. The most violent of the rebels were aiming to destroy the King, but the more moderate element, headed by Archbishop Stephen Langton, won the day. John was inveigled from his castle of Odiham to Windsor and thence, on 10th June, 1215, down to the water-meadow at Runnymede. There, as the world knows, the first successful attempt was made to curb the power of absolute monarchy.

The disaffected barons summoned Louis the Dauphin into England to their aid, and turmoil spread. John, having accepted Magna Carta under duress, probably meant to turn the tables on the barons when opportunity offered; but at the moment, faced with a foreign invasion, he needed loyal support and found it in the very man he had wronged, William the Marshal. As the Marshal's star rose, the King's waned, for Richard's passionate and erratic father was drawing near his end.

The chill caused by the soaking in the Wellstream, where his baggage train was lost, was exacerbated by his unwise diet in Newark Castle. On his deathbed there, John sent word to the Marshal that he placed his eldest son Henry in God's and his keeping, and begged him to forgive him the many wrongs he had done him. 'The Marshal has always served me loyally,' he said to those around him 'and has never acted against me, no matter what I said or did to him.'[14]

At his own wish they bore him across England to be buried in Worcester Cathedral. There his effigy still stands, alone before St. Wulstan's high altar; it shows a face ruthless but not uncomely, a beard trimmed and crimped – a small, neat man to be heartily feared, as he was by all his subjects save only by his faithful Marshal.

CHAPTER TWO

THE MARSHAL AND HIS DAUGHTER

RICHARD'S first seven years had been full of uncertainties and dangers precipitated by the actions of his formidable father. His next twenty-five were to be influenced strongly by the Marshal family, indirectly by its head, 'William the Marshal', and directly by his third daughter.

At John's death the threat of anarchy and of the country being overrun by the invading forces of the barons' French allies was very great. The Marshal seized the opportunity to preserve the dynasty in the shape of the nine-year-old Henry, who had been sent for safe keeping to the strong royal castle of Devizes in Wiltshire. With the other executors of John's will, the Marshal was now at Gloucester, and sent word for the little boy to be brought to him at once.

On 28th October, 1216, Henry was crowned in the Abbey Church. Archbishop Langton was not available to perform the coronation according to the traditional rights of Canterbury, for despite the statesmanlike course he had pursued over Magna Carta, he had been suspended from office by the Pope, who had completely misunderstood his motives and the underlying English political scene. Thus he had gone to Rome to plead his cause. A problem therefore arose as to who amongst the handful of higher clergy available should perform the ceremony – and what crown he should use, as the true one had been lost in the Wellstream disaster. After discussion it was agreed that Gualo, the Papal Legate, should preside, the Bishop of Wells dictate the oaths, and the Bishop of Winchester anoint and crown the child with a circlet specially provided by his mother.[1]

Someone had also to knight him, and this duty naturally fell to the Marshal. The innocence of childhood, so dependent on them, moved even the grim barons to tears before the 'little pretty knight' who took his oaths to maintain the honour of the Church, administer justice and observe the laws, kneeling before Gualo to do homage to the Holy See for the Kingdom of England and the Lordship of Ireland.

After the ceremony in Gloucester Abbey the King and the magnates went to the Great Hall of the Castle, where all of them, Henry included, pressed the Marshal to take upon himself the office of Regent. The old man pointed out that he was now over seventy and would not wish to take on so onerous a burden without the agreement of Ranulf, Earl of Chester, generally held to be the greatest baron in the kingdom. Ranulf's fame was almost as great as the Marshal's, and he was an even more popular figure – the Robin Hood of the north in the eyes of the townsmen and villeinage. The next day he arrived from Normandy. 'No, Marshal,' he said, having heard what was afoot, 'that cannot be. You are so good a knight, so fine a man, so feared, so loved and so wise that you are considered one of the finest knights in the world. I will serve you and carry out to the best of my power all the tasks you may assign me.'[2]

They had adjourned to a small room off the castle's great hall, where the discussion turned to the state of the realm and the chance of keeping the King's person safe from the enemy faction of disaffected barons and Frenchmen. The Marshal, his decision taken, was leaning easily with his back against the wall, a light in his eye – he was visibly inspired. If England were closed to him, Ireland was left. He could in emergency retire to Leinster; he would carry the King on his shoulders, 'one leg here and one leg there', from land to land and never give in.[3]

Even so, though the annals of Worcester Abbey describe him as '*custos regis et regni*', he evidently did not wish to be solely responsible for the young King's welfare, and shared the charge with the Bishop of Winchester. He now turned his attention to dislodging the French from the Kingdom. He had always liked the French; Philip Augustus, though his official foe, paid tribute to him on his deathbed, and during his lifetime permitted the Marshal to talk very frankly to him.[4]

It was now Philip's son Louis the Dauphin with whom the Marshal had to reckon. In the spring of 1217 the French entered the City of Lincoln and attacked the castle, held by its gallant hereditary lady castellan, Nicola de la Haye. The Bishop of Winchester, the militant Peter des Roches, was sent into the city after them clandestinely to reconnoitre, and came back with the report that there was an old gate partly blocked up which could easily be breached and about which the French knew nothing. The Marshal realized that if he could catch the enemy in the narrow streets of the city he would have them at his mercy; so he and his men smuggled themselves in through the disused gate. He had now been joined by his eldest son, William, formerly a baronial supporter. 'It was the happiest day of the old man's life; he was so excited he forgot his helmet and had to go back to fetch it before the fight.'[5] Up and down the narrow streets went the knights, some on foot, some on horseback, hacking and slashing with their broadswords, and in the end the English carried off a resounding victory. The whole thing was esteemed so successful and jolly that it became known as the 'Fair of Lincoln'.

In Kent Hubert de Burgh was sustaining a protracted siege in Dover Castle, which at that time consisted only of the great square keep and one ring of curtain towers. 'As long as I draw breath,' he said, 'I will not surrender to French aliens this castle, which is the key in the lock of England.' Nor did he. Louis eventually raised the siege, but a naval attack was launched from Boulogne under the command of a renegade English pirate called Eustace the Monk, who had terrorized the Channel for years and forced the men of Rye and Winchelsea to sail under his flag.

The Marshal turned up at Dover; on hearing of the fleet's approach he wanted to go to sea, but Hubert de Burgh would not let him, saying he was too valuable. Instead Hubert himself put to sea, commanding one wing of the fleet, while the other was led by Richard's namesake and half-brother, Richard Fitz John, the bastard son of King John by his mistress Suzanne. This elder Richard was a very dashing character, castellan of Chilham Castle near Canterbury, who had married the Lady Roese of Dover. He and Hubert allowed the French fleet to pass the port up-channel, then sailed out astern of them and approaching from windward broke open barrels of quicklime which was carried by the wind on board the French ships and partially blinded the crews. Running alongside, the English boarded the enemy, and to Richard Fitz John went the distinction of personally capturing Eustace the Monk, who had taken refuge in the hold of his ship. With an eye for effect Fitz John had Eustace's head chopped off just as the ship was coming alongside at Sandwich before the eyes of the rejoicing population.

Louis the Dauphin was allowed to withdraw to France: the Marshal was only too glad to see the last of him and his army and treated him with the utmost courtesy. Once the French had gone, the old Regent turned his attention to restoring the fortunes of the ravaged country, but he had little time left. His biographer describes his protracted illness in his manor of Caversham by Reading; how his five daughters came and sang to him, grieving at his incurable sickness, though Sybil, one of the youngest, was shy and would not sing until her father encouraged her;[6] how he called his Countess to his bedside just before his death with the words: '*Belle amie*, you are going to kiss me, but it is something we shall do nevermore.'

The Abbot of Nutley came to give him final absolution on behalf of the Legate; and so, in the spring of 1219, in his eightieth year, the Marshal passed away. His body was brought down the Thames to London and buried in the round Church of the New Temple in the presence of the Archbishop of Canterbury and many of the barons. 'Lords,' said Stephen Langton, 'you see what the life of the world is worth. Behold, all that remains of the best knight who ever lived. We have here our mirror, you and I. Let each man say his paternoster that God may receive this Christian into His glory and place him among his faithful vassals, as he so well deserves.'[7]

A few yards away from busy Fleet Street stands the Templar's Church, and there beneath the cupola lies the Marshal, his features almost as clear and distinctive as they were when the mason carved them, despite seven hundred years and the ravages of modern bombing. He lies with his hand on the hilt of his broadsword, in full chain-mail. He is very tall, like his son, William, who lies beside him. On the younger man's shield can still be detected the form of the blue-tongued lion of the Marshals on its field of *or* and *vert*.

William the younger was the eldest of five sons, whom fate was to carry off in quick succession, so that the name of Marshal rapidly became extinct and the hereditary office passed to the Bigods. The younger William, described by Paris as '*vir strenuus*', was – if not of the absolute unswerving probity of his father – an extremely able man, who was to be rewarded with the hand of Eleanor, the King's sister, later to become the wife of Simon de Montfort. Next in line to William was Richard, who succeeded him on his death in 1231; more ruthless and disputatious, he was at loggerheads with the King for years until killed in Ireland in suspicious circumstances. Gilbert, the third brother, was killed in a tournament at Hereford in 1241 when his stirrup-leather broke – an event which Matthew Paris graphically depicts in one of his marginal sketches.[8] Finally there were the two youngest brothers, Walter and Anselm, who died without issue in quick succession in 1245.

The Countess also produced five daughters, Maud, Joan, Isabella, Sybil and Eva. Isabella was born in the year 1200 in the great castle of Pembroke, and spent her girlhood in that sea-girt fortress until her father took her with him to Leinster when she was eight. They came back in 1213 to Striguil, or Chepstow, whence it was but a short ride to Gloucester. Even in her teens she was beautiful, and her father's chronicler, in a pun on her name, says she should have been called not Isabel but 'Vis a bel'.[9] Tall, flaxen-haired and blue-eyed, it is not surprising that she attracted the attention of Gloucester's Earl, the famous Gilbert de Clare; and they were married on St. Dionysius' Day, 9th October, 1214, in the Abbey Church of Tewkesbury, by the Abbot Peter, in the presence of the parents and family. In the course of sixteen years of happy married life she was to bear six healthy children to Gilbert de Clare.

Of all the Marshal children, it was she who most completely inherited the character of her father. Calm and brave, she was decisive in moments of danger, and was to exert upon her second husband, Richard of Cornwall, a steadying influence destined to mould him into the greatest English statesman of his time. When she first met him is not known; it was probably not at his brother's pre-coronation at Gloucester – he was then seven, she sixteen – but at the second ceremony at Westminster. But between eleven and twenty there is a great gulf fixed: he was still only a child, she already a mother and one of the leading ladies of the realm. As the years went by he admired her and desired her from a distance.

Somehow the death of the old Marshal seems to mark the decisive end of a long chapter of history. With him died the 'European' mentality of the English nobles common since the days of William the Norman. The barons were becoming more English and insular; Poitou was tenuously held, Gascony as far away and awkward of access; the immediate link, Normandy, had already gone. The violent offspring of Henry II were dead; and the boy-king on the throne was fired by very different ideals, especially by an immense piety and a love of the arts, so that his chief memorial remains, not the result of some feat of arms, but the rebuilt Westminster Abbey.

CHAPTER THREE

GASCONY AND CORNWALL

RICHARD remained at Corfe after the pre-coronation at Gloucester, being instructed by Acaster and acting as page to Peter de Mauley and the Demoiselle of Brittany; for after John's death the Marshal had lost no time in sending the Princesses Margaret and Isobel back to Scotland to King Alexander, whom John had contemptuously called 'the little sandy fox'.

On the morning of 7th March, 1220, a royal messenger arrived at the gatehouse of Corfe Castle with the command of the Council to Peter de Mauley to convey the Lord Richard to Westminster for the coronation of his brother. The preliminary ceremony at Gloucester had been something of a dress rehearsal, designed to bind the country together. Now that order was restored there was no further obstacle to the fulfilment of the coronation in the traditional place. On his deathbed the Marshal had entrusted the person of Henry to Pandulf, the new Papal Legate,[1] who had rather annoyed Hubert de Burgh and Peter des Roches by adopting a *de haut en bas* attitude towards them. Behind this ill-assorted triumvirate was Stephen Langton, 'in the minds of many men as well as in his own the spiritual successor of St. Thomas of Canterbury';[2] and it was he who was chiefly responsible for organizing this second coronation.

On Saturday, 16th May, Henry laid the foundation stone of the new Lady Chapel of Westminster:[3] probably his determination to rebuild the whole Abbey dated from that occasion. Richard reached London in time to be present at this ceremony and, of course, at the coronation the following day. Henry, seated in Saint Edward's chair, renewed his solemn oaths to maintain the customs, rights, liberties and dignities of the Kingdom, and received the homage of his vassals, 'in peaceful and splendid state'. Stephen Langton placed on his head Saint Edward's crown, seeming by its weight symbolic of the solidarity of his new power.[4] But as yet his power was illusory; he was still barely thirteen and in the hands of tutors – the Bishop of Winchester and Peter d'Aubigny – under whom he chafed. The following summer all was to change: Pandulf, the Legate, was to be recalled, and the King would emerge from tutelage and become the direct responsibility of the Justiciar, the bluff Hubert de Burgh.

The victor of Dover, though an exceedingly brave man, was regarded by the barons as an upstart, since he was only the son of a Norfolk squire. They were, moreover, angered that he had been made Earl of Kent and had married the Princess Margaret of Scotland. Nor were his activities as Justiciar calculated to make him loved, for he put down anarchy with a firm and ruthless hand. For instance, Fawkes de Breauté, one of King John's chief mercenary captains, castellan of Windsor and Bedford, had been condemned for unlawful disseisin of his neighbours' lands, but had seized the judge responsible and carried him off to Bedford Castle. Hubert promptly besieged it, eventually captured it, degraded and banished Fawkes, and summarily hanged fourscore of his supporters before the walls.

His mistrust next fell upon Peter de Mauley, whom he suspected of being a secret sympathizer with Fawkes de Breauté; and at Whitsun, 1221, he made him surrender the sheriffdom of Devon and Somerset and the castellanship of Corfe, in which capacity he had served John and the young Richard so well.

In Wales, Llewellyn was constantly in rebellion, and it became imperative for Hubert to be able to count on the loyalty of the new Marshal, William, whose strategically-placed county of Pembroke was virtually a Palatinate;[5]* to this end he was given in marriage no less a princess than Eleanor, sister of Henry III and Richard. She was young, and their marriage was comparatively short-lived,

* *Palatinate:* A palatinate was an earldom vested with royal privileges such as the counties of Chester, Durham and Lancaster.

In Germany such a holding was the Pfalzgrafschaft or County Palatine of the Rhine (see *post*).

and William Marshal's personality was then stronger than hers; for these reasons – though a beautiful and forceful person[6] – she does not make the impact on history as his wife that she does later as the wife of Simon de Montfort.

Despite de Mauley's removal, Richard remained at Corfe, to which he had returned after the coronation. He spent two more years there as a page, and was promoted squire on his fourteenth birthday. He spent the night of 4th January, 1225, on his knees in vigil before the High Altar in Saint Edward's Abbey. The following morning, his sixteenth birthday, he received Communion from Archbishop Langton, and then walked in procession to Westminster Hall, where his brother awaited him in full regalia, the Marshal and Justiciar beside him. Kneeling before the dais, Richard received from the eighteen-year-old King the accolade of knighthood.

There were other honours in store. On 13th February he found himself again kneeling in Westminster Hall, this time to receive the Earldom of Cornwall during pleasure; and a month later, on 25th March, a commission (the chief of three) to recover the lost lands in Gascony and Poitou seized by Louis VIII of France, bestowing on him the title of Count of Poitou in favour.[7] The other two commissions appointed William Longespée, Earl of Salisbury and Peter d'Aubigny, the King's ex-tutor. The former, Richard's uncle, was of almost equal military ability to the old Marshal; he was to be responsible for planning the campaign, though Richard was nominal leader of the English force.

Immediately after receiving his knighthood Richard had commissioned the heralds to prepare his arms. In heraldic parlance they were argent, a lion gules couronné or within a border sable bezanty. Some wit said the bezants were '*les pois*', the peas of Poitou; others, with more reason or tact, said that they represented the Cornish tin mines. These arms are still to be found in many places, notably in the crossing at St. Albans Abbey, in Westminster Abbey's nave, and at Hayles and Beaulieu.

The expedition set sail on Palm Sunday, 1225, with a company of sixty knights,[8] and landed at Bordeaux after an uneventful voyage. 'There, in the presence of the assembled citizens, the archbishop and nuncios of the kingdom, Richard the King's brother handed over letters from his brother to the archbishop and citizens, in which the King prayed humbly that all those faithful to him in those parts would support his brother amicably, standing by him equally with help and advice, to enable him to regain the lost territories.'[9] Matthew Paris continues that they gladly agreed, and it was evident from the monetary help given to Richard that the sending of this expedition under his brother's command was the best move Henry could have made to cement his power in Gascony.

Richard, Longespée and d'Aubigny steadily reduced by siege those Gascon castles which withstood them, the Earl of Salisbury using direct and ruthless methods as an example to others. Saint Macaire, on the Gironde near Langon, fell, and they then moved north to besiege Bergerac. When this too fell, Richard was able to write home that only La Réole now held out and that he was turning his full attention to it.[10] La Réole stands some fifty miles south of Bergerac, the Garonne in those days flowing at the foot of the castle's mount. Throughout the heat of the long southern summer the siege dragged on, the garrison sustained by the support of the wily Count Hugo de la Marche who saw fit to accept Louis VIII's commission to hold the castle against the English.

After John's death his widow Isabella of Angoulême had returned to France, and soon afterwards – to the astonishment of Europe – had supplanted her own daughter Joan and married Count Hugo de la Marche, the son of the man to whom she herself had been betrothed twenty years before. The tiresome circumstance that Count Hugo had thus become their stepfather, was destined to dog Richard and Henry throughout their Gascon and Poitevin campaigns. Richard now obtained a safe-conduct to go to La Marche, which lay in north-eastern Poitou, and visit his mother and Count Hugo; but though Isabella was clearly proud to see her son commander of the English army, she and Hugo were deeply embroiled in the plot to keep a foot in both camps. When, therefore, Richard came to take his leave and asked point-blank whether Hugo would assist him in Gascony, he received an equivocal answer and rode away disappointed.

In addition to La Réole he had another problem much farther north, in Poitou itself. This was the great seaport of La Rochelle, held by the troubadour Savaric de Mauléon, once a mercenary captain of John's but now serving King Louis. Richard made little headway, and when he paused irresolute before the walls he was irked to see Savaric parading the battlements and hear him strumming his lute.

Richard initially had hopes that Henry III would be able to secure some useful political alliances. Henry had entered into secret negotiations with Count Raymond of Toulouse, the sworn enemy of Louis, and – following John's precedent – was also conducting clandestine diplomacy with the German princes in the hopes of staging a pincer movement like the one which so nearly succeeded before Bouvines.

If further encouragement was needed it was to be found in the shape of 'one Master William, surnamed Pierrepoint, expert in the arts of astronomy, who was one of the counsellors of the King',[11] and who now foretold the death of Louis VIII. The Papacy, however, intervened to dash Henry's hopes, strictly enjoining him not under any circumstances to molest Louis, who was their chosen instrument in the Crusade against the Albigensian heretics.* Raymond of Toulouse, on the other hand, had incurred Papal displeasure and had been excommunicated. Henry III and his Council mulled over the Pope's threatening epistle and decided it would be wiser to let Richard carry on without any diplomatic action.[12]

The besiegers of La Réole were meantime in a sorry plight. Disease, egged on by carrion thrown down by the defenders, played havoc with their health; and by October Longespée lay sick

* For close on a century southern France was riven by religious schism under various forms. Albi was regarded as the centre of heresy and the Papacy preached a holy war against it, one of its chief henchmen being Simon de Montfort's father. Basically the heresy was a branch of Catharism, rejecting, *inter alia* the idea of purgatory. The Inquisition put it down mercilessly, but flickers o resistance continued until 1241.

with dysentery. Early next month they carried him down to Bordeaux and put him on a ship for England. The voyage was terrible, with great autumnal gales sweeping the Bay of Biscay, and the ship was continually driven off course. Dysentery was followed by pneumonia; and although they eventually reached Cornwall after Christmas, by February the great soldier was dead. Fortunately his wife, the Countess Ela, stood by him to the end, successfully withstanding the pressures of Raymond de Burgh, Hubert's nephew, who – during the long period of her husband's voyage – importuned her with protestations of love and assertions that she was now a widow.[13]

Shorn of his uncle's military experience, with his forces falling sick about him, Richard's prospects looked bleak indeed. Suddenly, however, the whole situation was changed by the striking fulfilment of William Pierrepoint's prophesy. Louis VIII died in Auvergne and was succeeded by his son, Louis IX, a child of twelve. Instantly the barons began to waver. Hugo de la Marche, suddenly emboldened, refused to attend the new King's coronation. Savaric de Mauléon found equally suddenly that he was once more the liege man of the King of England. Henry put out feelers, accompanied by bribes, to entice other Poitevin magnates back to his side.[14] The future of French overlordship in Poitou hung in the balance, when there came upon the scene a remarkable and determined woman.

A considerable emancipation of women had taken place in the early years of the thirteenth century, influenced largely by Eleanor of Aquitaine. The widow of Louis VIII, Blanche of Castile, was of equal stature with the best of them, and was the mother of one of the most remarkable men who ever sat on the throne of France. Domineering and determined, 'her wisdom and resolution rallied all that was best in France to the loyal protection of the young King.'[15] Throughout her life she was a stateswoman, the only member of her sex whose political stature was so great that a Pope was prepared to listen to her plea for reconciliation between himself and the Empire.

With her finger on the pulse of contemporary events, Blanche

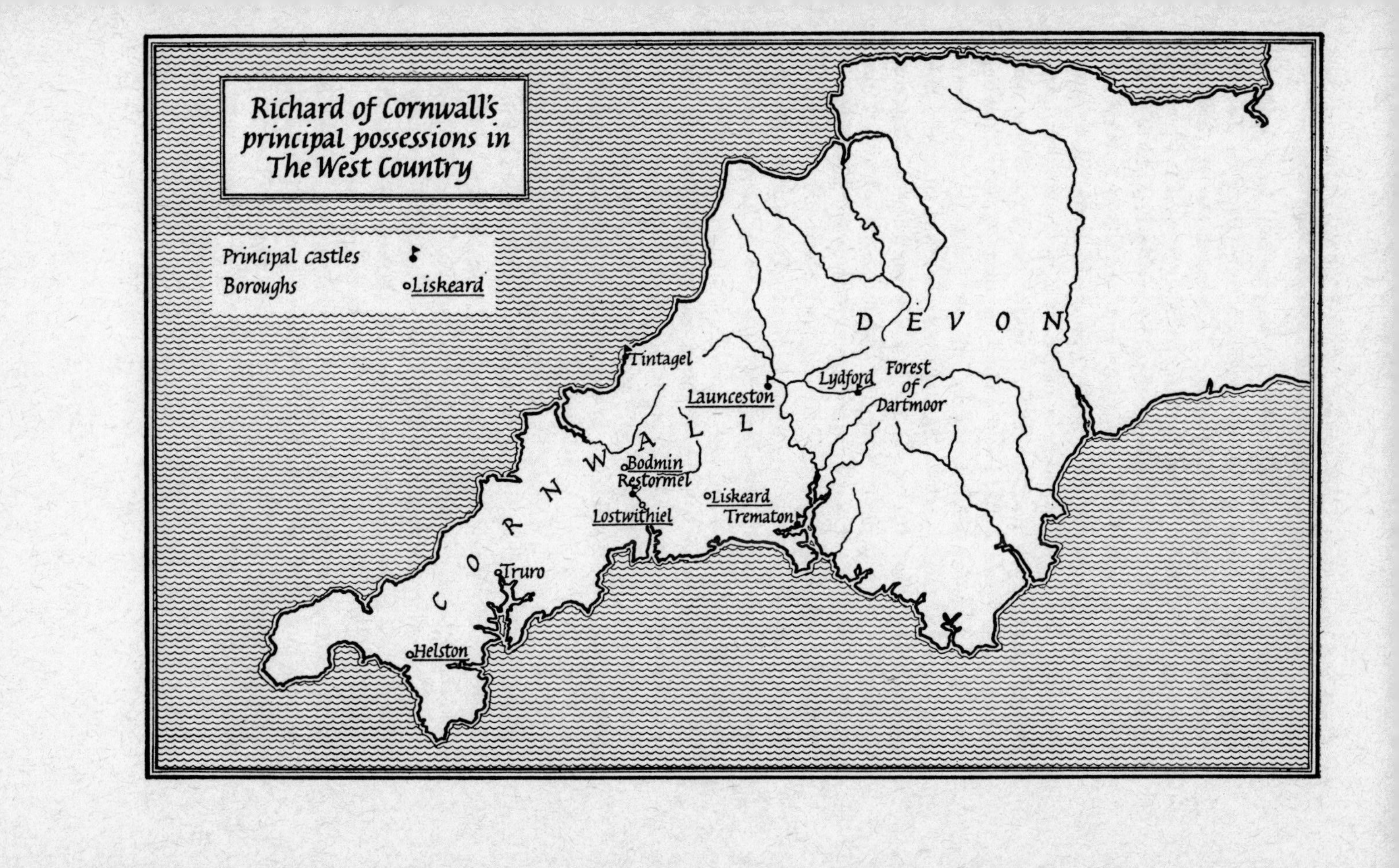
Richard of Cornwall's principal possessions in The West Country
Principal castles
Boroughs
Liskeard
DEVON
CORNWALL
Tintagel
Launceston
Lydford
Forest of Dartmoor
Bodmin
Restormel
Lostwithiel
Liskeard
Trematon
Truro
Helston

realized that treachery in Poitou must be checked. In February, 1227 she led her forces south-westwards from Paris to Tours; thence she moved to Loudun, where she paused. She dispatched her emissaries to the Poitevin nobles currently gathered at Thouars, a few miles to the west, to invite them to join in a series of conferences. These took place at Curçay, and resulted in a truce between the Poitevins and the King of France. Richard of Cornwall saw his opportunity; he had done all he could in Gascony and was in no state to pursue a war in Poitou now that the fickle nobles had changed sides once more. He sent his envoys to Queen Blanche, and the two met for the first time in the Castle of Vendôme, where they signed a truce to last until a fortnight after St. John the Baptist's Day. Apparently the Earl of Cornwall and the Queen Mother of France took an immediate liking to each other. In later years, she was to receive him most handsomely on his visits to Paris, especially when he passed through on the way to his Crusade. Both were astute enough to know that they had saved the day with honour; the truce was particularly welcome to Richard's disease-ridden army.

The English came into Dover on a tranquil May morning of 1227 and saw the figure of Hubert de Burgh, the new Earl of Kent, upon the quay to greet them. It was indeed a welcome sight, even if Philip d'Aubigny and some of the others of the ancient aristocracy were jealous of his rapid preferment.[16] Hubert's new Maison Dieu, a hostel for pilgrims, just outside the walls of Dover, was practically finished, and he showed the Earl of Cornwall round. Thence Richard followed the familiar road over the bare downs to Canterbury, through the tortuous alleys of the city, filled with exultant townsfolk, to the Castle. There he changed into more magnificent attire in order to return to the Cathedral and visit the Martyr's shrine in the company of Stephen Langton.

King Henry and his magnates met Richard at Blackheath, and escorted him into London; the bells were pealing in the city, which the populace had decorated in Richard's honour. The Mayor met them at London Bridge with an address of welcome, and at Westminster Abbey a service of thanksgiving was held for Richard's

William Marshal the Elder, father of Richard of Cornwall's first wife, from the effigy in the Temple Church, London

The grave-slab of Isabella Marshal, now in the Lay Brothers' Refectory, Beaulieu Abbey

Henry III's tomb in Westminster Abbey

The Seal of Simon de Montfort

safe return and victorious campaign in Gascony. The fact that the campaign in Poitou had proved abortive did nothing to lessen the warmth of his reception, and at Westminster Hall on the morning of 13th May, before the nobles and magnates, Richard was advanced to the full title and dignity of Earl of Cornwall in fee.[17]

CHAPTER FOUR

MARRIAGE AND MONTFORT

TO EVALUATE Richard's achievements in Gascony it must be remembered that the position of the English fiefs in France was very uncertain. Gone were the satisfactory days when England and Normandy were united. Poitou had been a natural geographical sequel to the south, and Gascony a further extension south again. Since John had been beaten out of Normandy by Philip Augustus the keystone of the edifice had gone. During the long absences of the English King, the Poitevin and Gascon nobles were in the unpleasant position of being face to face with a new and militant French monarchy, now no longer content with being mere Kings of the Ile de France, the area round Paris, but determined to push their authority south and west to the coast. The nobles often held their fiefs of two masters, and who can blame them for constantly changing sides.

Richard's achievement was to give new heart to the Gascons, so that they still looked down the Gironde and across the sea for their trade and their overlord, and not across country to Paris. Had he not conducted his campaign when he did it is almost certain that Gascony would have fallen to Louis VIII; as it was, he laid the foundation on which Simon de Montfort was later to build years of firm government of the province.

Directly the rejoicings at his return were over, Richard decided to pay a rapid visit to Cornwall, which he had never seen. Throughout his life he had an eye to castles which were militarily defensible, good to look upon, and pleasant to inhabit. Such a one confronted him at his first contact with his new county; the Earl was deeply impressed by Launceston, rising to a crown of stone on the hill-top ringed by the little town. He determined to make his seat of government in it and to extend its buildings considerably. His vassals were required to present themselves to do homage for their fiefs in its hall. Before they did so he made a quick tour of the other three principal fortresses – first Tintagel, on its sea-girt headland, which was a royal castle; and then two others which were held of him by vassals – Restormel, home of the Cardinans, and Trematon, above the River Lynher by Saltash, held by the Baron de Valletort. It was at this juncture that Richard discovered that the manor of Tamerton, which should have properly belonged to the Earldom of Cornwall, had in fact been granted by his father to Walram the German, one of his many foreign mercenary soldiers of fortune, and now constable of Berkhamsted.[1]

Throughout his life Richard, in common with most great men of his time, had very decided ideas on property and could not stomach anything which he regarded as filching; his reaction was direct and immediate. He seized the manor and required the bailiff, in his master's absence, to do homage to him for it at Launceston Castle. This done, he returned to London; but the news of his exploits had gone before him and Walram was already at Westminster, making complaint to Hubert de Burgh.

The Justiciar prevailed upon the King to hear the dispute, and on 7th July Henry summoned his brother before him. Richard, 'speaking reasonably and eloquently without any advocate', pleaded that the manor belonged to him by right and that he would submit himself in the matter of judgement of the King's court and the magnates.[2] This was an unfortunate choice of phrase; at the mention of the word 'magnates' the King and the Justiciar, who regarded themselves as capable of ruling without baronial interference, became most indignant, and Henry, 'addressing his brother in a most imperious and indiscreet voice, ordered him to surrender the manor at once or leave the realm'.[3]

Richard replied hotly that he would not surrender to the German what was his by right, and left the Hall to go to his lodging. 'Then the Justiciar, ostensibly feeling that the Earl might disturb the peace of the kingdom, advised the King that when his brother was asleep that night he should be seized by armed men and placed in close confinement.'[4] Fortunately for Richard he had friends, who overheard Hubert's plot and warned him; 'hearing this, he left the city secretly with only one knight accompanying him, and did not draw rein until he reached Reading'. Here, at the Marshal's castle of Caversham across the Thames, he was among friends; hearing that the Marshal himself was at Marlborough, he pushed on westwards after a short rest, and came down to the castle 'to his friend and sworn confederate'.

William the Marshal listened gravely to Richard's story. Round him in Marlborough Castle were assembled a number of other great nobles, including Ranulf, Earl of Chester, none of them well-disposed towards the upstart Justiciar. 'In a short while there collected at Stamford with horses and men, the Marshal, Earl Richard, Gilbert de Clare, Earl of Gloucester, William de Warenne, Earl of Surrey, Humphrey, Earl of Hereford, William, Earl of Ferrers and William, Earl of Warwick, together with many barons and a huge gathering of armed men, and informed the King with threats that he must right the wrong done to his brother, the blame for which they imputed not to him but to the Justiciar.'[5]

Faced by such a formidable array of force, Henry was not prepared to stand his ground. He fixed 3rd August as the date to meet them at Northampton, and 'the parties being met there on the said day the King gave to his brother Earl Richard all his mother's dowry, adding all those lands in England which by right belonged to the Count of Brittany, together with all the lands belonging to the recently deceased Count of Boulogne, and so they went their way reconciled'. Richard had gained far more than one West Country manor, and the King had shown himself incapable of standing up to a determined baronage. As a result of this episode Richard came into ever closer association with the Marshal family, while the King's distrust of the overbearing Justiciar grew steadily. On the surface, peace was temporarily restored; and the King and Richard went down to Dover for the ceremony of granting the charter to Hubert for the Maison Dieu. But in fact relations between Henry and Hubert were never the same again.

They were not improved by the death of Archbishop Stephen Langton the following year.[6] He had exercised something of a restraining hand upon Hubert. With him out of the way and Peter des Roches on Crusade in the Holy Land, the Justiciar was free to exercise almost completely unrestricted influence over the King.[7] An example occurred that same year, when the barons of Normandy besought Henry to come over and resume his ancient rights as their overlord. It was a chance, for Louis IX was still only fifteen and his mother had her hands full enough without embarking on a major defensive campaign to preserve what Philip Augustus had won. Henry paused irresolute and sought the Justiciar's advice; de Burgh was most emphatic. Henry did not go and the opportunity was lost.

Instead, within a year Henry was about to embark on a much more unproductive campaign in the adjacent province of Brittany. His reasons were mainly political, designed to draw attention away from his unpopular policies in support of the Papacy in its quarrel with the Empire. Henry had allowed himself to become embroiled in this in the spring of 1229, when the Pope's chaplain, Stephen of Agnani, had arrived in England bearing a list of charges made by the Pope against the Emperor. These were mainly accusations of malpractices by Frederick II during his Crusade, and the Pope demanded a tithe from all laymen and clerics in England, Wales and Ireland to further his 'holy war' against the Hohenstaufen. Although the barons made their opinions very plain at an acrimonious Parliament at Westminster, the King gave way. Wide powers were given the Papal Nuncio, who was permitted to introduce usurers into the kingdom.

Hence the diversionary war in Brittany. It was the second string to his bow, for – faced with the barons' resentment – he had first intended to recoup his popularity by going to Normandy after all, seeing himself as the saviour of his barons there and as the conqueror who would recover all the lands his father had lost. He therefore assembled the entire nobility of England at Portsmouth, with so many knights that everyone was amazed;[8] but when he came to the watergate at Portchester Castle and saw the ships riding at anchor, he realized that they were far too few to convey so large a force. Moreover, they were insufficiently victualled. It was a dreadful humiliation, and in his fury the King turned upon Hubert de Burgh, whom he held responsible for the fiasco. He called him an old traitor and, drawing his sword, would have run him through had not Earl Ranulf of Chester stepped between them.[9]

The expedition was therefore called off; but, fortunately for Henry, on 7th October, Pierre Mauclerc, Count of Brittany, arrived with a plea for help against the Queen of France. He did homage to the King as his overlord and received in return all his rights in England, which Henry had recently granted to Richard to hush up the Tamerton affair.* It was agreed that the King would lead an expedition to Brittany the following Easter.

Hubert was not going to be caught again. This time he collected too many ships; so that when Henry, accompanied by Richard – whom he had prevailed upon to join the expedition – arrived at Portchester, they saw the harbour crammed with craft. Nothing had been spared to render the expedition magnificent. The King's carpenter had been paid extra for panelling the cabins; and to ensure that the sailors were all in good shape, one Simon Wistlegray received 100 shillings to pay the wages of the mariners 'and others keeping the King's great ship'.[10]

Awaiting Henry at Portchester Castle was a magnificent regalia which he had ordered to go to war. No less than £108 4s. 5d., a vast sum at that time, had been paid to William of Haverhill and William the King's tailor for the robes of white silk. In addition there were a crown, a sceptre and gloves.[11] The old warriors muttered that this was not a campaign to recover a throne, but they were ready enough to drink the Gascon wine awaiting them at Portchester and on board. John de Colemere, the King's clerk, had received £105 for seventy tuns, 35s. for conveying them from Southampton to Portsmouth, 17s. 6d. for loading and unloading them, and 8s. 9d. for barring and cooping them. Later he received

* It is odd that the withdrawal of lands which had been granted to Richard as a peace-offering provoked no outburst from him. If it did, none is recorded.

£32 15s. for a further twenty-one tuns 'against the King's coming passage to parts beyond the sea'.[12]

When they eventually set sail on 1st May there were no less than 450 knights on board the fleet. Matthew Paris provides a marginal sketch of the royal ship, its mainsail bearing the three royal leopards, King Henry and two of his nobles in the waist, and the helmsman aft at the tiller.[13] They landed at St. Malo after a four-day passage.

Perhaps it was the fact that he was going to Brittany which stirred Henry's conscience and caused him to make a liberal parting gift to the Demoiselle Eleanor, still held in Bristol Castle – a robe of scarlet, tunic, supertunic, cloak, and furred and fringed cape; while her two maids were to have two robes of green trimmed with rabbit skin. Her countrymen now came to do him homage, hoping for his aid against Queen Blanche; but although he had a chance to show himself military master of the province, and though he had two outstanding captains with him in the shape of Ranulf of Chester and Gilbert de Clare, Henry was again unready. He spent weeks feasting splendidly in St. Malo before starting on a slow, leisurely and colourful progress south through Dinan and Rennes to Nantes. Ranulf and Gilbert went off on their own and made some productive forays in Northern Brittany; but Henry again hearkened to the advice of Hubert de Burgh, who told him to keep his forces intact and not to risk an open encounter with the French. If this seems out of keeping with the character of the defender of Dover, it must be remembered that he was virtually drunk with power. The military opportunity was there, had he chosen to seize it, for the young King Louis had approached Nantes and captured the castle of Oudun just to the east, at the confluence of the rivers Loire and Havre.

Instead of attempting to beat Louis back up the Loire, when he was within a few miles of him, Henry proceeded on southwards through Poitou, achieving nothing concrete. Eventually they arrived at Bordeaux, where the royal brothers were pleased to encounter their mother, Isabella of Angoulême. After Richard had conducted Henry round the scenes of some of his Gascon exploits, they returned northwards once more. The only positive action on their line of march was when Henry actually decided to besiege the famous castle of Mirebeau, north-west of Poitiers, the scene of one of his father's spectacular military feats in which he had released Eleanor of Aquitaine, then a prisoner in the keep. The young King was as successful as his father had been, though there was no beleaguered lady to release.

Well-pleased with this success, Henry decided to rest on his laurels. In the heat of July he and Richard found themselves once more in Brittany, where the continual feasting took its toll. Arrived at Redon, the brothers both fell ill with food poisoning, and so remained very wretchedly for a month. It was fortunate that Louis had his hands full with troubles with his own barons, and so was unable to mount an attack upon the English at this crucial time. The King and the Earl eventually recovered, and Henry had already ordered a return to St. Malo and the ships, when news of a fresh disaster reached them.

Gilbert de Clare had been 'mopping up' in the distant parts of Brittany, had captured Douarnenez, and was returning north-eastwards, when he died suddenly at Penros on St. Crispin's Day – leaving his body to the Abbey Church of Tewkesbury. 'On the following Saturday his family brought him to Plymouth and he was borne hence through the midst of Devon, Somerset and Dorset to his manor of Cranbourne and so to Tewkesbury.'[14]

The King meanwhile returned to Portsmouth 'after withstanding many perils of the sea, on the seventh of November, having consumed an endless amount of money, caused the death of innumerable nobles, stricken by illness or weakened by hunger, and reduced others to extreme poverty'.[15] Thus damningly Matthew Paris indicts Henry's military incapacity. Practically nothing had been achieved at enormous cost, and one of the best soldiers in England had been lost; Gilbert de Clare was buried before the high altar in Tewkesbury Abbey and his widow retired to the Abbot's protection.[16]

Richard had probably seen her in Brittany when she set off on her tragic journey to Plymouth with her husband's body. His decision to marry her must have been taken then; it was reinforced at Christmas when, during the revels at Westminster, Henry remarked to his brother that it was time he found him a wife and that he had a very suitable match in mind. Richard realized that he must act at once or be tied to a wife of the King's political choosing. As soon as he could he took his leave and rode off down to Striguil to consult the Marshal.

Meanwhile Ranulf, the Earl of Chester, had remained behind across the Channel. He had fortified the castle of St. James de Beuvron, near Avranches, which he held by right of his wife, and 'filled it with knights, arms and food'.[17] This in itself might not appear to be an event of great importance, but in fact it was to be of profound significance for England, because it gave a certain unknown French knight his opportunity.[18] His name was Simon de Montfort, of the great family whose ancestral seat was at Montfort l'Amaury, south-west of Paris. Being aware of Ranulf's reputed love of fair play, the young man presented himself at St. James de-Beuvron. The earl received him kindly and, having heard his suit, decided to cross to England with him and help him lay his claim before the King.[19]

Ranulf's readiness is the more surprising since what Simon wanted was one of his own principal holdings, the Earldom of Leicester. These lands had belonged to Simon's grandfather, Robert, but had been seized by King John in 1207. Eight years later, at the time of Magna Carta and the invasion of the Dauphin, John had committed it to the Earl of Chester at the request of the Pope, nominally to be held for the use of Simon the Crusader, young de Montfort's father. It is very probable that John had not the slightest intention of returning it to him, but his death in 1216 and that of Simon the Crusader two years later effectively prevented his intentions being put to the test.

The Earldom therefore remained in the keeping of Earl Ranulf, though the young Simon, third son of the Crusader, had had his eye on it for several years. His elder brothers Amaury and Guy were satisfied respectively with the family stronghold and lands of Montfort l'Amaury, and the Pyrenean county of Bigorre; the former released to Simon all his rights to their father's inheritance in England while Simon released to him all his rights in France.* Thus young Simon, like William the Marshal before him, had little left but his sword and a great deal of daring. So, to quote his own words, in 1229 'I went to England and prayed my Lord the King that he would restore me to my father's inheritance. He answered that he would not do it because he had given it to the Earl of Chester and his heirs by charter. Whereupon I returned without finding grace'. Then by a lucky chance Earl Ranulf came to St. James de Beuvron 'and there I prayed that I might find his grace to have my inheritance, and he graciously agreed and the following August took me with him to England and asked the King to receive my homage for the inheritance of my father to which, as he said, I had greater right than he'.

Henry, even when confronted by Ranulf, fully prepared to surrender what was his, still obstinately prevaricated, until Richard of Cornwall stepped forward and added his plea in Simon's favour. This turned the scales, and on the thirteenth of the month Henry ordered the sheriffs of four counties to give full seisin to Simon, as the King had received his homage for the honour of Leicester which belonged to him by hereditary right. Though the title was not yet formally bestowed, Simon de Montfort could enjoy the lands and revenues of his father's earldom.

Meanwhile the Marshal had received with delight Richard's proposal, and agreed that there was no time to be lost: as the marriage would take place without the King's consent, it must – he declared – take place under his own protection, to guard against Henry's almost certain anger. Richard went off to Tewkesbury to woo Isabella. 'Vis a bel', now almost thirty-one, was of astonishing, mature beauty.[20] She did not require much persuasion, and early in the New Year, in consultation with the Marshal, the wedding plans went forward. Isabella was to be conveyed under escort to her

* Amaury, though not a particularly good soldier, was appointed Constable of France in 1230 and retained this high office until his death. This may well have influenced Henry III's ultimate change of heart in Simon's favour: a younger and impoverished brother would be preferable to having the Constable of France lord of the great Earldom of Leicester, thereby opening the door to the King of France's influence in English affairs.

brother's strong castle of Caversham, and thence on the eve of the wedding to his manor at Fawley, remotely situated in the Chilterns between Henley and Marlow. After the ceremony the Marshal would again escort them to Richard's manor of Cippenham, where they would spend their honeymoon. Cippenham lay a short way across the river from Windsor, so that they would be near enough to his brother should he be willing to receive them, but discreetly far enough away to keep their distance should the need arise.

At noon on 13th March, three days before Palm Sunday, the small, secluded Church of Fawley witnessed the unparalleled event of the marriage by the Abbot of Tewkesbury of the heir to the throne to the sister of the Earl Marshal.[21] The manor had been a hive of activity for days, with tailors, seamstresses and armourers all at work. There were many barons there, including the Marshal's four brothers, and many villeins and serfs. Among the latter must have been someone with a contagious disease, of obscure nature; but nobody paid him any attention.

Gay and carefree, the cavalcade rode away after the wedding along the ridge of the Chilterns and down to the flat lands of the Thames Valley; and so they made their way to the manor of Cippenham, a timber structure protected by earthworks and moats. A palace of the Saxon Kings had once stood here; it was now a comparatively unpretentious place, very different from the great thundercloud of Windsor Castle away in the distance.

The news of the wedding had already reached the King there. His reaction was one of unbridled fury; and he would have descended on Cippenham and arrested his brother there and then, but for the intense efforts of some of the bishops then at Windsor and of Eleanor – his and Richard's sister. She had helped Richard prepare Cippenham Manor for the reception of the bride, and was determined not to let her elder brother mar the couple's happiness. Eventually the peacemakers won the day: the King accepted the inevitable, and invited Richard and Isabella to a belated wedding banquet at Windsor Castle on 13th April.

For Isabella it was a great moment. Thanks to her young husband she was now a Plantagenet and accepted by them as one of themselves. The King, his ill-temper forgotten, was charming to his new sister-in-law. Her brother, the Marshal, sat beside them at the High Table; but, as he rose to pledge the newly married couple, to the horror of all present he collapsed and died. The illness was traced to the wedding at Fawley.[22] 'The King, when he realized that the Marshal was dead, wept and exclaimed "Ay me, will the blood of the blessed martyr Saint Thomas never be avenged?"'[23], seeing in the event another judgement on the Angevin house.

The Marshal was carried to London and buried in the New Temple beside his father. His death cast a cloud over Richard and Isabella, and they withdrew to their estates. In August the King granted his brother the Stannaries – the tin mines of Devon and Cornwall – in fee, and also the vast honour of Wallingford with the castle which was to become his favourite home. A further charter confirmed an earlier grant to Richard of the honour of St. Valery, whose headship was at Beckley in Oxfordshire, and of the honour and castle of Eye in Suffolk.

CHAPTER FIVE

FAMILY PROBLEMS

FROM THE MOMENT of the Marshal's death things began to go wrong for Richard and Isabella: for the next four years they were to undergo domestic trials which tested the strength of their love for each other and for their respective families.

Isabella conceived almost immediately, but she had a troublesome pregnancy. On 2nd February, 1232, at her manor of Marlow on the Thames, she presented Richard with a son, whom they christened John after his grandfather.[1] William Marshal had been succeeded by his younger brother Richard, a dashing young man whom Paris describes as '*vir nobilis pectoris*'.[2] Relations between him and Henry III were far worse than those between Henry and the elder brother, and the King was not only reluctant to grant him the Earldom of Pembroke, but even dallied over his appointment as hereditary Earl Marshal. But what rendered the year 1232 particularly hazardous was Henry's growing antagonism to Hubert de Burgh. He had become progressively more impatient of his tutelage and interference, and a series of quarrels culminated in Hubert's fall and degradation from office in the summer.

Stripped of his post of Justiciar, Hubert would have been imprisoned in the Tower and possibly executed, had it not been for the intervention of Richard of Cornwall and Richard Marshal, who upbraided Henry with gross ingratitude to the man who had been instrumental in saving his kingdom. The best bargain they could strike was for Hubert to be imprisoned in Devizes Castle in Wiltshire – heavily chained by the King's personal order – and for each of four earls (Cornwall and the Marshal themselves, with the Earls of Warenne and Lincoln) to appoint a knight to be specially responsible for guarding Hubert. Richard's choice was Sir Richard de Punchardon, a knight of North Devon.[3] The Calendar of Patent Rolls grants to the four knights sixteen pounds, that is four pounds each, for their wages for this office from the Sunday after St. Martin's Day until St. Stephen's, 'both days being counted'.

The King had virtually agreed to Hubert's imprisonment far from London under duress. He bided his time to get even with the two Richards, who were now engaged in a campaign in Wales, where they had fortified the castle of Radnor and left a strong garrison in it. Henry summoned a Council for 11th July, 1233, at Westminster, but the two Richards and many other magnates boycotted it. Undeterred, the King tried again, and fixed a date in August; and on this second occasion Richard of Cornwall attended. Henry had already decreed a muster at Gloucester later in the month for an expedition to Ireland. This was another example of his policy of diversionary campaigns to draw attention off from present ills; but it was rather spoiled, as things turned out, by a foolish piece of mistiming. He brought a large force of foreign mercenaries into Dover on the sixteenth of the month, ostensibly to assist in the Irish campaign; but the wary barons rightly suspected that they were really for use against themselves. Richard Marshal, however, took another view: he was sure that because of the forthcoming Irish campaign Henry would need all the help he could get, and so would not alienate those who had recently opposed him. He therefore set off for Westminster from Wales full of confidence.

Richard of Cornwall had left Isabella at the manor of Woodstock; she was again pregnant, and expecting her second child early in September. Moreover, the health of baby John was giving them both cause for worry. Before he left for Westminster her husband imparted some confidential information to her about the Marshal. It was difficult to be loyal to both his own brother and to hers, but – knowing that the Marshal intended to spend the night at Woodstock on his way to the Council – he chose the means by which he could best salve his conscience. 'Now when the earls and barons of

England were making their way to London in great numbers to attend the Council fixed for August, Richard Earl Marshal and others came to seek the hospitality of his sister Isabella, the wife of Richard the King's brother. She asked him where he was bound and he replied that he was going to the Council at Westminster. To which she replied; "Know, dearest brother, that a trap has been prepared for you; if you go you will be seized by your enemies who will bring you to the King and to the Bishop of Winchester, so that they may do with you what they did with the Earl of Kent." The Marshal could scarcely credit the woman's words (for he was a high-minded man) although the lady described the capture and the captive with such convincing arguments. But when eventually the Earl Marshal did give credence to what his sister said, he broke off his journey, the night being far advanced; and turning, did not draw bridle until he was safe once more in Wales.'[4]

This was typical of Isabella, who could always be decisive in an emergency. Nevertheless the family crisis had its effect on her. She moved once more down to Marlow where, on 9th September, she gave premature birth to a baby girl, who was baptized Isabella to commemorate mother and grandmother.[5] A bare fortnight later little John died. Isabella, rising hastily from childbed, was present with Richard when their firstborn was buried before the High Altar of Reading Abbey.[6]

After her successful deflection of the Marshal, Henry III had pursued him into the Marches and spent some time quite ineffectually besieging him in his castle of Usk, making himself ridiculous by his incompetence while Richard strolled about on the wall-walk mocking him. Henry besought a truce: if the Marshal would surrender Usk Castle for fifteen days only, peace would be restored and the King undertook to return the castle to him. Richard Marshal unwisely agreed, withdrew to Striguil as an earnest of good intentions, and waited. But Henry did not keep his part of the bargain, and once in possession of Usk declined to return it. The Marshal understandably remained in Striguil, smouldering with wrath. His opportunity for revenge came quickly.

A few weeks after the death of Isabella's child a spectacular event shook the country. Hubert de Burgh escaped from Devizes Castle, swam the moat, and took sanctuary in the near-by parish church. On Henry III's order, sanctuary was violated. Hubert was seized at the altar and dragged back to the Castle where he was again cast into the dungeon, laden with more chains than before. There he would have remained but for the intransigent opposition of the Bishop of Salisbury, who declared that not even the King could violate sanctuary, and insisted on Hubert being returned to the church. If the King failed to do so, he would be excommunicated. This presented Henry with an agonizing choice; how could he, the exponent of piety, the visionary who would build a new Westminster, risk excommunication? In a very short while Hubert was back in church.

The way was now open for the Marshal's master-stroke. One October night a party of his knights burst into the church in the small hours, rushed Hubert out to a horse, and rode off at top speed, not drawing rein until they had him in the safety of the walls of Striguil. Henry, ridiculed and distrusted by the barons, looked for support elsewhere. He put out feelers to entice his brother back into the royalist camp. Richard wavered, and eventually gave in; he could have found no better way of drawing opprobrium on his own head. The Marshal's adherents were disgusted. Early in 1234 a party of them, headed by Richard Siward, fell upon Richard's manor of Beckley, one of his favourite houses and the headship of his honour of St. Valery, and sacked it as a reprisal for his defection from their cause.

The Marshal himself, hearing that Hubert de Burgh's son Richard and other royalists were ravaging his estates in Ireland, sailed over to Leinster. The royalists sent some Templars as their emissaries to him, and it was agreed to meet on the Curragh to discuss a truce. When the Marshal demanded the return of his castles as a preliminary to any discussion, they attacked him and his knights; he was seriously wounded, and died on 16th April of the same year.[7]

The King professed to be heartbroken when the news reached him, but it was widely suspected that his tears were crocodile.

Ugly rumours began to circulate that the Marshal had been murdered at his instigation, and a major scandal ensued. Richard of Cornwall regretted his recent change of front and contemplated taking up arms against his brother again. When Henry got wind of this, he forbade him to take part in any journeys without his licence. This precaution, extended to all the baronage, was, of course, a favourite with medieval kings, who regarded the tournament as the easiest way for rebellious subjects to collect the ingredients of revolt.

Isabella and Richard were at Marlow again together in the autumn when, on 10th October, the day after Isabella's thirty-fourth birthday, their year-old baby girl died: she was buried beside her brother John before the High Altar of Reading Abbey.[8]

The parents were in despair. What followed has been roundly condemned by some writers, who see in it an indication that Richard decided that a wife nine years older than himself who could produce only sickly children was no good to him. He wrote to Pope Gregory IX asking whether he should seek a divorce from Isabella on the grounds of consanguinity. The consanguinity was rather far-fetched, and Richard's manner of approach suggested that he did not expect the Pope to agree, in which he was perfectly right. In view of the great affection shown by Richard and Isabella for each other throughout their nine years of marriage it seems very likely that she was party to the letter, seeing in the loss of her two children evidence of some fundamental sin meriting divine punishment.

While they were awaiting the Pope's reply, a letter of a different sort arrived. It was a love-poem written with all the polish of the troubadour schools of Provence, couched in Cornish mythology, the hero being unmistakably a thin disguise for Richard. The authoress was the Lady Eleanor of Provence, second daughter of the Count Raymond Bérenger and the Countess Béatrice.[9] The county of Provence embraced the ancient kingdom of Arles, which in turn was the westernmost component of the Holy Roman Empire. Count Raymond's overlord was thus not King Louis of France but the Emperor Frederick II; nevertheless, throughout his reign, Raymond Bérenger strove to free himself progressively of imperial influence. The Hispanic nature of his name is due to his descent from a branch of the house of the Counts of Barcelona, and in Provence he was the fifth to bear it. He had only been four years of age at the death of his father, Alphonse II, in September, 1209; and for the first ten years of his reign he had been under the tutelage of his mother, the Countess Garsende. Directly he achieved his majority Raymond Bérenger struck out on his own. His effigy in the Church of Saint-Jean-de-Malte at Aix-en-Provence shows a face more cultured than that of the average medieval noble; though dressed in chain mail he is holding, of all things, a rose. Beside his effigy is that of his wife, Béatrice de Savoie, her long hair falling down upon her shoulders; he had been betrothed to her when she was only fourteen years of age. Their eldest child, Marguerite, had similarly been only thirteen when she married Louis in the Cathedral of Sens.

Raymond Bérenger was an enlightened and able man, who reorganized the administrative and judicial system of Provence, and maintained his county against all comers. His, says Busquet, was 'the greatest and most fruitful reign of any of the Counts of Provence, which transformed it into a modern state. In addition he made Provence, by the delicate mondanity of his comtal Court, into the principal centre of the literary civilization of the troubadours'.[10] Here indeed this spirit found its most enlightened expression; but its apogee was now past, as many of the lands west of the Rhône where the tongue was spoken had had the spirit all but smashed out of them by the Albigensian Crusade. At Raymond's principal castle of Tarascon on the Rhône, however, the troubadour spirit was still alive, and his daughters learned at their father's knee how to turn a polished phrase. Eleanor, the second girl, was twelve years of age when she wrote her poem to Richard of Cornwall. Her mentors in composing it had been her father and his poet-chamberlain, Romeo de Villeneuve.[11] It was a daring thing to do, and the most charitable interpretation that can be put on Eleanor's action is that she did not know that Richard – fifteen years her senior – was married to Isabella Marshal. Her father doubtless knew it, and was flying a kite in the hopes of catching Henry of Winchester.*

Raymond's plan succeeded perfectly. Richard showed Isabella the poem. Coming when it did, it underlined their foolishness in contemplating divorce; and Isabella, in wry amusement, advised her husband to send it to his bachelor brother. The result was magical; touched to the heart, the romantic King 'immediately sent prudent men into Provence with letters expressing his most heartfelt desire to contract marriage with the Count's daughter Eleanor. The Count was an illustrious man, excelling in military virtues. He had married the daughter of the Count Thomas of Savoy, sister of the present Count Amadeus of Savoy, a woman of remarkable beauty. She had borne her husband daughters of great charm, the eldest of whom, Marguerite, had married Louis, King of the French. And so it was the younger virgin of this most lovely race whom the King of England sought as his wife through those self-same ambassadors'.[12]

Henry was in fact the last of the children of John and Isabella to marry. His younger sister, Isabella, had contracted that same year, 1235, the most eligible marriage in Europe. Early in the spring imperial messengers had come to London, seeking a bride for the Emperor Frederick II. They had evidently inspected Isabella minutely, for they reported back to their master that she was 'in every way suitable for the imperial couch' and that they were particularly taken with her grace, sweetness and beauty. The Emperor, impressed by the report, sought her hand, and sent for her to join him as soon as possible. King Henry was determined that she should have a magnificent trousseau, and personally supervised its collection down to the smallest detail. He also sent the sheriff of Norfolk 'to purvey ten good ships against the transport of the King's sister Isabella, and to furnish them with good mariners and other necessary armaments'.[13] The two brothers then went down to Dover to bid her a glittering if lachrymose farewell on 15th May.

* It was the practice for medieval Kings to be referred to by the name of the town in which they were born.

A few weeks later, in June, the Pope's reply to Richard's letter arrived. In unequivocal terms, Gregory IX stated that Richard had no cause for divorce and should remain united with his wife Isabella. She was already expecting their third child, and retired to Richard's castle of Haughley, in the honour of Eye in Suffolk, for the confinement. On 12th November they were rewarded by the birth of a fine, lusty, baby boy whom they christened Henry in honour of his uncle and grandfather. He was to become the apple of his father's eye, a man of great promise destined to succeed him as King of Germany.

On receipt of Henry III's offer of marriage, Raymond Bérenger and Béatrice accepted with alacrity on behalf of Eleanor. The young princess was escorted up through France by her uncle, William of Valence, and on arrival in Paris was lavishly entertained by her sister, Queen Marguerite, her brother-in-law, King Louis IX, and the dowager Queen Blanche. Thence the party proceeded to Wissant, where they embarked and, aided by favourable winds, 'came with rapid course before they were expected into the port of Dover. The King hurried down to Canterbury to meet them and rushed to embrace his returning ambassadors. Then, having seen the damsel, and accepted her for himself, he married her at Canterbury, the ceremony being performed by the Archbishop Edmund, assisted by the bishops who had arrived with the damsel, on the nineteenth of February, in the presence of many magnates, nobles and prelates. On the twenty-fourth of the same month the Lord King arrived at Westminster and on the following day, which was a Sunday, in a ceremony of great splendour in which he wore his crown, the coronation of Queen Eleanor took place'.[14] So the second daughter of the House of Provence gained a crown. She was to be happily married to Henry for many years, and was to be the mother of one of the ablest of English kings, who was devoted to her; but her domineering personality alienated her from the mass of the people and made her a most unpopular queen.*

Delighted with his dark and beautiful wife, Henry wished to be at peace with all men. Hubert de Burgh was restored to all the

* See genealogical Table of the family of Provence.

lands he had held before his fall; and later the 'three castles', Skenfrith, Llantilio and Grosmont, guarding the Monmouthshire passes into Wales, were also granted to him. Typically, after grossly ill-treating Hubert, Henry was smitten with remorse; but his anger did not remain buried for long. It burst out again against Hubert when he discovered that de Burgh's daughter Meggotta had been secretly married without the King's consent to Richard de Clare, Earl of Gloucester, Isabella Marshal's son by her first marriage.* Once again Hubert was put on trial; the result was inconclusive, but a great deal of bad blood was stirred up.

The King's remorse extended also to the Marshals. Richard had been succeeded by his younger brother Gilbert, and Henry had issued letters patent 'making restitution to Gilbert Marshal, Earl of Pembroke, in pursuance of the King's remission to him of the anger and indignation conceived against him on account of the late war between the King and Richard Marshal, Earl of Pembroke, his brother, and the King's restitution to him of his inheritance in England, Wales and Ireland, of his castle of Striguil, which he handed over for the security of his fidelity to Edmund, Archbishop of Canterbury. And it is the King's will that this grace, which he has made to him on account of the death of Earl Richard, shall not be an occasion of hatred between Earl Gilbert and the magnates of Ireland and England, and the King releases to the said Gilbert and his brothers the indignation he had against them on the said ground'.[15] Henry, in other words, though considerably more to blame than Richard Marshal for the 'indignation', was seeking to bury the hatchet.

His relations with his brother likewise improved. In July he joined Richard and Isabella at Wallingford Castle for a peaceful and pleasant summer interlude.† The Cornwalls were steadily extending their Thames-side castle which now presented a double

* See genealogical Table of the family of Marshal.

† Shortly before, in June, 1236, Richard had been at Winchester where, together with Gilbert Marshal, he had taken the Cross – that is, undertaken to go on Crusade. Paris tells us that as evidence of his determination to go he had his woods cut down to pay for part of the expenses of his journey. He did not actually set out for another four years.

circlet of curtain walls and new domestic buildings within, rising to a crown in the great keep on its lofty mound. Richard was spending considerable sums on improving the interior decoration and military equipment of Wallingford, which was always one of his favourite castles. He and Isabella divided most of their time between it and Berkhamsted in the Chilterns, and here, too, they were assiduously at work. Berkhamsted was also a motte-and-bailey castle in plan, with a shell-keep on a tall mound, the whole protected by the encircling arms of a moat fed from near-by springs. The bailey was very extensive, divided into inner and outer wards, and in the latter Richard and Isabella erected a chapel on whose decoration they lavished considerable sums. The Hall and lord's quarters lay near by, and these two came in for special expenditure. It would seem that Isabella rather preferred Berkhamsted to Wallingford, and took if anything more trouble over her rooms there.

The year 1237 passed moderately quietly, with the couple engaged in the unspectacular pursuits of a country lord and lady. Richard appeared to be close in the King's counsels, and in December was at Westminster when he, Simon de Montfort, the Earl of Lincoln and the Archbishop of York attested the payment of a thousand marks by Brother Geoffrey, the King's almoner.[16] It was, therefore, to his utter astonishment that Richard learnt, early in 1238, of a certain ceremony which had been performed in almost complete secrecy. 'The sister of the King of England, the former wife of the younger Marshal, married Simon de Montfort, at which the Earl of Cornwall was mightily incensed; the marriage took place in the King's small private chapel at Westminster on the nineteenth of February'.[17]

It is quite evident that Henry kept the marriage from his brother until he could present him with a *fait accompli*, for instead of choosing Westminster Abbey, the venue was his private chapel in the Palace. Whether 19th February was deliberately chosen because it was a year to the day after his own marriage is uncertain: probably this has some significance, as Richard would not have suspected Henry of any such intention on his anniversary.

The principal reason for Richard's rage was that his brother had not chosen to consult him when he married their sister off to the man who had been his close friend – with whom indeed he had been conducting the kingdom's business. Furthermore, Eleanor was of course the widow of Isabella's brother, William Marshal the younger, and after his sudden and tragic death she had made a vow of perpetual chastity. This was now broken; and among those who were utterly scandalized was the saintly Archbishop Edmund Rich of Canterbury, who left England shortly afterwards, never to return. In short, the whole affair was handled with complete lack of tact by Henry from start to finish, and dragon's seeds were sown whose bitter harvest he himself was later to reap in full measure. As to Eleanor, she was to prove a devoted, loyal, determined wife. Probably she had little to say in the matter, in accordance with the fate of medieval ladies to be given in marriage where their fathers and guardians chose; but she also was probably nothing loath, for sixteen is young to make a vow of perpetual chastity, and Simon was a striking and heroic figure.

In his fury Richard took up arms against his brother alongside the discontented barons, disgruntled by this special preferment of Simon de Montfort, who in eight years had risen from obscurity to marry a princess. No actual fighting took place, but Henry wrote to the Constable of Dover and the burgesses of the Cinque Ports warning them not to obey Richard should he seek to give them orders in the King's name.

There now occurred the second major tergiversation of Richard's life, the reasons for which are very hard to find. He had been the prime mover in the rebellion, yet no sooner had Henry agreed to sign the 'Provisions' which the barons had drawn up, than Richard – at the psychological moment – deserted the baronial cause, so that the whole force of the King's submission was lost and the 'Provisions' were never put into effect. Having three times been the leader of the baronial party in its opposition to the King, Richard now became a King's man for the rest of his life. In baronial eyes his conduct was shameful. When he had been wronged over Tamerton they had helped him; he had suddenly deserted

Richard Marshal in 1233; and now he did it yet again, after it had suited him to side with them when he was enraged by his brother's behaviour. Though the barons were intelligent enough to appreciate his worth in years to come and to regard him as the prudent statesman and sheet-anchor of the realm, a bad reputation dies hard in the popular mouth. Twenty-five years later, on the battlefield of Lewes, the men-at-arms were to sing mockingly:

> 'Rickard, though thou be ever trickard,
> Tricken shalt thou nevermore.'

The key to Richard's repeated return to the royalist cause despite temporary excursions on to the barons' side is probably to be found in the personality of Isabella. Though the continual quarrels between her husband's brother and her own must have been very painful to her, and she sought, as at Woodstock, to save her own family from disaster, it may be inferred that she steadily moulded Richard's character to be a mirror of her father's and to prize loyalty to the Crown above everything else. In years to come he was to sacrifice even his own German Kingdom for the sake of bolstering up his brother's tottering régime.

CHAPTER SIX

THE VICTIM OF JAUNDICE

IN MAY, 1239, Queen Eleanor gave birth to a son, for whom his father chose the name Edward, after the saintly Confessor whom he so much admired.[1] On 20th June the baby was baptized in Westminster Abbey, and Richard of Cornwall and Simon de Montfort, two of the godfathers, bore him from the font on their shields.[2] Everything seemed set fair, with Richard and Henry reconciled, and Simon basking in royal favour. Again they reckoned without the unpredictable King. A bare month later, when Simon and his Countess were again at Westminster, this time for the churching of Queen Eleanor, Henry turned on him without warning, called him excommunicate, and accused him of seducing his sister before their marriage. He went further, and screamed that Simon had bribed the Pope to free Eleanor from her vow of chastity. Richard, intensely embarrassed at this scene in the Abbey, tried to stay his brother's torrent of words, but to no avail. Henry now accused Simon of financial sharp practice, and de Montfort – realizing that he was in danger – fled to France with Eleanor and his household that very night. It was not a moment too soon, for Henry had already made plans for his removal to the Tower, and only the steadying counsel of Richard stayed his hand for long enough for Simon to make good his escape.[3]

Too late the fickle King repented of his outburst, but by then Simon was safe in Montfort l'Amaury and unlikely to recross the Channel again. Henry, unable to make amends to Simon, turned instead to Richard, and, as a mark of gratitude for his mediation, granted him the Forest of Dartmoor and Lydford Castle in fee.[4] This was a very worth-while gift, as the Moor was rich in tin deposits and venison, and Lydford was the headquarters of the

Stannaries, the administrative centre of the tin industry. Hitherto the boundaries of the Forest, the 'feresta' or royal chase, and those of the surrounding lords' lands over which the inhabitants of border parishes enjoyed common rights, had been very loosely defined.[5] This was not good enough for the careful Richard, who decided to have the boundaries of his new lands delineated in an orderly manner.

Taking advantage of his brother's good humour and goodwill towards him, Richard went down to spend Christmas at Winchester in his company. Isabella remained behind at Berkhamsted, for she was already eight months pregnant with their fourth child. Though she could not manage the journey to Winchester, far less the one much farther westward which Richard intended to take, she was much more confident than she had formerly been. Richard therefore took his leave of her, content that all would be well.

With him to Winchester went his ward, young Baldwin de Redvers, whom he had just successfully married to his step-daughter, Amicia de Clare, Isabella's child by her first husband. It did not take a great deal of effort on the part of Richard to persuade Henry to grant Baldwin the Earldom of Devon, which had been held by his family since Henry I's time.[6] The young man's grandfather, another Baldwin, had been the first to bear the title, and had been in royal favour at first. He founded St. James's Priory, near Exeter, and extended the castle of Plympton, but on taking up arms against Stephen had most of his fortress razed for his pains. The headship of the Devon earldom was then moved to Okehampton, and thither Richard now accompanied the newly-married Earl and Countess directly after the Christmas festivities were over, on the day after his thirty-first birthday. Having seen them settled into their fine castle crowning the hill above the West Okement, Richard made a brief sortie to visit his Cornish estates. On the way back he visited his new castle of Lydford – a square, grim and unembellished keep high above the deep, dark gorge through which the River Lyd foamed violently on its way down from the high Moor to join the Tamar. Round about the castle stood the hovels of a little village, once a Mint town of the Saxon kings but now the homes of a few poor serfs. The castle had a tolerable hall on its first floor, and the lord's chambers were adequate, if lacking in comfort; but below the ground floor in a lightless pit certain poor captives were confined, men who had infringed the Stannary laws and had been sent thither by the judgement of the tinners' court which sat twice yearly on Crockern Tor, far out by the West Dart.

Richard, however, had no time for prisoners. He came swiftly to the business in hand. The castellan of Lydford was William Brewer, a staunch henchman of his father, but generally very unpopular. Nevertheless, he could be trusted completely, and Richard marked him out to lead the team of knights who, he planned, would conduct a Perambulation of the boundaries of the royal forest the following summer. He arranged with Brewer that he would prevail upon his brother to grant authority for twelve trusted knights, accompanied by monks to act as scribes, to undertake the journey.

To brief Brewer and several of the knights who had already gathered at Lydford, Richard went up with them on to the peak of Yes Tor, or Ernestorre, the mountain of eagles, as it was then called.[7] Thence he indicated the great round mass of Cosdon Hill where the Perambulation should start, and sketched out a rough itinerary. To follow it even today, from tor to tor, twisting up one river and down the next, over miles of trackless waste, would be an exceptional undertaking: in the thirteenth century it must have presented a journey into the unknown. In the event, however, the knights and scribes overcame all difficulties and left behind a document which is still the basis of the boundaries between the Duchy of Cornwall lands and the Commons.[8] But Richard was not to be there to see, even had he intended it.

A messenger came up from Okehampton with news from Berkhamsted which was to change the whole course of his life. In the words of Matthew Paris, a few days previously 'the most noble lady Isabella, Countess of Gloucester and Cornwall, was taken dangerously ill of the jaundice, and when her time was come (for she was heavy with child, and about to give birth) she lost consciousness. Then, after having had her ample flaxen tresses cut off and made a full confession of her sins, she departed to the Lord, taking with her a baby boy, born alive but short-lived, who was immediately baptized with the name Nicholas. When Earl Richard, who at that time had gone into Cornwall, heard this, he broke down, groaning and weeping, and grieved inconsolably; returning at great speed, he caused the body of his wife to be buried in his presence at Beaulieu, the house which King John had founded and built and delivered to the Cistercian Order.'[9]

This description does not sound like that of a man who cared so little for his wife that he was prepared to divorce her on a flimsy pretext. He apparently intended to be buried beside her, having already founded a chantry at Beaulieu and made provisions for prayers to be said for his soul after his death; for this reason he declined to allow her to be buried at Tewkesbury beside her first husband, although she had apparently wished it. The Prior of Tewkesbury, Brother Henry de Siptune, who had been present at her deathbed, was, however, permitted to take Isabella's heart to Tewkesbury, where he buried it before the high altar in Gilbert de Clare's grave.[10] A sad postscript is provided by the Liberate Rolls for 7th February, 1240, according to which four hundred pounds of wax were delivered by Brother Geoffrey, keeper of the King's wardrobe, to Earl Richard by the King's order; they were to make candles for the masses to be said for Isabella's soul.[11]

So passed Isabella Marshal, leaving behind her a husband far better fitted than before her advent to assume a major position in the affairs of state. Of all the qualities she had brought to him the most valuable was wisdom. With her death the first division of his life ended and the second, and most important, which led him to kingship, began.

PART TWO

THE KING OF THE ROMANS AND SANCHIA OF PROVENCE
1240–1261

CHAPTER ONE

AN EVENTFUL FRENCH JOURNEY

ISABELLA's death caused Richard a profound shock. His immediate reaction was to go abroad to forget, and to atone for his sins by undertaking the Crusade for which he had taken the Cross at Winchester four years before. This decision taken, he made sure that no detail was forgotten, and the winter and spring of 1240 were for him a period of hectic activity. He committed his five-year-old son Henry to his brother's care, went to St. Alban's Abbey to ask for prayers for his Crusade, rapidly toured his estates, and finally, in May, took his leave of the Council of Clergy at Reading. Their sorrowful farewell shows that he was already looked upon as the sheet-anchor of the realm: 'When all the prelates saw this, they burst into tears, and said to Earl Richard; "Why, Earl, our only hope after the King, do you desert us? Why do you leave us thus desolate? Rapacious aliens will invade us in your absence."'[1]

Richard's mind was made up, and he said as much: he embarked from Dover on 10th June, the King coming to see him off. With him went his Chief of Staff, Thierry de Nussa, who advised him to travel to the Mediterranean overland and embark at Marseilles; and also, among others, the Earl of Salisbury, Richard's personal friend Philip Basset, and his old mentor – the former castellan of Corfe – Peter de Mauley. Seventy knights bachelor went with him as well, but not Simon de Montfort, although they had originally intended travelling together. Simon did eventually go, but independently, making his way down through Lombardy and embarking from Brindisi, leaving his wife Eleanor behind there in a castle of the Emperor's.[2]

Richard arrived in Paris shortly before Midsummer Day and

was received sumptuously at the French Court by three of the most remarkable people of the time: King Louis, his Queen Marguerite, and his mother, the dowager Queen Blanche. The latter had doubtless spread her good opinion of Richard, acquired at their meeting at Vendôme twelve years before, about the royal household. Blanche was a forceful personality in a century of outstanding members of her sex. To quote Régine Pernoud: 'If there was ever a period where woman's influence triumphed, it was the thirteenth century in which it seems that all the truly feminine virtues reached their full fruition.' Certainly the French Queen Mother had been an able administrator and politician, had brought up her son Louis to be saintly, of transparent integrity, but in no way a milksop. She was withal physically attractive, and inspired the troubadour Count Thibaut of Champagne, King of Navarre, whose passionate verses were, however, tempered with the courtly respect proper to the tradition of the troubadours encouraged by Eleanor of Aquitaine. Blanche was in fact the granddaughter of Eleanor, for her mother was none other than that other Eleanor, daughter of Henry II, who married King Alfonso VIII of Castile. A mixture of Spanish and Angevin blood thus flowed in Blanche's veins, and produced this determined but not unattractive character.

Her besetting sin was the habitual possessiveness of mothers who bring up sons alone. She could not bear to share Louis with another woman; and after her son had married Marguerite in 1234, the young couple were put to all sorts of ruses to spend a brief while in each other's company. 'Queen Blanche did not want to allow her son to be in his wife's company, save at night when he went to lie with her. The place where he liked to live best was Pontoise, because there the King's chamber was on the top floor and the Queen's immediately below, and the couple thus arranged to meet and talk in a newel stair which led from one chamber down to the other, and arranged between them that when the doorkeeper saw the Queen coming towards the chamber of the King her son, he would strike the door with his rod, and the King would come running back to his chamber so that his mother should find him in it; and the doorkeeper of the chamber of Queen Marguerite did

Blanche de Castille, Louis IX's mother, from the effigy in the Abbey of Saint-Denis

The Emperor Frederick II, Richard of Cornwall's brother-in-law, from the statue known as 'Der Reiter' at Bamberg Cathedral, Germany, erected *c.* 1230 and said to represent Frederick II

Louis IX (Saint Louis), King of France, husband of Marguerite de Provence

Marguerite de Provence, sister of Sanchia, Richard's second wife and wife of King Louis IX of France, from a statue in the Louvre modelled 150 years later by Jeanne de Bourbon

the same when he saw Queen Blanche coming so that she should find Marguerite inside.'[3]

Marguerite, as dark as her husband was fair, 'was, as a woman, what King Louis was as a man – typical of her time; she was the feudal lady *par excellence*. She was tender, gracious, compassionate, but she was conscious of her rights and held on to them firmly. First and foremost she was a lady, a princess and a Queen.'[4] The same writer, Boutaric, has called her one of the most gracious figures in the history of France. She was also a woman of courage, resourcefulness and piety, as can be detected clearly from the pages of Joinville, Louis's faithful seneschal, and from those of her confessor, Guillaume de Saint-Pathus. Her character emerges strikingly from several incidents which took place during Louis's Crusades.

Some years after Richard first met her, when she was returning from the Holy Land with King Louis, the ship was in great danger of foundering. She was on the point of entering the King's cabin to ask him to pray for deliverance, when Joinville suggested to her that she should make a vow to Saint Nicholas. This she did and vowed, if they were saved, to give a ship of silver, with five marks each for herself, the King and the three children, to the Saint, Joinville to be the witness of her promise. She went away and prayed and came back in a short while to tell Joinville that Saint Nicholas had answered her prayer and they would be saved. So it was indeed, and 'on return to France she had the ship made, with herself, the King and the three children in it, the seamen, the mast, the rigging, the rudder and the sails all fashioned in silver. When it was ready she sent it to me at Joinville to bring to Saint Nicholas, and so I did.'[5]

Later during the same voyage she was awakened one night by the smell of burning. One of the ladies who slept in her quarters had carelessly let her candle fall over, and the coverings of Queen Marguerite's bed were alight and the fire was beginning to spread. She leapt up on the instant, seized the burning clothes, and ran out on deck, stark naked, and threw them overboard, thereby doubtless saving the ship and her company.

Some years afterwards, during King Louis's second Crusade, when she lay in childbed at Damietta and heard of her husband's capture by the Egyptians, 'before she lay down she made everyone leave her chamber save her old knight of eighty summers (an ancient and trusted man who slept at the foot of her bed); she knelt down before him and begged him a boon; the knight swore to grant it to her and she said to him; "I charge you, by the faith you have sworn me, that if the Saracens enter the city, you will cut off my head before they can capture me." The knight replied; "Be assured I will do so, for I had already decided I would kill you before they should capture us."'[6] Three days later her baby son, Jean Tristan, was born; and the same day she learnt that the merchants who had followed in the wake of the Crusaders were evacuating the town in haste. She called the chief of them to her bedside and begged him to have pity on her and not leave her; when they murmured about the shortage of food if they stayed, she organized the purchase of all foodstuffs in the town and the rationing of them on condition that the Italian merchants would remain. They agreed and Damietta was saved. Later she was able to go to Acre and meet her husband when he was released from captivity. 'Both,' says Régine Pernoud, 'in equally dramatic circumstances showed themselves capable of playing their parts to the full, incarnating what the Knight and the Lady could mean to the Middle Ages.'

The third of the remarkable trio who gave Richard an unforgettable reception in Paris, Louis IX himself, had 'the face of an angel', with fair hair, blue eyes and a clear and almost girlish complexion which he had inherited from his grandmother, Isabella of Hainault, so different from his dark, half-Spanish mother. From Blanche he had inherited political wisdom and an almost choleric temper, which, however, he contrived to keep very tightly within bounds – so great was the self-discipline which he practised on himself throughout his life. He never swerved from the path of absolute fairness and drove his policy almost to a fault. He regarded himself as the servant of the people and not as the Lord's anointed entitled to exert absolute monarchical sway.

Saint and mystic, he demanded a high standard of integrity and devotion from those about him, but was nevertheless tolerant and understanding of their faults. He was the friend of the poor, not in the smug sense in which that phrase was used in the nineteenth century, but practising what he preached; regularly, paupers were invited to sit at his table and share his meals, and he would visit and feed in hospital lepers whose condition was so loathsome that his barons and churchmen shrank from accompanying him. From the rich he demanded a high standard: if they committed crimes, he remained implacable to any plea that they should receive greater mercy or be punished in greater privacy than the poor.

At the time of Richard's visit Louis had not adopted quite the severe garb which was his invariable wear after his return from his Crusade. Joinville describes him at one of his great feasts as 'clothed in a cotte of blue satin, a surcoat and mantle of scarlet satin trimmed with ermine'. Elsewhere he mentions him wearing a white cotton hat, 'which suited him very badly'. Though Louis's taste may not always have been impeccable, his wife was a leader of fashion, and, with her sisters, set female taste throughout a wide area of Europe. Eleanor of Provence had introduced into England the cyclas, a long sleeveless brocaded over-robe, and the practice of wearing an ornamental chaplet of flowers in the hair to brighten a gloomy winter's day. Raymond Bérenger's daughters neglected no detail to render their clothing more glamorous; the girdle, hitherto worn at the waist, with the material of the upper part of the gown bulging over it, on them followed a sloping line from the hip-bone to a point in front. The bulge disappeared and the gown was held down in small pleats, while the corsage under it flattered the figure. Nor were legs neglected: 'if the lady's feet and ankles be beautiful, she may hold up the robe in front, under pretence of stepping out briskly.'[7] Richard, who had already admired his brother's wife, now had cause to admire Marguerite of Provence. A similar beauty was shortly to come his own way.

King Louis saw him off with great ceremony, after renewing with him the truce between the kingdoms of England and France. He unstintingly admired Richard's determination to go on Crusade, and had long ago decided to follow the same route himself when he could. Indeed, within a short while of Richard's departure he set about fortifying the port of Aigues-Mortes as a special point of departure for the Holy Land. He had other projects nearer home which he confided to Richard. A little less than a year before, on 19th August, 1239, he had received in Paris one of the most precious of all Christian relics, the Crown of Thorns. The Latin Emperor of Byzantium, Baudouin II, had come to France to seek his help against the infidel, and Louis had negotiated with him the transfer to France of the Crown and a large section of the True Cross. The former was already in Paris, Louis having gone as far as Villeneuve-l'Archevêque, fifteen miles beyond Sens, to meet the procession bearing it; and had borne it back to Paris on his own shoulders, simply clad in a rough cotte, and barefoot. It was housed temporarily in the Chapel of Saint-Nicholas in the Palais-Royal on the Ile de la Cité, where Richard was now staying. Negotiations were still proceeding for the reception of the True Cross, which was temporarily in the keeping of the Knights Templars in Syria. Once it arrived, Louis was minded to have built for both relics a special chapel in the precincts of the royal palace, which would incorporate the very latest architectural advances.

Louis gave Richard his Marshal to accompany him to the boundaries of his dominions, which in 1240 reached nearly, but not quite, to Lyons. That great city, forming part of the Duchy of Burgundy, was loosely attached to the Holy Roman Empire, so loosely in fact that the Pope, when the sworn enemy of the Emperor, was able to stay there in perfect safety for some months. The King of the French provided the Earl of Cornwall with barges for his voyage down the Rhône, and, after an hospitable reception at Lyons, the Crusaders set off. Tying up for the night at Vienne, however, they encountered trouble. 'Having gone aboard his ships at Vienne, he proposed to sail down the Rhône in them to Arles. But the citizens of Vienne and others from near by asked Earl Richard if he would sell them his barges, for which they were prepared to pay triple the normal price. When the Earl refused, saying that he was no merchant, the citizens seized the ships by force.'[8]

Vienne lay outside the domain of the King of France,* being technically in the Empire, and owed allegiance to Count Raymond of Toulouse, whose fiefs stretched from the foothills of the Pyrenees across the south of France, and even across the Rhône. Just south of Avignon the great river became the boundary between the County of Toulouse and that of Provence, and so continued down to its mouth. As a result, the castle of Tarascon, one of the principal seats of Raymond Bérenger, faced a hostile castle of Beaucaire, held by Raymond of Toulouse, across the river, as the two houses were intermittently in conflict for years.

In 1232 Raymond of Toulouse's forces had devastated the area round Tarascon and Arles, and a ban of excommunication had been pronounced against him by the Archbishop of Arles, to be lifted only when, in 1237, Raymond again infiltrated into Provence, when revocation of the ban was used as a lever to get him to withdraw. The matter was further complicated by the appointment by the Emperor Frederick of an Imperial Vicar for the Kingdom of Arles and the County of Vienne, ousting the Archbishop of Arles from his city – one of the direct consequences of which was the excommunication of Frederick by the Pope on 24th March, 1239. Shortly before the excommunication, Raymond Bérenger had received the homage of the Archbishop of Arles and of Aix-en-Provence, had entered the former city and had driven the Vicar Imperial out. The Archbishop returned, and on 24th July con-confirmed to the Count jurisdiction over Arles. Raymond promptly appointed a viceroy to rule for him.

In the words of Raoul Busquet: 'This success illustrates the policy of the Count of Provence, prudent, attentive to detail, imperturbable when set on his course, bold when the decisive moment struck. It marks the culminating point of his reign and the final eviction of the Emperor from the affairs of Provence.'[9] It

* *Kingdom and domain:* A distinction was drawn between the Kingdom, the actual possessions of the King, and the domain, which was the dominions dependent on him. Basically the Kingdom of France at the beginning of the thirteenth century consisted only of the Ile de France with Paris, the Orleannois, Bourges and Rheims. The domain included the counties of Blois, Flanders, Champagne and part of the Duchy of Burgundy. Philip Augustus added Normandy in 1204.

also unleashed a fresh state of guerrilla warfare between Raymond Bérenger and Count Raymond of Toulouse, who had had to surrender Languedoc to Louis by the treaty of Meaux in 1229, and had hoped to recoup himself from the fat lands of Provence.

Into this explosive situation came Richard of Cornwall, disgruntled and robbed by Toulouse's vassals in Vienne, only to behold, when he came in sight of the twin towns of Beaucaire and Tarascon, his stolen barges tied up beneath the protecting walls of Beaucaire Castle. Hearing of his approach, Raymond Bérenger 'in rejoicing and exultation' hastened out to meet him and received him hospitably in Tarascon Castle. Paris suggested that he had an axe to grind and hoped to gain Richard's financial support against the the Count of Toulouse. Richard had too much at stake in his Crusade to take any such step at present, but at least Raymond got his barges back for him under threat of hostilities with Toulouse, who saw fit to apologize belatedly to Richard for the theft of the ships.

Tarascon Castle's impressive bulk rises directly beside the Rhone. In its great hall Richard met the Countess Béatrice and her third daughter, Sanchia. Fortune's wheel was turning inevitably; here was the very place where Eleanor had concocted the love-poem to him, and here he now was confronted with a girl whom the chronicler describes as of incomparable beauty. It was a dark and lovely French face to take in his memory on Crusade.

Richard now made a pilgrimage to Saint-Gilles, the Benedictine Abbey where the tomb of the saint lay. Here another trap was in store, in the shape of the Archbishop of Arles, sent specifically by the Pope to forbid Richard to proceed on his Crusade. In point of fact the Pope wanted him to compound his interest in the Crusade for a monetary payment to help the Frankish Empire of Byzantium. Perhaps the Pope imagined that Richard, who had just seen the marvellous relic which Louis had obtained for his help to that same Frankish Empire, might be persuaded. Crusading to the Holy Land was in any case in Papal eyes becoming too secular, too much of a nobleman's jaunt. Not for nothing was the inn at the gate of Nottingham Castle named 'The Trip to Jerusalem'. But for

Richard this was no trip to Jerusalem; he was quite sincere and determined, standing to gain nothing materially from it. It was in fact a pious exercise, in some respects an atonement for past sins, something done in honour of Isabella's memory. If anything more had been needed to clinch his determination, it was now forthcoming; for the legate and the Archbishop of Arles strongly advised him, if his mind was made up to sail to the Holy Land, to avoid Marseilles and embark from Aigues-Mortes. This port in the low-lying Camargues west of the Rhone, not yet improved and fortified by Louis, was, however, known to Richard's retinue as a haunt of disease in high summer, and the object in seeking to divert him there became apparent.[10]

Richard, angered by this ecclesiastical duplicity, administered a deliberate snub to the Papacy by sending Robert de Twenge, a knight of his entourage noted for his hostility to the Pope, as ambassador to the Emperor Frederick II – partly to acquaint him of the events in Provence, and partly to express his regret at being unable to postpone his Crusade any longer and visit the Emperor in Italy. Then, having fitted out and victualled his ships at La Roque, he sailed in the middle of September out into the Mediterranean.[11]

The manner of such a Crusader's embarkation is graphically described by Joinville. The large ships, '*les nefs*', could carry 500 to 800 persons or 100 horses, and had three classes: first, which was in the after-castle, reserved for persons of high rank, second in the tween-deck, and third on the open deck itself. Each passenger was allowed a long box to serve as a trunk (or, in unhappy circumstances, as a coffin), a small barrel of fresh water, a chamber-pot and a lantern. The horses required in the Holy Land were placed in the hold; and its hatch, which at sea was below water-level, sealed. Then, when his hour-glass indicated that sailing-time was approaching, the master called to his sailors for'ard: 'Are you ready to sail?' They replied: 'Aye, sir; let the clergy and priests come forward.' The master ordered them up on to the after-castle to sing the 'Veni, Creator Spiritus', while all the passengers knelt on deck. Then, when the hymn was finished, the master cried: 'Make sail, and God speed us!' and the royal ship led the fleet to sea.[12]

CHAPTER TWO

THE CRUSADER

GROUSSET, a modern Frenchman writing about Richard's exploits in the Holy Land, is as complimentary as were the contemporary chroniclers of seven hundred years ago. Richard's Crusade, he writes, 'had the happiest results. Brother-in-law of Frederick II, he conducted himself as official delegate of the Emperor-king, but, unlike him, refused to be drawn into local quarrels; he behaved like a wise arbiter and a dispenser of justice. Because of this, he was able to resuscitate and exercise the royal function without holding the actual title.'[1] In other words, Richard was the last man really to wield authority in the ancient Frankish Kingdom of Jerusalem which had existed since the capture of the Holy City in July, 1099, and the election by the barons of the 'most pious of their number', Geoffrey de Bouillon, to the royal title.*

The situation which Richard found when he landed at Acre on 11th October, 1240, after a voyage of nearly a month from La Roque, was one of confusion and anarchy. To quote his own letter addressed to Baldwin de Redvers, Earl of Devon, the Abbot of Beaulieu and Robert the clerk: 'In the Holy Land discord has replaced peace, division has replaced unity, civil war has replaced concord. The two Fraternal Orders, set up in the days gone by for the defence of their common mother, are now quarrelling in her bosom, for they are swollen with pride from the excess of their

* After the disastrous battle of Hittin in 1187 Jerusalem itself again passed into Saracen hands, leaving only three enclaves on the coast, respectively round Acre, Tripoli and Antioch, in the hands of the Christians; but these were still referred to as 'the Kingdom of Jerusalem' or more simply 'Outremer'. The Crusade of Richard Cœur-de-Lion did not result in the recapture of Jerusalem, but he did obtain from Saladin free access for Christian pilgrims to the Holy City.

riches.'[2] Grousset observes that 'from the very moment of his disembarkation the English Prince found himself the buffer between the Hospitallers who wanted him to adhere to the peace with Egypt and the Templars who were trying to draw him into the Damascan alliance'.[3]

This dissension between Hospitallers and Templars was the crux of the ills which beset the Holy Land, but there were many other contributory factors to the state Richard described, going back over a long period of time through an undergrowth of plot and counter-plot. The shadows of France and the Empire fell across his path, as they were to do throughout his life.

A hundred years after its foundation the Frankish Kingdom of Jerusalem had suffered a severe decline from its former glory. The Crusade of Richard Cœur-de-Lion had made great changes, however, and by the year 1220 the Franks had succeeded in winning back a great deal of the lost territory along the coast, including Acre, Jaffa, Caesarea and Sidon. Inland, however, they had practically nothing left in Galilee, and Jerusalem itself was in the hands of the Saracens. The King of Jerusalem, Jean de Brienne, undertook a campaign against the Sultan of Egypt, which proved disastrous; he was compelled to make peace, and returned empty-handed to Syria, whence he sailed for Europe to complain to the Pope and the Emperor that the main blame for the disaster in Egypt could be laid at the door of the Papal Legate. Pope and Emperor promised that there would be no recurrence; the former had for long years nursed the vain hope of getting the latter to go on a Crusade himself.

The great Hohenstaufen, however, although he had taken the Cross at Aachen in 1215, was not particularly interested. If he had been, the disaster in Egypt might have been averted. However, he was by no means averse to becoming King of Jerusalem, an idea which the aged Pope Honorius, who had been instrumental in obtaining Frederick's election, still cherished. The Pope had therefore proposed in 1225 that Frederick should marry Isabella, the only daughter and heiress of Jean de Brienne, and the Emperor had agreed with alacrity. Jean de Brienne, a simple, uncomplicated man, was dazzled by the prospect; for him such a solution presaged the assured safety of the Frankish Kingdom in the Levant.[4]

Thus, on the death of Jean de Brienne in the same year, it was the Hohenstaufen who became King of Jerusalem through his first marriage. Soon afterwards he felt constrained to visit his new kingdom and was in Palestine from 1228 to 1229, leading what Grousset describes as an 'excommunicate, islamophile and anti-Frankish Crusade', and Pernoud calls 'the Crusade without Faith'. For it did not now suit the Papacy's book for Frederick to go; much less did his methods appeal to Rome. Vastly in advance of his generation, a politician of Machiavellian stature, philosopher, savant, logician, doctor, he rapidly obtained a rapprochement with the Saracens. In modern eyes he would be classed an able diplomatist: then his behaviour was considered scandalous.[5] To save offending his Saracen friends he deliberately let the fortifications of Jerusalem be run down. At the same time he was playing off the Sultan of Egypt against the Sultan of Damascus. When he returned to Europe in 1229 he had succeeded in obtaining a truce with the former, Malik al-Kamil, under which Jerusalem was returned to the Franks and no attack was to be made by either side for ten years.

When the ten years were approaching their end, in July, 1239, the new Pope, fearing a fresh Saracen assault on Jerusalem on the expiry of the truce, sent his henchmen to preach a new Crusade in France and England. The result was two Crusades in quick succession – those of Thibaut of Champagne and Richard of Cornwall, the former landing at Acre on 1st September, 1239.

From the moment when the ill-prepared French expedition under the troubadour Count blundered into the Holy Land, a succession of the most frightful mistakes was to be committed. The first was the psychological error of making the voyage at all without first preparing the political ground. 'If Frederick II's Crusade of 1228 had been at fault in the negligence of its military preparations, the entire enterprise being risked on diplomatic preparation alone, Thibaut's Crusade ten years later was guilty of exactly the opposite.' The poet Count, titular King of Navarre, who sighed for the beautiful Queen Blanche, was anything but a politician; and he had with him the flower of French chivalry – bored with life at home, and bursting to prove itself and find an outlet for its energy. In Thibaut's company were Hugo, Duke of Burgundy, Amaury de Montfort (Simon's brother), the Count Henri de Bar, Raoul de Soissons and many another famous name.

Grousset observes that it is a perpetual besetting sin of the French race to try to make up for general unpreparedness by last-minute military improvisation, and this was only too true of Thibaut de Champagne. Any diplomat worth his salt – and certainly one of Frederick's calibre – would have sought out the weak spots in the Saracen princes' family tangle, and made advantageous alliances with one section against the other, as had been the regular policy of the kings of Jerusalem of old.[6]

The arrival of the French Crusaders was the signal for the Saracens to regard themselves as freed of any obligation placed upon them by the Treaty of Jaffa between them and Frederick; and, just as the Pope had feared, they attacked Jerusalem. Frederick had left the city almost unfortified as an act of deliberate policy. Practically the only remaining strong-point was the citadel, or Tower of David, and this fell to the comparatively small forces of Al Nasir Dawud of Transjordan, who arrived from his castle of Krak of the Desert, and subjected the Tower to a mangonel siege lasting twenty-seven days. When it surrendered he magnanimously allowed the Frankish garrison to withdraw to the coast.

This was the grim news which greeted the French Crusaders on landing. A council of war was held at once between Thibaut de Champagne and the local Frankish chiefs, including the Archbishop of Tyre, Pierre de Sargines, the Grand Master of the Temple, and the Count of Jaffa, Gautier de Brienne. They all gave Thibaut conflicting advice, some counselling him to attack Egypt, others Damascus. The policy on which Thibaut finally decided was the worst of both worlds – to refortify the ruined castle of Ascalon and then seize Damascus. As Ascalon belonged to the Sultan of Egypt he contrived to alienate both the most powerful

Sultans at once. Moreover his authority over his followers was really illusory, and the proud French barons, in search of glory, decided to branch out on their own.

First of these was Pierre Mauclerc, Count of Brittany, who was apprised by his intelligence that a huge Saracen caravan, consisting mainly of cattle, was on its way to Damascus to revictual the city. Together with Raoul de Soissons and a hundred other knights he ambushed it in a defile and returned to Jaffa on 4th November loaded with food and booty.

Though in general hailed as a great achievement, Mauclerc's master-stroke excited the jealousy of the proud Count Henri de Bar, who decided to make as big a name for himself. His plan was to attack an Egyptian detachment which had just arrived at Gaza, and among the band of dashing and foolhardy young nobles who joined him were the Duke of Burgundy and Amaury de Montfort. Although they made their preparations in secret, on the evening of 12th November – just as they were giving their horses a final feed of hay, and were preparing to mount – Thibaut de Champagne accompanied by the Count of Brittany and the Grand Masters of the Templars, Hospitallers and Teutonic knights rode up in an attempt to dissuade them. All their eloquence was in vain, and the Comte de Bar and his knights galloped off towards Gaza.[7]

'It was a fine, clear night, with a full moon and stars giving great brilliance.' Despite the advice he had received from the Count of Jaffa not to proceed too near the enemy positions, the Comte de Bar pressed on into the sand-dunes of the coast. The French knights took no precautions at all; they sent out no scouts, but dismounted in a sandy hollow and sat down to eat. They had taken care to bring bread, cooked meat, cheese, fruit and wine – all the ingredients for a jolly Gallic picnic.[8]

The inevitable happened. Amazed despite themselves at the French foolhardiness, the Saracens fell upon them as they lay at a disadvantage. The friable sand of the dunes gave the French little foothold to defend themselves, surprised in the middle of their midnight repast. The Count of Jaffa and the Duke of Burgundy escaped; Henri de Bar went down, fighting bravely; while Amaury de Montfort with 600 others was captured and led off to prison in Cairo.

On the receipt of this dreadful news a quarrel broke out between Thibaut de Champagne and the Templars and Hospitallers as to what should be done next. As a result of their indecision they withdrew without refortifying Ascalon, and returned to Acre. They fully expected the victorious Saracens to pursue them, but in fact they were too preoccupied with a palace revolution in Cairo. Al-Nasir of Transjordan had been reconciled with Salih Aiyub of Jazira, and had helped him to depose Al-Adil and make himself Sultan of Egypt in his place; in return he promised Nasir assistance to drive out his uncle Ismail from Damascus, whence he himself had been dislodged.[9] Aiyub made a triumphal entry into Cairo on 19th June, 1240, and in gratitude to Nasir for his support made a public announcement that he would place him on the throne of Damascus.

The usurper Ismail was naturally terrified; his only hope was to ally himself with the Franks. In return for military aid against Aiyub and Nasir he promised to restore to the Franks all the old kingdom of Jerusalem as far as the River Jordan, and – as an earnest of his good intentions – handed over a great slice of territory from Sidon to Tiberias. This was just the moral uplift which the Frankish army, idling about in Galilee, needed; so Thibaut marched back to Jaffa to defend Syria against the Sultan of Egypt.

He reckoned without Pan-Islamism. True Moslems regarded the alliance with him as frightful treachery on the part of Ismail; and, although initially it was crowned with success, and Nasir was sent packing back into Transjordan, yet when they reached Gaza, Ismail's forces deserted *en bloc* to the Egyptian enemy. Thibaut de Champagne decided to make an immediate separate peace with Egypt and, leaving the unfortunate Ismail to his fate, he concluded a treaty with Aiyub. The troubadour had lost his head completely, and the French Crusade collapsed. He made a rapid pilgrimage to Jerusalem and embarked at Acre for France on 30th September,

1240, unhappy and disillusioned. All the remaining French forces went with him, except the Duke of Burgundy and his personal vassals, who stayed behind intending to refortify Ascalon. Matthew Paris suggests that the departure of the King of Navarre and the Count of Brittany was also hastened by jealousy of Richard of Cornwall, whom they knew to be on the way, and who, as they rightly suspected, would succeed where they had failed.

The chronicler of St. Albans also tells us that the Saracens tried to discover the future by casting lots, and this showed them that a second Christian army was approaching their shores, led by a certain young English nobleman. '"Is he of that same magnificent race as the man who terrorized the whole Orient?" asked the Saracen prince. "He is his nephew, and bears the same name," answered the soothsayer. "And what manner of man is he? How powerful?" "His fortune is greater, but his skill in war is less; nevertheless he will carry through to the end whatever task he has set himself." Upon hearing this, dismay and despair filled them all.'[10]

Eleven days after Thibaut's departure, Richard's ships came alongside at Acre. 'At the same time Earl Richard came sailing safely and cheerfully to the Holy Land with all his fleet and associates and landed at the port of Acre on the twelfth day after Michaelmas. He was received with great rejoicing by a procession of clergy, the princes and knights greeted him with respect, bells rang, the churchmen chanted, the people applauded with drums, zithers and singing, for in his arrival they saw the answer to their prayers, and exultantly stretching their hands to the stars cried out "Blessed is he that cometh in the name of the Lord."'[11]

The rival Templars and Hospitallers hurried to gain his ear; but though courteous, he calmly ignored them and made up his own mind. Having heard all that they and the other Frankish nobles, headed by Gautier de Brienne, Count of Jaffa, had to tell him, he decided that the key to the situation lay in completing the refortification of Ascalon. A year before, this would have been foolish; but now, with the changed fortunes of the Saracen princely house, it paid handsomely. It fitted the pro-Damascan policy of the Templars, and tipped the scales as far as further aggression by Egypt was concerned by making it perfectly plain to Aiyub that Richard was determined to defend what was left of the Kingdom of Jerusalem at all costs. The Duke of Burgundy was delighted to see Richard on his arrival at Ascalon. The work of repairing the ruined castle now went forward with a will; and no sooner was it completed, in March, 1241, than – as Richard had anticipated – emissaries from Al-Salih Aiyub arrived from Cairo to ask him to ratify the treaty with Egypt which Thibaut had set in train but left unfinished.

This was exactly what Richard wanted. The Duke of Burgundy, the Grand Master of the Hospitallers, and the Count of Jaffa all advised him to accept. The leader of the Saracen emissaries was none other than Nasir, and the treaty and its corollary provided Matthew Paris with the subject matter for one of his most striking drawings which gives us the best picture of Richard still extant.[12]

In this drawing Richard and Nasir appear in the centre, kneeling facing each other, clasping their right hands, their shields in their left hands, and their helmets behind them. Both men are in chain mail. The Saracen is bearded, the Englishman clean-shaven, with brown hair parted in the middle curling back from his temples. Behind him stand some of his knights, while behind Nasir is the castle of Krak of the Desert filled with Saracens.

A few pages farther on in the same manuscript is another expressive picture, a direct sequel to the first, showing the release of French prisoners as a result of the treaty concluded between Richard and Nasir. Scantily clad in loin-cloths they are emerging from the dungeons of Cairo shedding their chains; their expressions betoken wonderment at their good fortune and dazzlement at seeing the sun once more.[13]

Once again the de Montfort family was especially in Richard's debt, for foremost among those released was Amaury. The scanty clothing of the French prisoners was not poetic licence on Matthew's part, for we read that 'the Sultan restored their liberty to Count Amaury and the other knights and returned to them all their honourable clothes. They rode through the whole of Cairo and then returned home. In exchange the Qadi received the Moslem prisoners taken by the Franks.'[14]

Not content with releasing the living, Richard also turned to the dead, whose bones still littered the dunes at Gaza, and ensured that they received Christian burial in the cemetery at Ascalon. 'When the French throughout the realm of Gaul heard that Earl Richard had performed this pious work of burial of their loved ones, amid all his other problems, they swore to give thanks and undying praise to him.'[15] French indebtedness to him was to stand him in very good stead before the world was a year older.

Richard, writing home, reports with some satisfaction that the return of the French prisoners took place on St. George's Day, a subtle touch calculated to emphasize the English achievement. He had reason to be pleased with himself. Not merely was his treaty a psychological victory, a return to the 'moral appeasement' for which Al-Kamil and Frederick II had worked so diplomatically, it was also a territorial masterpiece which at one stroke returned to the Franks more than half the old territories of the Kingdom of Jerusalem, interior and coast combined – only part of Samaria and Hebron being excluded.[16] He had achieved this with singularly little loss of life; though among those who died during his Crusade was, sadly enough, old Peter de Mauley, his one-time custodian. There had, moreover, been no major battles.

If any further proof of his statesmanship were needed it was to be found in his choice of governor of his newly-restored castle of Ascalon. This was Gautier de Pennepié, whom Frederick II had left as his bailiff in Jerusalem. By his deliberate choice of an imperial officer to control this important coastal fortress, which he himself described as 'the key by sea and land to the Kingdom of Jerusalem', he kept Ascalon out of the hands of the warring factions of the Hospital and the Temple, and made it an effective bulwark against Philistia and so against the Sultan of Egypt.

In the last ten days after the return of the French prisoners, Richard made a quick pilgrimage in smock and staff to Jerusalem

Acon sive tholomaida:

Cxpiani

Come Britañ

Nazer dñs crac.

fedus initū.

Sarraceni

Crac.

XI

The treaty between Richard and Nasir, from Matthew Paris's *Chronica Majora* MS. 16. C.C.C.C.

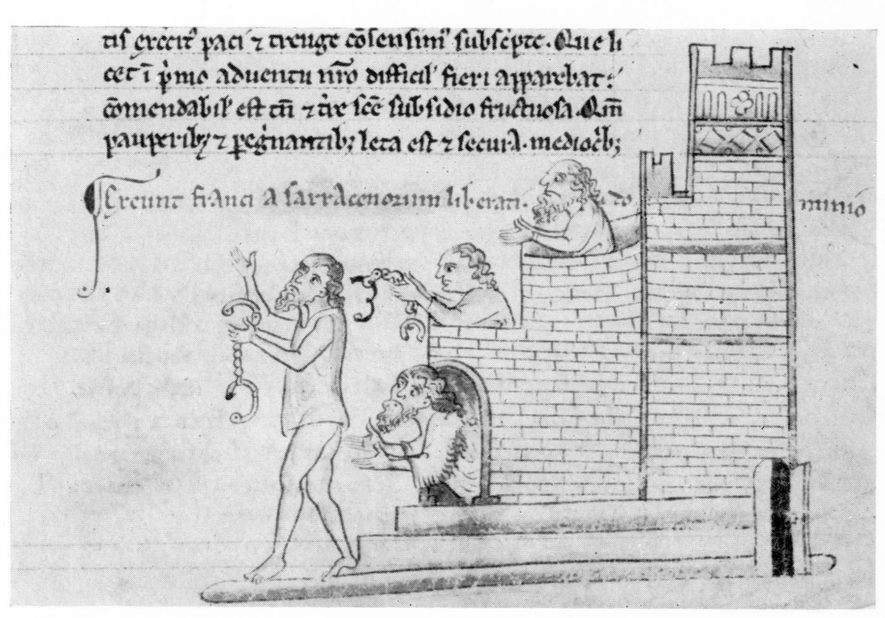

The release by Richard of the French prisoners of the Sultan, from Matthew Paris's *Chronica Majora*, MS. 16. C.C.C.C.

Frederick II's state elephant sent to meet Richard of Cornwall in the streets of Cremona on his return from the Holy Land, from Matthew Paris's *Chronica Majora*

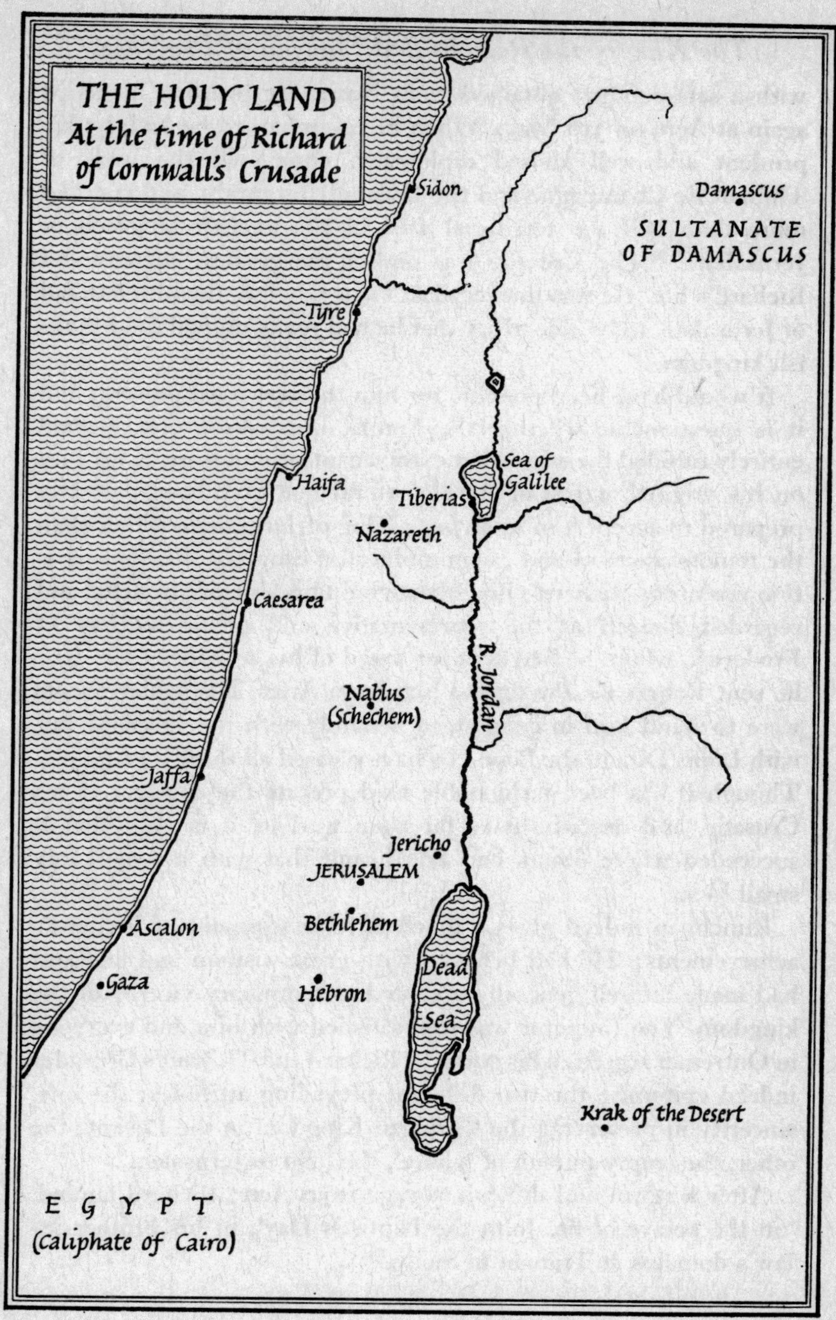
THE HOLY LAND
At the time of Richard of Cornwall's Crusade
Sidon
Damascus
SULTANATE OF DAMASCUS
Tyre
Sea of Galilee
Haifa
Tiberias
Nazareth
Caesarea
R. Jordan
Nablus (Schechem)
Jaffa
Jericho
JERUSALEM
Bethlehem
Ascalon
Dead Sea
Gaza
Hebron
Krak of the Desert
EGYPT
(Caliphate of Cairo)

with a safe-conduct obtained from Nasir. He boarded his ships again at Acre on 3rd May. 'When he re-embarked he had, by his prudent and well-advised diplomacy, completed the work of Thibaut de Champagne and the Duke of Burgundy, and restored more than half the territorial area of the ancient kingdom of Jerusalem.'[17] The Crusade was one of the greatest successes of Richard's life. He was the very last Prince, before the ultimate fall of Jerusalem, to be able to say that he had really unified the Frankish kingdom.

It would have been possible for him to exert regal powers; and it is questionable whether the Franks – in whose eyes he had entirely fulfilled the somewhat extravagant promises made for him on his original arrival at Acre – would not have been perfectly prepared to accept him as *de facto* King of Jerusalem, rather than the remote absentee and excommunicated Emperor. Such usurpation was not in Richard's line; throughout his Crusade he acted and regarded himself as the representative and plenipotentiary of Frederick, whom he had kept informed of his activities ever since he sent Robert de Twenge to him from Arles. His achievements were to stand him in good stead not only with the Emperor but with Louis IX and the Pope. To have pleased all three was unique. Though it has been fashionable to deprecate the conduct of his Crusade, and describe it as far from warlike, it is clear that it succeeded where others had failed, and that with a remarkably small loss.

Runciman indeed gives a much fairer assessment of Richard's achievements: 'He had behaved with great wisdom and tact and had made himself generally accepted as temporary viceroy of the kingdom. The Emperor was well satisfied with him and everyone in Outremer regretted his going.'[18] Richard and Thibaut's Crusades indeed epitomise the two different prevailing attitudes: the one, sincerity in preserving the Christian Kingdom in the Levant; the other, the empty pursuit of 'gloire', the 'trip to Jerusalem'.

After a storm and difficult voyage from Acre, Richard landed, 'on the octave of St. John the Baptist's Day', in his brother-in-law's domains at Trapani in Sicily.[19]

Simon de Montfort remained behind with the Duke of Burgundy. He too was held in such high esteem that some of the nobles of Outremer petitioned the Emperor, soon after Richard's departure, to appoint the Earl of Leicester governor of the Kingdom, but nothing came of it. It was, however, a significant indication of his power as a leader of men, even though his achievements in the Holy Land had been overshadowed by those of Richard. In the following year, 1242, Simon re-landed in his native France.

CHAPTER THREE

TO PARLEY WITH SAINT LOUIS

THE EMPEROR FREDERICK II prepared a welcome fit to gladden any weary Crusader's heart. After the flies and rotting corpses of Gaza, Richard revelled in baths, blood-letting and sleep, while to entertain him two Saracen girl-jugglers danced on rolling spheres. Matthew Paris gives a spirited drawing of these damsels, dressed in diaphanous robes of pale green, and perching precariously on their orbs.

More entertainment was to come. To delight Richard, Frederick produced his state elephant which paraded majestically through the streets of Cremona, bearing on its back a wooden platform on which were musicians playing a variety of instruments.[1] Whether Frederick also offered his brother-in-law the use of his oriental harem, the chronicler of St. Albans discreetly does not say. The Emperor did, however, permit him to see his sister, the Empress Isabella; and the way in which Matthew Paris describes the meeting makes it clear that this was a great concession even to a near relative.

Isabella, whose selection by the Imperial emissaries had been so colourful, and whose trousseau had been so ornate, was now a virtual prisoner in her own court. Guarded by eunuchs, she was allowed no visitors save, exceptionally, Richard. It was small wonder that she died shortly after he left; for his visit, with his first-hand stories of the Crusade, and his news – though rather stale – from England, must have been one of the few brighter moments in her repressed and monotonous existence. Evidently the personality of Frederick was so forceful that nothing Richard could say would better his unfortunate sister's lot.*

* Frederick's first wife, Isabella de Brienne, had fared little better and died after a bare year of married life.

In gratitude for all the kindness shown him, Richard undertook a peacemaking mission which, had it succeeded, would have prevented his own election to the throne of Germany. That possibility he could not then foresee, and he went to Rome in an endeavour to heal the breach between the Emperor and the Pope. Few other peacemakers could have been as acceptable as he, yet the intractable old Pope Gregory, the Cardinals and the Curia, received his overtures with ill-concealed contempt. Mortified, Richard returned to the Emperor empty-handed; but it was some consolation that Frederick said he had expected no other result. The breach between the Papacy and the Hohenstaufen was too wide for anyone to bridge. Even a later attempt by the 'most Christian Prince in Christendom', King Louis, and his enlightened mother, met with no greater success.

After spending some four months at the Emperor's Court Richard set out for home, Frederick giving him his Marshal to accompany him to the limits of the Empire. The chroniclers do not say at exactly what point the Marshal took his farewell, nor is there any record of the precise route Richard took. Subsequent events, however, point clearly to his having called again at Tarascon to visit the Princess Sanchia: it was an opportunity not to be missed after an absence of a year.

Sanchia's features are not perpetuated for us by any remaining effigy or picture, but the chroniclers agree on her dazzling beauty. At her coronation at Aachen sixteen years later she was still the cynosure of all eyes.[2] Extremely intelligent and clear-headed – as is shown by her epistolary style – she was also very ambitious; and having seen her two elder sisters become Queens she longed to do the same herself. An improbable story is told of the three elder sisters, Marguerite, Eleanor and Sanchia, having become respectively Queens of France, England and Germany (which could not have been before 1257, after which there is no record of their all three having met) insisting on the youngest, Beatrice, sitting on a stool at their feet to mark the difference in rank.

As yet, Sanchia was not married. It must, however, have come as a shock to Richard to learn that this beautiful girl, whom he already loved for her own sake and not for any potential territorial gains,[3] had been betrothed by proxy at Aix-en-Provence on 11th August, 1241, to the Count Raymond of Toulouse, her father's ancient enemy. This was a purely political match, designed to heal the breach which had led to such bitter fighting in Provence for so many years. Raymond had been married before and his previous marriage had just been annulled. The betrothal was the direct sequel to a treaty made between him and Raymond Bérenger on 2nd June.

Richard took no positive steps then, but – probably intending to get Henry's backing – hastened home. He arrived at Dover on 7th January, 1242, where his brother, Queen Eleanor, and a great gathering of nobles were awaiting him. As soon as his ship came alongside the two brothers rushed into each other's arms.[4] A slow and joyful progress followed, taking a week to Canterbury and a further fortnight to London, where the bells were ringing and the streets had been decorated by the populace with trappings and branches in Richard's honour.[5] The fame of his positive achievements in the Holy Land had long preceded him, and the Londoners were eager to acclaim him as a national hero – an honour accorded last to his famous namesake and uncle.

He was not left long in peace to make plans for his marriage. Henry immediately urged him to accompany him on a campaign to recover the territories in Poitou now threatened by Louis. This was a foolish venture, the blame for which can be laid squarely at their mother's door. Isabella of Angoulême, still very beautiful – 'a splendid animal rather than a stateswoman'[6] – completely dominated her husband, the Count Hugo de la Marche. Henry and Richard were therefore placed in the unfortunate position of being unable to disregard any demand or request of the fickle and untrustworthy Count; for their mother was always in the background, and they were forced to assume honesty on her part at least. The campaign in Poitou on which the brothers soon embarked was caused principally by Isabella considering herself insulted by the King of France.

Joinville describes how King Louis had taken the castle of

Saumur and held a great feast in the hall 'which it was said the great King Henry of England had built for his major festivals'.[7] Here Louis knighted his brother Alphonse, and a fortnight later, at Poitiers, invested him with the title of Count of Poitou, which Henry III had granted to Richard in 1225.

Alphonse received the homage of Hugo de la Marche, who was Count of Angoulême in the right of Isabella.[8] This would have been galling enough for the ex-Queen, but Louis and his mother kept her waiting three days before they would receive her at their court in Poitiers and, when they did at length do so, did not invite her to sit down. As John's widow she considered herself of equal status,[9] and flew into a fury, shutting herself up in the castle of Angoulême and refusing to emerge until Hugo agreed to her demands that he should send off urgent messages to her son imploring him to come and drive Louis out of Poitou. Henry had always treasured dreams of recovering Normandy; it was unthinkable that he should let Poitou also slip out of his grasp. So when Hugo, declaring himself the English King's liege man, bombarded him with pleas for military aid, he rapidly imposed a new scutage on his unwilling barons. Hugo had promised him all necessary military and pecuniary aid, and Henry believed him. Richard, wiser than Henry, did not view the proposed expedition with any favour at all; yet the granting of Poitou to Alphonse stuck in his gorge. His mother had taken care to see that he was apprised of it. The barons were even less enthusiastic, and very grudgingly paid the new scutage, thirty marks on each knight's fee, which Henry imposed to cover the costs of the campaign. In their view the King's stepfather was dragging him into an unnecessary war in time of truce in order to settle a personal vendetta of his wife's.[10] They were very right, for Louis had no wish to provoke a conflict with anyone; indeed his reign stands out as one of the most prosperous and peaceful in all French history. What Isabella depicted to Henry as encroachments were to Louis the natural admission of overlordship by men who held fiefs from him and were therefore already his vassals.

Henry's preparations were typical. He made a pilgrimage to

various shrines, including his favourite priory of Bromholm in Norfolk, and spent much time and money ordering himself splendid apparel and having his ship fitted with painted, panelled cabins. Brittany had not taught him a lesson. Eventually the royal brothers sailed out of Portchester on 15th May, 1242, with a force of six earls and 300 knights, as well as thirty barrels filled with silver.

Two days later they arrived at the Pointe Saint-Mathieu, on the westernmost tip of Brittany north-west of Brest. It was Sunday, so they came ashore to hear divine service at the Abbey on the headland, and sailed on next day to the mouth of the Gironde, landing at Royan on the Poitevin side to be received honourably by Reginald de Pons and other local magnates. Reginald was as untrustworthy as Hugo; they were both to desert the English cause together.

Hugo, meanwhile, had been unable to contain his impatience at the slow arrival of the English, and had begun hostilities on his own.[11] This was awkward, since Henry and Louis were still nominally at peace as a result of the truce renewed between Louis and Richard in Paris in 1240. As soon as Henry learnt of Hugo's activities, therefore, he wrote to Louis on 16th June advising him that the treaty was to be abrogated as from the eighteenth.[12]

Louis was busy besieging Hugo's castle of Fontenay, but found time to send Henry a courteous reply, suggesting that he should not involve himself on behalf of the Count de la Marche. When it was clear that Henry was too much under his stepfather's influence to pay any heed, Louis addressed his nobles, expressing his doubtless sincere grief that he was compelled to fight a relative, whose wife and his were sisters. Fontenay now fell to him and among the prisoners taken was none other than one of Count Hugo's sons. The French barons were for hanging him and his retainers at once, as an example to others; but Louis observed, with his usual magnanimity, that the young man did not deserve to die for supporting his father, nor did his henchmen for following their lord faithfully: instead, he would send them as prisoners to Paris.[13]

Fontenay is in the Vendée, the sandy, heathy country on the

coast just north of La Rochelle. Some fifty kilometres to the south-west the river Charente debouches into the sea near Rochefort; farther inland it comes out of the hillier country through the narrow valley of Taillebourg, twelve kilometres or so north of the large town of Saintes, where the vineyards cover the hillsides. Between Saintes and the Gironde estuary lies the triangle of land called the Saintonge, and across this Henry and Richard now made their way from Royan, where they had landed, to Pons, where they met Count Hugo. The news of Louis's capture of Fontenay reached them, and Henry realized it was vital for them to hold the pass at Taillebourg against him, to prevent him passing from the coastal-belt into the hills. He asked Reginald and Hugo what plans they had for ensuring the safety of Taillebourg: they were very reassuring. Their friend and ally, Geoffroy de Rançon, the third of the great magnates of Poitou, would, they said, hold the pass against all comers.

Henry, lulled into a false sense of security, did not hurry. He actually by-passed Taillebourg, without bothering to confirm the truth of his allies' statements, and marched farther down-river to a point close to the castle of Tonnay. There, in a meadow beside the Charente, he pitched camp and began to enjoy what he considered to be the true sport of campaigning – feasting and granting honours to supposed friends. Among those whom he knighted were two more sons of Count Hugo, the King's half-brothers. After six days' dalliance, he learned that Louis was approaching rapidly from the north. It behoved him to get to Taillebourg first to reinforce Geoffroy de Rançon; so, relying on the advice of Count Hugo, he advanced under cover of night and pitched his tents on a meadow opposite Taillebourg whence a high-arched bridge led across the Charente to the town and castle perched on its rock.[14]

When day broke an astonished and horrified Henry beheld across the river, a stone's throw away, the pennants and ensigns of a vast French army, and enough tents to make a large town.[15] Above them flew the oriflamme, signifying no quarter to the enemies of France.

Conflicting communiqués were current in those days as now:

Matthew Paris had it that the English had by that time 1,600 knights to the French 4,000, while Joinville patriotically claimed that Henry had twenty men to Louis's one. As Joinville was only seventeen at the time, and as his account of what happened does not accord with other sources, it is probably wiser to believe Paris. Joinville's version was clearly embellished by hearsay, for he wrote that the French forces crossed the bridge and attacked the English, which in fact was just what did not happen.[16]

Henry, after one glance, realized that the pass and castle had fallen; and there was no sign of Geoffrey de Rançon. He turned on Count Hugo. '"My Lord Count and father,' he said reproachfully, "where is your promised help now? When we were still in England we received your messengers and letters patent, assuring us that when necessary you would provide all the soldiers we needed to resist the King of France, and money too." Richard agreed, adding: "I have your letters patent here in this very camp." To this the Count de la Marche retorted, "I never signed any such letters." "Father, what did I hear you say?" cried the astonished King. "Did you not keep sending us impassioned pleas, begging me to come here? Where is what you promised?" At this the Count Hugo swore a horrible oath: "I never did any such thing. Impute it to my wife, your mother. By the throat of God, I am guiltless of her machinations."'[17]

As the full force of Hugo's treachery broke in on him, Henry paused irresolute. Not so Richard. He saw very clearly the only possible action which could be taken to save the King and the English army, and going to his tent had his squire strip him of his armour and put upon him the pilgrim's smock which he had worn at Jerusalem. Then, taking his staff in his hand, he set off alone across the bridge to parley with King Louis.[18]

The narrow valley lay peaceful; it was Sunday morning.[19] The two armies watched him in almost complete silence until he reached the enemy sentinels, when a great shout rang out, and in a moment all the French knights were cheering him. Many came and knelt before him, acclaiming him as their liberator in the Holy Land. It was a touching and emotional moment.

They brought him in to Louis, who received him honourably, despite the very different circumstances from their last meeting. Richard explained that he had come to beg a truce. Louis replied that he would grant him one till the morrow, partly because he was his kinsman, partly because it was Sunday, but principally because of his action in the Holy Land whereby he had found such favour in France.[20] As Richard was about to leave the royal tent King Louis rose and kissed him, saying: 'My Lord Earl, I have granted you this truce that you may deliberate – for the night brings counsel with it.'

Richard recrossed the bridge to the English camp and spoke to Henry privately and urgently: 'Quick, quick, away with us or we shall all be taken prisoner.' They could do nothing during daylight which might attract attention, but the moment the sun went down they began breaking camp; and when it was completely dark the army moved silently off, led by the King himself on a fast charger. It was little more than a disorderly rabble of angry men and hungry, unmanageable horses,[21] but at least it was an effective withdrawal. When day broke King Louis looked again to see if he were dreaming when he beheld the meadows across the Charente empty.

He wasted no time, but pursued the English army southwards to Saintes. Here a considerable battle took place on 22nd July among the vineyards. The position was not nearly so favourable as the level meadows at Taillebourg would have been, and the vines hampered the attackers. In the end the French were victorious, and the English withdrew. A number of them, however, including Simon de Montfort – an unwilling recruit to Henry's forces – acquitted themselves well, and held the French off long enough to enable the King to make good his escape to Blaye on the Gironde, whither Louis did not bother to pursue him. Poitou was, after all, by now irretrievably lost to the English.

Count Hugo de la Marche, meanwhile, deserted Henry, 'having' as Matthew Paris says disgustedly, 'exhausted the King's treasury'. Realizing that it was high time he changed sides, Hugo sent the Count of Brittany and the Archbishop of Saintes secretly to Louis to ask for terms. Those he got were hard but, considering his behaviour, more than fair, and after some hesitation he decided to comply. Geoffroy de Rançon, who (he would have had Henry believe) was his ally who would have held the pass at Taillebourg, was on the contrary his bitterest enemy. He was among those at the French court at Poitiers who witnessed the ultimate humiliation of the proud Count Hugo and Isabella of Angoulême, kneeling with their children before King Louis to beg for mercy. Geoffroy, whom Hugo had wronged deeply, had sworn never to have his hair cut like a knight until the Count were defeated, and had worn it long like a woman. Now, seeing the de la Marches on their knees, he called for a barber and had his hair cut short forthwith before them all.[22]

After this disastrous campaign Henry withdrew to Gascony, where he spent the rest of the summer frittering away what treasury he had left, and quarrelling with his nobles, Richard among them. An open breach arose between the two over Henry's unjust treatment of William de Ros, a north-country knight who could not afford to continue his campaign. This was, however, only the last straw, coming on top of Henry's mishandling of the military situation, the loss of Richard's county of Poitou, and especially the tactless and toothless alliance which Henry had just concluded with Raymond of Toulouse, the man to whom Sanchia was betrothed.

A bitter argument ended with Richard withdrawing in heat from the Court at Bordeaux, and deciding to go off on his own to Tarascon to supplement the work of Pierre d'Aigueblanche, the Bishop of Hereford, whom he had already commissioned to go to Raymond Bérenger on his behalf with a formal offer for Sanchia's hand.[23] He now decided to get married there and then, if he could, and set out for Provence. Shortly before he reached Toulouse, however, he learned that Henry was preparing a trap to seize and imprison him. Accordingly Richard returned secretly to Bordeaux, and in the nick of time took ship with the Marshal and certain others of his friends, and sailed off down the Gironde for England.[24]

Having eluded one danger he was to encounter a much greater. Off Ushant his ships ran into a violent Atlantic storm. The little fleet was scattered, some vessels being driven on to the coast of

Brittany; but Richard's drove on at the mercy of the gale, in great danger of foundering. In the stress of the storm he prayed to the Virgin, vowing that, if saved, he would found an Abbey in her honour on his lands in Gloucestershire.[25] His prayer was answered. Somehow the master contrived to bring the ship round Peninnis Head and into the lee of Porth Enys in the Scillies. Matthew Paris, whose knowledge of the West Country was evidently hearsay, charmingly wrote that 'Earl Richard barely escaped death by reaching a certain island near Cornwall, which is called Scilly, being distant from Cornwall by the same space of sea as Dover is from Wissant, and encompassed on all sides by the ocean'.

CHAPTER FOUR

MARRIAGE TO SANCHIA

THE DATE of Richard's departure from Bordeaux was early in October, for he had witnessed a charter there on 30th September; but by 16th October he was well under way and Henry – as usual after his outbursts of anger – was feeling remorseful. On that day he issued a mandate to the Archbishop of York, Regent of England in his absence, 'to put at the disposal of Richard, Count of Poitou and Cornwall, who has stood by the King beyond the seas and is now returning home with his licence, houses, castles, forests, parks, stews and tanks, and to instruct, on behalf of the King, John de Frethorn to let the Count have two of the King's goshawks of the King's gift, and to put the other goshawks at his disposal. The King also wills that Henry de Haverill place the King's falcons at his disposal.'[1]

Before Richard could enjoy these peace-offerings he had had to endure the dangers of the ocean. Now, from Scilly, a fishing craft ran him to Newlyn while his own ship was licking her wounds; and so he made his way eastwards through his own county and among friends, from one castle to the next. At Restormel above the Fowey valley he was greeted by his aged vassal, Andrew de Cardinan, and his young and beautiful daughter Isolda, destined to become the most eligible heiress in Cornwall. It was probably Richard who gave her as a present the pet monkey whose skull is still preserved at Restormel Castle. Thence he called on the monks at Bodmin, paused briefly at his favourite Launceston, rode to Lydford to receive the report of his Perambulators, and thence to stay with his former ward, the Earl of Devon, at Okehampton. Baldwin had been one of the recipients of his long letter from the Holy Land; he was to remain a firm friend of Richard throughout his life.

His West Country calls completed, Richard put on more speed to come to London. On arrival there he learned that the news of his projected marriage to Sanchia had preceded him and was not at all favourably received by the baronage. They viewed with alarm the prospect of the arrival of a second Provençal princess, having bitter experience of the number of foreign relatives of Queen Eleanor who had been granted lands by the King and given high offices of state.[2]

Family news from France was likewise bad. Count Hugo de la Marche had been accused by a French knight of complicity in an attempt on the life of King Louis. In his rage he had challenged his accuser to a duel, but was brought to trial by his peers. Hearing the news, his wife, Isabella of Angoulême, mounted her horse and galloped to the castle where the trial was being held; and there – hearing that things were going against Hugo – she snatched the wimple from her head, tore it to shreds and stamped on it.[3] Then 'the Countess Isabella, former Queen of England, being smitten in her conscience by so much evil, fled to the sanctuary of the Abbey of Fontevrault, where she eked out her existence as a nun. For many of the French and indeed the Poitevins pursued her with implacable hatred, asserting that she should be called not Isabel but most impious Jezebel'.[4]

The shock of Hugo's trial was too much for her passionate nature, and her reason was unhinged; when she died three years later, as a lonely recluse, in remorse and shame, she gave orders that to expiate her sins she was to be buried not in a magnificent tomb but in the common grave at Fontevrault.

Meanwhile Pierre d'Aigueblanche, Bishop of Hereford, had been successful in his mission. Raymond Bérenger annulled the betrothal of Sanchia with the Count of Toulouse, accepted Richard's marriage proposal, and sent Sanchia, in the early autumn of 1243, to England in the care of her mother, the Countess Beatrice. The Count of Provence does not seem to have been over-fond of his third daughter; in his will of 1238 he made her a dowry of only 2,000 marks, compared with 10,000 each given to Marguerite and Eleanor, but he thought better of it later and added another 3,000.[5]

By his own admission, Beatrice, the youngest of the four, had always been his favourite. A compensating reason may have been that no extensive dowry was necessary to cement a political match between Provence and England in this case. That had already been done with Eleanor, and Richard's and Sanchia's was a love-match pure and simple.

Marguerite de Provence entertained her mother and sister with lavish delight when they reached Paris. On 14th November, 1243, they landed at Dover with what Matthew Paris disapprovingly describes as 'great magnificence and overmuch ostentation', although he admits that the Countess Beatrice was 'of great charm and beauty, wise and affable'.[6] At the King's command many of the English nobility awaited her arrival on shore. Henry also commanded the citizens of London to decorate the city from London Bridge to Westminster with banners, hangings and other ornaments, and to remove 'all mud, filth and offensive matter from the travellers' sight'. Many nobles from remote parts of England and neighbouring parts of Scotland also came to meet the Countess and her daughter by the King's command.[7] The inference is that the demonstrations of enthusiasm were not entirely spontaneous.

The marriage of Richard of Cornwall and Sanchia de Provence in Westminster Abbey on St. Clement's Day was one of the most splendid occasions of the century. At the end of the service Richard dowered his wife at the Abbey door with a third part of all his lands, and the castle and manor of Berkhamsted.[8] The wedding feast was, to quote Matthew Paris, stupendous; indeed, he modestly says that if he gave details of all the magnificence his readers would be bored; but 'in brief the royal kitchens prepared no less than thirty thousand dishes for the diners.' Eyes and thoughts of the beholders were dazzled by the unheard of richness of the occasion, the glittering line of royalty – the King, the bridegroom, the Queen 'sister of the bride Cincia (she changed her name, and is now known as Scientia) and the Countess Beatrice of Provence, as well as innumerable other magnates'.[9] Whether this alteration in the bride's name were true is doubtful: it always baffled the medieval chroniclers, who served it up in various forms – Schenchia, Sehenchia, Sancia, Cincia and even Sench – while to the French she was Sanche or Sancie. The King went out of his way to be charming to his new sister-in-law, and well he might, for however much the English resented her impecunious relatives, they could not but admire the great beauty of the new Countess of Cornwall. Among the guests at the wedding feast were Simon de Montfort and his Countess; for he had returned to England shortly before, bringing with him his wife and three sons, Henry, Guy and Simon, the eldest now six, the youngest three.

The Calendar of Patent Rolls contains an amusing little postscript to the sumptuous wedding feast: 'Notification that the service of the King's buttery which the barons of London did for the King on Sunday the feast of St. Cecilia this year at Westminster, when Richard Earl of Cornwall espoused Sanchia, daughter of the Count of Provence, was done voluntarily at the instance of the King and not of debt, and lest this should be to the prejudice of them or their heirs hereafter the King has caused these letters to be made.'[10]

The matter of Richard's and Sanchia's lands and finances were also regularized in a most careful covenant:

> Made on the morrow of St. Andrew at Westminster between the King and the Earl his brother touching all the demands and rights which the Earl says he has in all lands, castles, counties, honours and knights' fees as well in England and Ireland as in parts beyond and this side of the seas, which King John, their father, ever had when he was Count, and touching which the Earl has submitted himself to the will and disposal of the King.
>
> The Earl quit-claims the King and his heirs all demands and actions, right and claim which he had to this day in whatever of the above King John had when he was Count, saving the County of Cornwall, the honour of Wallingford, the honour of Eye, with all castles, towns and advowsons of churches which he had on the day of the covenant made between the King and him touching him and Lady Senchia his wife and the heirs of their bodies. He also quit-claims the King the right and claim which he had in Gascony by reason of the gift which the King made him of it at Saintes or by any other reason unless the King confer Gascony on him again of his mere liberality.

And for all this the King grants that he or his heirs will grant to him and Senchia his wife and the heirs of their bodies land to the value of 500.l a year in escheats* that may fall in England. And this as soon as the said escheats fall in, except castles and ancient demesne belonging to the Crown, by extent made by juries of the vicinage, and so that the King shall hold no escheats in his hands until this is done, to hold for their lives, with reversion on the death of either. And in the meantime they shall have 1,000 marks a year at the Exchequer of London, the proportion of the said escheats to be deducted therefrom as they receive them, to wit for every 100.l of land 200 marks shall be deducted at the Exchequer, and so soon as the full amount of 500.l of escheats is assigned, the 1,000 marks at the Exchequer is to cease. Also at every assignment of an escheat the King shall make them a charter, and at the end one charter of the total.[11]

The King also saw to Sanchia's provision should she become a widow; for on 4th January, 1244, while he was doubtless still full of good Wallingford Christmas cheer, he granted 'to Senchia, wife of the Earl of Cornwall, the King's brother, that in the case of his death, while she and her heirs by her survive, she shall have the custody of all the lands which the said earl has appointed to the use of the said heirs, during their minority; but in case of her death during such minority the custody of the said lands shall revert to the King'.[12]

These documents, bearing the imprint of the careful financier which Richard had become, cemented the prosperity of himself and his wife. Already the King had been frequently in his debt and had raised loans from him for all sorts of purposes; in 1239 he had borrowed £100 from Richard for work on the Tower of London, and as the years passed this reliance on Richard as banker grew. The stage was now set for his assuming the role of financier of the realm.

The London festivities over, the Court, including the Montforts, went down to Wallingford to spend Christmas with its newly-

* *Escheat :* The reversion of a fee to the Crown or overlord if the owner died intestate without heirs.

Demesne : This word, from which 'domain' is derived, basically meant the land close to the manor house or castle which the lord kept in his own hands. Hence by extension a royal manor.

Ancient demesne : Specifically crown land at the time of Domesday Book.

married lord and lady. In the prevailing atmosphere of bonhomie the Countess of Provence took the opportunity to approach the King about the lack of a marriage-portion for Eleanor de Montfort when she married Simon. The beautiful and talented Beatrice wanted to do the King's sister some good in return for all the benefits showered on her own relatives; and the King, who admired her greatly, granted her wish. The most spectacular evidence of her success was the grant of Kenilworth Castle to Simon; this, coupled to Odiham, meant that there were placed in the hands of the Earl and Countess of Leicester two of the finest castles in the realm which in later years were to prove the two principal pivots of Simon's power.

CHAPTER FIVE

FINANCIER OF THE REALM

THE FESTIVITIES at Wallingford over, the Countess Beatrice 'with many other English and Provençal nobles of both sexes' returned to London at the feast of the Circumcision so that they could celebrate Saint Edward's festival there before she returned home. 'Which being done, the Countess directed her course seawards to return to her native parts, the King and a large number of the magnates of the realm accompanying her to the coast. But before the Countess could board her ships at Dover, messengers reached her with the doleful news of the illness unto death of her husband, the Count Raymond of Provence. When the King heard this, he grieved inconsolably and offered prayer and alms to God to have mercy upon him.'[1]

Raymond Bérenger, on his deathbed, called his youngest and unmarried daughter Beatrice before him and said to her: 'Dearest daughter, you have always been the most loving of all your sisters to me; I know that by God's will all my daughters save only you have been married nobly and exaltedly in the eyes of all Christendom. To you therefore, the only one yet to be married, I give and leave in my will all my lands, treasure, castles and possessions. For your sisters are not poor and I have made provision for them elsewhere.'[2] This was in fact the law of Provence, that daughters who had already received dowries could have no part in the estate of their father.[3] Sanchia, as we have seen, had come off less well than her elder sisters, and considerably less well than Beatrice, which doubtless encouraged her to support Richard's careful moves to amass wealth for her in England.

The immediate result of Raymond Bérenger leaving everything to Beatrice was that a Provençal noble endeavoured to carry her off, and would have succeeded but for King Louis's intervention. A horde of suitors suddenly appeared for this eligible young woman. The Emperor demanded her for his son Konrad, and sent a naval squadron to parade ostentatiously on the coasts of Provence to indicate that he would not be trifled with. Raymond of Toulouse, baulked of Sanchia, had already had discussions with Raymond Bérenger about the possibility of his marrying Beatrice, and now came forward openly, only to be frustrated by the opposition of the Pope, who regarded him as far too sympathetic towards the heretics of Albi. James of Aragon wanted her for his son Pedro, and sent his forces to threaten Aix-en-Provence by land, as Frederick had by sea. Finally, however, the choice fell on none of these, but on a suitor whose candidature was supported by Pope Innocent IV – King Louis's younger brother, Charles of Anjou.[4]

Meanwhile in England another member of the house of Provence had been delivered of a son – Queen Eleanor, who, on Saint Marcellus's Day 1244 gave birth to a second boy, 'and the King in his joy bestowed the name Edmund upon him'.[5] This was the future Crouchback, sometime puppet King of Sicily.

'About the same time rumours of bad news from the Holy Land increased so that it was feared that the whole territory would be lost; Earl Richard, from his natural generosity, sent about a thousand pounds to the Hospitallers.'[6] But it was in vain; since Richard's departure four years before, there had been no authoritative hand guiding the destinies of the Kingdom of Jerusalem. Frederick, the titular monarch, and the Pope, who were the most interested parties, continued to quarrel, and the Sultan Aiyub of Egypt quietly made his plans. That same year a band of Khwarazmian Turks fell upon the Holy City and defeated the Frankish garrison, while a similar disaster befell a Christian force at Gaza attacked by the Saracens under the Emir Baibars Bunduqdari. All Richard's work was undone; and Frederick, though he wrote at length to Henry III bewailing the loss of Jerusalem, did not attempt to return to the Holy Land. Only King Louis, desperately ill with malaria, determined to take the Cross, and did so just before Christmas, 1244, as soon as he was strong enough even to speak.[7]

Richard was sick at heart at the news from Palestine, but he had his hands full at home, working on his brother's behalf. In the summer he went north, and on 13th August negotiated a treaty with Alexander of Scotland at Newcastle, by which the King of the Scots delivered the castle to him.[8] With Richard safely out of the way, it was the opportunity for the Welsh; and an attack was mounted by their Prince David, against whom Henry sent only a feeble detachment because his treasury was, as usual, empty. He needed loans from his brother; but unfortunately, when Richard did take a hand, ugly rumours started to circulate. He was said to have retired to his castle of Tintagel, feigning illness, in order to plot there secretly with David of Wales. It was suggested that the desire to receive a relative – for David was Henry and Richard's nephew – was merely a pretext for the meeting; but that the real motive was Richard's wish to do a deal with the Welsh, and to obtain for himself the County of Chester, which he had already sought of the King. It was added that Henry, prevailed upon by Eleanor of Provence, had refused to grant it to him, whereupon Richard, out of pique, had entered into treacherous liaison with the Welsh.

All this has the ingredients of a first-class Court scandal. The mystique of Cornwall is still great; in the thirteenth century it was as remote as the moon. To rumour-mongers it must have been very spicy to picture Richard skulking on his cliff-top while David's ship slunk into Padstow, and then the two of them conferring in secret in a dark and windswept tower above Merlin's cave.

Matthew Paris scornfully deflates the rumours with the voice of reason: 'This is not worth believing, for when the King had run short of money in the construction of his castle of Gannock, and in paying the army, the same Earl, moved by generosity and brotherly compassion came to the King's aid to the tune of three thousand marks.'[9] Certainly there was no overt sign of discord between the brothers then; and in November Richard was appointed one of a committee of twelve to report upon the reform of the realm. It was the Parliament of the barons who appointed him, and this in itself is evidence of the trust they reposed in him in comparison with the erratic King.

In the early part of 1245 the country was in a turmoil about Henry's favour to the Papal agent, Master Martin, whose exactions were the source of great bitterness. Master Martin's visit got off to a bad start, as Paris describes sarcastically; 'a certain messenger of the Pope, weighed down with many Bulls, landed at Dover. Directly the constable of that port learned of his intentions, he took all his letters off him and imprisoned him in the castle of Dover. When Master Martin heard this he hastened to the King, complaining. The King denied that he was the author of this act, and returned the letters seized from the messenger at Dover to Master Martin'.[10] It was not the last time that the logical actions of the officers at the ports were interfered with by higher authority for political ends, nor the last time that such interference brought its own reward.

The barons decided that this was not good enough, and took the law into their own hands. Martin was in reality nothing more than a collector of taxes for the Pope against the Emperor, with whom baronial sympathies were much more attuned. That same summer the barons collected Master Martin, informed him that they might possibly succeed in escorting him to Dover before his throat was cut – though they were not very sanguine – and agreed to his immediate plea for an escort to the coast. In blatant panic throughout the journey, Martin was thankful to escape across the Channel. Matthew Paris, though a monk and a good churchman, believed in the independence of the national church, and devotes one of his most scathing passages to Martin's rapacity.

The incident was one of the first stirrings which indicated that the barons were not prepared to sit passively by and let Henry III act against their interests. By the following spring he had taken the point sufficiently to join with his Parliament in protesting against Papal exactions from the English clergy. Richard's attitude in the matter was equivocal: at one point he was backing the barons against Master Martin, at another he and several bishops threatened Henry in order to make him comply with Papal demands. It is an inescapable fact that Richard's generally admirable character is marred by occasional tergiversations of this nature, and equally inescapable that they occurred for personal ends. At the present juncture he was grinding two axes; obtaining monies still due to him for his Crusade, and preparing to fulfil the vow made at sea three years earlier.

He and Sanchia spent Christmas in London with Henry and Eleanor. The year had witnessed the sudden extinction of the male line of the Marshals. The end had come with the sudden deaths of Walter and Anselm, the two youngest of the sons of the great Regent. Gilbert, who succeeded Richard as Marshal, was killed at a tournament at Hereford in 1241, while Richard of Cornwall was still away on Crusade. Gilbert was succeeded by Walter; but 'in the same year (1245) on the eighth day of December Walter Earl Marshal went the way of all flesh and was buried at Tintern, not far from Striguil, where many of his illustrious predecessors are entombed. And a little later, that is to say on the third day before Christmas, Anselm the next younger brother of the same Earl did likewise'.[11] There remained the three surviving daughters, each of whom was married to one of the principal Earls of the realm, and the great Marshal estates were divided amongst them. The sole link left with Isabella, apart from her three sisters, was Richard's young son Henry, now ten years of age. He had just become a page in his father's household, and seems to have been on very good terms with his stepmother; a discordant element was however introduced when Guy and Simon, the young sons of Simon and Eleanor de Montfort, were brought into Richard's *familia* in a similar capacity. Memories of Isabella were also evoked by a visit which Richard and Sanchia paid to Beaulieu the same summer. Attended by the three pages, they accompanied King Henry and Queen Eleanor when Bishop William Raleigh of Winchester dedicated the church of the great Cistercian Abbey which King John had founded forty-two years earlier.

Isabella's was the only royal grave in the newly-dedicated Abbey; a leaden coffin shaped to her figure had been placed beneath the slab. Matthew Paris writes that 'when the dedication of the said church had been accomplished with the greatest solemnity, Earl Richard took with him about thirteen monks from the said church to a certain house of the Cistercian order which he had founded from his own wealth, to dwell therein. This House, which lay not far from the Priory of Winchcombe, in a pleasant enough spot, was built by the said Earl for the redemption of his soul in accordance with the vow which he had made when in peril of the sea, and was endowed very abundantly by him. It is impossible to believe that all this could have happened without God's help.'[12]

The Abbey referred to was Hayles, which indeed lay in a pleasant enough spot, a well-watered valley sheltered beneath the western escarpment of the Cotswolds, tactfully screened by an intervening hill from Winchcombe, lest the Prior there might feel jealous of a great new House rising hard by.

Here at that time stood the small parish church of Hayles, some hundred years old, a mill, and a few farms making up Richard's manor. 'About thirteen monks' whom Richard brought from Beaulieu actually meant the Prior of Beaulieu, released by the Abbot there to become the first Abbot of Hayles, and twelve brethren – one of whom was the master-mason, Brother John 'Cementarius', under whose guidance the beautiful Cotswold stone began to rise rapidly on the plan of nave, transepts and choir, very similar in design to the mother house in the New Forest. The only permanent building available for the royal party to occupy was the mill, and therefore they had to be content with tents. It was a somewhat rough and ready existence and Richard did not stop long, but rode off to London on his brother's business, leaving Sanchia in charge. She was in advanced pregnancy, so discomfort was added to responsibility in the makeshift conditions.

Sanchia was probably not sorry to leave Hayles for Wallingford. 'The same year also Cincia, Countess of Cornwall, the wife of Earl Richard, gave birth to a son. After her childbed the King and Queen and many of the nobles of England gathered at Wallingford on the day of her churching and celebrated the occasion with a banquet, at which Earl Richard, rejoicing, gave thanks to God for so much favour.'[13] But his joy was short-lived; for the baby, of whose name we cannot be sure, but who was probably called after Richard, died after living a bare month. It was, as in the case of Isabella's first two children, almost certainly the result of another disturbed and over-strenuous pregnancy; and, if so, this was the price of Hayles. Nevertheless, Sanchia was always kindly disposed to Wallingford, the birthplace of her firstborn, and it was to the Prior there that she wrote an account of her later experiences as Queen of Germany.

The years 1246–7 provide a remarkable illustration of two of Richard's chief characteristics, piety and business acumen. After the foundation of Hayles he turned to the more mundane matter of supervising the re-coinage of the realm. At a gathering of magnates, or Parliament, at Oxford, in April, 1247, bitter complaints were made that because of the clipping of all coins under twenty marks in value it was a commonplace to find that three pieces were needed to provide the correct weight of two.[14] The King therefore ordered the withdrawal of all such old coins, which were to be pierced to show they were no longer legal tender. On 14th April he appointed Richard to take charge of the complete re-coinage of the country. Several mint towns in England were appointed to issue the new coins, but the actual date of introduction varied from place to place.[15] As to who was responsible for the debasement of the coinage, it was proved unquestionably to be principally the work of the Jews and Flemings; but, luckily for the Jews, Richard gave them his protection, for they were at this juncture much too useful for him to allow anything to happen to them.

In his typically meticulous way he made sure that he had all the powers he needed, and the craftsmen required for the task. On 12th July, 1247, the King granted to Richard 'that he may make new money in the King's name in England, Ireland and Wales from All Saints, in the thirty-second year of the reign of King Henry III, for twelve years, on condition that the King have a moiety of the exchange and mint. Grant also that before any partition of any profit the Earl and his assigns or executors shall receive so much by tale of the new money as they put of their old money to make the new money. Grant further that the King will cause to be observed all laws, compacts and customs belonging to the mint ancient and approved or to be approved for the common utility for the period.'[16] On 28th August at Windsor the King issued power to one Rayner of Brussels 'to conduct from beyond the seas into England at the King's expense all ministers knowing of any kind of minting or exchange of silver, to do in the realm what belongs to the office of each, and to receive the wages according to the approved customs of the King's exchange and to stay in safety there and return'.[17]

Richard originally provided the necessary capital and undertook to farm the mint for twelve years. He was given complete powers to do so. He set up seventeen local mints, each staffed with its own officials, who were supplied from London with dies and enough new coin to begin their work.

Between them they made an excellent job of it, and Earl Richard – by judiciously farming the mint – lined his pockets nicely. The populace was not so fortunate. Travelling to the exchange offices, which were often more than a day's journey from their homes, they found that instead of receiving a new coin in exchange for an old on a *per caput* basis, their old coins were weighed, and they received only the equivalent of the weight of the old ones back in the new currency. For every pound, the officials deducted a charge of thirteen pennies; and the unfortunate citizen found himself with about two-thirds of his original wealth.

This struck home at the same time as a general rise in the cost of living, and rightly or wrongly engendered a great wave of public resentment against Richard, 'who was regarded as the soul of the whole transaction.'[18]

As far as Richard was concerned, the re-coinage came at a useful time, for he had recently made the unpalatable discovery that finds of tin in Germany were bidding fair to rival the trade of his Cornish mines, hitherto undisputed suppliers of the European tin market. Henry had moreover declared as recently as 4th July, 1247, that he stood 10,000 marks, or say £7,000, in his brother's debt. Therefore on 20th July, at Marlborough, Richard prudently obtained 'a bond in 1,000 marks payable next Michaelmas which by order of the King he delivered as a loan in the Wardrobe to Peter Chacepore, Keeper of the same Wardrobe';[19] that is to say of the King's privy treasury. A tithe had thus been redeemed; the re-coinage provided a source of income with which to offset the loss of the tin mines.

As a further supply Richard fell back on his Crusade tax, which had never been adequately collected, although it should have been paid to him in 1240 when he was in the Holy Land. The tax had been granted by special authority of Pope Gregory, and King Henry had issued a half-hearted order to the Bishop of both Provinces for its collection while Richard was still refortifying Ascalon. This had not had much effect, and Pope Innocent had repeated the demands in 1244 through Master Martin. Richard now wanted the money to get on with the construction of Hayles. He kept pressing the Pope, who issued another letter to the English clergy and appointed two more emissaries, John Sarrazenus and Giles de Vocumb (later replaced by Bernard de Nympha) to go to England to drive up the laggards.[20] Coming so soon after the extortions of Master Martin, this was calculated to make Richard more unpopular than ever. The Pope's emissaries wrote to the Bishop of Lincoln, Robert Grossetete, on 4th June, 1247, fixing 19th August as the date for all archdeacons of his diocese to appear at St. Mark's Church in London to report on what progress they had made. Grossetete ordered the archdeacons to report to him on the thirteenth before they set off. In the event, said Matthew Paris, Richard collected 'enormous sums, and it was said that one archdeaconate alone produced six hundred pounds'.[21]

It required a further Bull from Innocent at the end of the year really to get things going. Preachers for a new Crusade moved through the country, and priests and monks in white robes carrying crosses and banners went in procession to meet them, accompanied by a great throng of laity. The preachers themselves received the Crusading vows of the people, only to sell them indulgences from them a few days later. The money from these indulgences paid Richard's crusading tax[22] and also met some of the Pope's own demands. It was not a pretty picture, very different from the real

Crusade which Louis was preparing across the water. Richard of course could argue that it was all in a pious cause, namely the construction of Hayles.

This contradictory streak in his character again exhibited itself in the matter of the tomb of Archbishop Edmund Rich of Canterbury. The saintly Primate had gone to France in chagrin and disgust after the marriage of Simon de Montfort and Eleanor, and had been buried at Pontigny in Burgundy;* but in 1247 Louis had arranged his translation to a more worthy grave in the Abbey there. Richard, who was his particular admirer, was ill at the time and was very upset when the news reached him that the translation had taken place in his absence. He prayed to Saint Edmund Rich for recovery from his illness, and in due course got better. In gratitude, he vowed to have the front part of the new coffin made of precious ore.[23] In the eyes of baronage and common people this was sheer extravagance for which they had been mulcted.

The opportunity for Richard to visit the saint's shrine in person was now forthcoming because of the second Crusade of the King of France. Louis IX announced that before his departure he would clear his conscience by making restitution to any he had wronged. Henry III jumped at the offer, putting quite the wrong construction on it, and sent Richard to France to ask for the return of Normandy. No one in his right mind could possibly have anticipated success – Richard certainly did not; but he liked Louis, and it provided him with a good excuse to go to Pontigny. He even took young Henry with him,[24] but apparently Sanchia stayed at home.

Richard knelt at the saint's shrine, offered thanksgiving for his recovery, and gave the Abbot the promised new coffin-front of precious ore, and also a bracelet worked with gold and precious stones.[25] Then 'on the day of Saints Simon and Jude he returned from parts beyond the sea, bringing his son Henry with him'. Small wonder that the people labelled him hypocrite, 'ever trickard', when he was kneeling at a saint's shrine while his extortioners were preaching an empty Crusade. But according to his own lights he was an honourable and logical man.

* See p. 55.

An unexpected criticism was, however, awaiting him on his return, in the shape of a bitter reproach from his brother-in-law the Emperor, who upbraided him with having used his Crusade tax to get money to export to Frederick's enemy, the Pope, and with having accepted much of the proceeds at the hands of the same enemy's officers. Frederick had every reason for his suspicions; Matthew Paris speaks of Richard 'secretly and cautiously making good the Pope's financial stringency'.[26] Richard could hardly argue his way out with his brother-in-law, in whose eyes any support for the Holy See was now a direct affront.

There was indeed a vast difference between relations obtaining in 1248 between the Emperor and the Pope, and those which had attended Frederick's coronation at Aachen in 1215, when he was the Papal nominee, regarded as the saviour of the Empire, chosen to replace the fallen Otto. Dissensions over his delay in going on Crusade had been sharpened by the nature of the Crusade when it eventually came; and though the first ban of excommunication had been lifted because of his services in the Holy Land, it was reimposed because of his policies in Germany.

Frederick had no love for Germany; he disliked its climate and regarded its people as barbaric, his whole inclination – reflecting the character of his Sicilian mother – being towards Italy. His aim was to place the German part of his Empire under the rule of his sons. Having let his eldest son Henry die in prison, he persuaded the German electors to choose as 'King of the Romans' his son by Isabella de Brienne, Konrad. For this the Pope had a Crusade preached against 'the son of perdition', and decided to set up his own anti-King in Germany. In 1246 the choice fell on Heinrich Raspe, Landgrave of Thuringia, who was duly elected by the three Rhenish Archbishops 'at the Pope's command'.[27] The principal Elector and Archbishop of Cologne, Konrad von Hochstaden, was violently anti-Hohenstaufen, and readily swung the other two ecclesiastical electors against Frederick and Konrad. Heinrich Raspe was short-lived, dying a year later; but the Pope, 'skilled as he was in the fierce excitements of conflict unburdened by scruple',[28] swiftly commanded the Archbishops to choose a successor in the shape of William, Count of Holland, who was duly 'elected' on 3rd October, 1247.

Three further years of unrelenting discord followed, and then a higher Power than the Papacy decided the outcome. In December, 1250, Frederick II died, leaving a vacuum which in five and a half centuries of the Empire's further existence no one of quite the same calibre was ever again to fill.

'*Stupor mundi*', the wonder of the world, Matthew Paris called him. His features can still be studied in the statue called 'Der Reiter' outside Bamberg Cathedral, which – though not, like those of Louis IX, constituting 'the face of an angel' – are yet arresting and full of character, purpose, and indeed beauty.[29] Frederick has been described in this century as 'the greatest European between Charlemagne and Napoleon'; and as being, 'of the long line of Germanic successors of Charlemagne, the only one with a genius and frame of character that are not those of a Northern or a Teuton; a love of luxury and beauty, an intellect refined, subtle, philosophical; a sensualist yet also a warrior and a politician, a profound lawgiver and an impassioned poet'.[30]

His removal from the scene was a shock for Central Europe. With him the Hohenstaufen dynasty virtually ceased to exist, though his sons and grandsons struggled on manfully for some years. The time was ripe for another to take its place. Far ahead of his century, a prince on the Renaissance pattern who would have delighted a Machiavelli and made a worthy Metternich, 'the greatest human force in the Middle Ages passed in and out of history like a comet which shines and is gone'.[31]

CHAPTER SIX

POWER POLITICS

EUROPEAN EVENTS were meanwhile marching steadily upon Richard of Cornwall. English interest in events in Germany was certainly lively: the magnates followed the fortunes of William of Holland,[1] and were duly impressed by the foundation of Cologne's new Cathedral[2] – an event which gave a considerable stimulus to Anglo-Rhenish trade. The death of Frederick II, however, evoked the profoundest interest of all. Although Richard was as interested as anybody in the question of the succession, it may be that he did not see himself in that connection as yet, whatever secret thoughts his wife harboured on the subject. In the early part of the year 1250, at all events, while Frederick yet lived, Richard was preoccupied with more interesting events nearer home. Soon after Christmas, 1249, Sanchia had been safely delivered at Berkhamsted of a baby son, whom they christened Edmund after Richard's much admired Saint of Canterbury.[3]

When Sanchia was up and about again he took her over to France, 'travelling with a huge retinue, eighty knights arrayed in magnificent robes and many of his household, taking with him the Countess his wife and Henry his eldest son, so that the French marvelled at such a wonderful and honourable spectacle. Queen Blanche hastened to meet them with great honour and reverence'.[4] She was still Regent of France, for King Louis was attacking Damietta at that very moment. But the objective of Richard's journey was not Paris, despite their sumptuous welcome there; for he was following his old road of ten years earlier as far as Lyons, whither he had been invited by the Pope. They dined together on 6th April and had long private conversations together afterwards.

The air of mystery surrounding them was as dear to the 'Press'

Raymond Bérenger of Provence, Sanchia's father, from the effigy called 'le Chevalier à la Rose' in the Church of St. Jean de Malte in Aix-en-Provence

Beatrice de Savoie, Countess of Provence, wife of Raymond Bérenger and mother of Richard's second wife, Sanchia, from the statue in the Church of St. Jean de Malte, Aix-en-Provence

Konrad von Hochstaden, Archbishop of Cologne, from the effigy in Cologne Cathedral

of 1250 as a similar event would be today. Matthew Paris speculated avidly on what the subject matter could be, and suggests that it was possibly the offer to Richard of the Imperial Crown.[5] If this were so, Richard kept his own counsel, and nothing more was heard of it for six years, though Sanchia clearly had the idea in her mind when she met her sisters in Paris four years later. It seems more likely that the conversations marked the start of the 'Sicilian business'; for the Pope was determined to break the remaining Hohenstaufen hold on the island kingdom, and had Richard in mind as a suitable candidate. The astute Genoese lawyer, who as a Cardinal had been one of Frederick's bitterest opponents, now chose to ignore the existence of Frederick's sons. If we find it strange to think of the Pontiff conversing with an English Earl in an imperial provincial city, we must remember that the isolation of the Pope had not yet come about, and that it was customary to see him moving around among his flock in Europe.

If Richard gave him an answer it was presumably an equivocal one, for he succeeded in fact in procrastinating on the Sicilian issue for two years. Yet on his return to England he received a triumphant welcome. 'On the Monday before Rogation-tide, Earl Richard landed, returning from the Roman Curia; and when he reached London he was received with honour and reverence no less than that which had been shown to him in parts beyond the sea.'[6] Paris discourses at some length on the honour shown Richard by Queen Blanche and by the Pope. Well might the Queen favour him, for Henry III had given his brother 'power to prolong the truce with Louis King of France for sixteen years or more',[7] and on the very day when Richard and the Pope had dined together at Lyons Louis had fallen into the hands of the Sultan of Egypt. Anything which Blanche could do in her son's absence to preserve peace in France was vitally urgent.

Soon after his return Richard was in demand twice in quick succession as an arbiter in disputes, the first between the talented and crafty Abbot of Westminster, Richard de Crakesley, and the Mayor and citizens of London. The latter implored the King to protect the freedom of their charters against the Abbot; and when

Henry, to whom Westminster was sacrosanct, turned a deaf ear, they took their troubles to Richard and Simon de Montfort, who interceded successfully on their behalf.[8]

The second case was that of Henry of Bath, itinerant justice and privy counsellor of the King, who was accused of corruption and amassing himself a fortune during his eyre.* The King accepted the version of Henry's accusers and charged him with high treason. 'Henry of Bath, realizing the danger of his position, accompanied by the Bishop of London, Philip Basset and others of his special friends, went to Earl Richard, and so convinced him, as much by their prayers as by their financial gifts',[9] that they would set the whole realm in uproar if he did not intervene, that he used all his eloquence on his brother, at first to no avail for 'the King's fury and indignation did not abate'. As the Earl withdrew, he observed: 'We cannot leave the nobles of the Kingdom in the lurch when they are in the right.' Henry, however, fixed 17th February, 1261, as the date by which Henry of Bath must surrender to his will, and when he did not do so he took up arms against him. Once again Richard came forward, and by dint of greasing Henry's ever-empty palm got him to withdraw his condemnation of the justice.[10] On 8th July, at Woodstock, the King 'released Henry of Bath and his household of the King's indignation and rancour for all manner of trespasses until the Sunday after the Translation of St. Thomas the Martyr this year'.[11]

For over a year Richard turned to his estates, but kept an eye over his shoulder for European events. Pope Innocent returned to Italy from Lyons in 1251, now that Frederick was dead, in the hopes of driving out Manfred, the Emperor's bastard son, who had been nominated Regent of Sicily and had taken the field against Papal forces. But demands on the Pope by the Lombard cities exhausted his treasury, and he was unable to proceed with his designs. To make matters worse Konrad IV – Manfred's half-brother and King of the Romans – now arrived in Italy from Germany and consolidated Manfred's successes. The Pope

* *Eyre:* A circuit of itinerant judges, holding courts in different counties, just as assize judges go on circuit nowadays.

therefore continued to put out feelers to Richard about the Sicilian crown, but Richard was for the moment otherwise engaged.

The autumn of 1251 saw the fruition of another of his plans. 'On the ninth of November of that same year, the vigil of Saint Leonard, Earl Richard caused the Church of Hayles to be dedicated with great solemnity. He had founded it with great magnificence, and had raised the buildings according to the vow he had made at sea when, returning from Gascony, he had almost failed to reach port in Cornwall. There were present at this memorable dedication the Lord King and Queen and many magnates and prelates of England; there were indeed thirteen Bishops, each celebrating Mass at his own altar on the day of dedication, and the Bishop of Lincoln solemnly chanted Mass at the High Altar. It was Sunday, and the quality dined that day with the bishops splendidly and amply on meat; the clergy and monks dined off fish of great number and variety. There were also more than three hundred knights present. If I should fully describe the magnificence of this feast and the number of guests, you would say I had transcended the limits of truth. But when I, Matthew Paris, sought to be informed on this matter, lest I should insert anything false in this book, the Earl affirmed with absolute certainty that, including the whole cost of the banquet, he had expended ten thousand marks on the construction of this same church, adding the following memorable and commendable words; "Would to God that I had expended all the money I have spent on Wallingford Castle in so wise and salutary a manner."'[12]

This description underlines the importance of Matthew Paris's testimony of Richard's life, inasmuch as on numerous occasions he had direct access to him, obtained information from him first-hand, and doubtless reported an actual conversation.[13] Richard loved magnificence: his wedding feast, and now the dedication of Hayles, were so splendid as to stagger the beholders. The same was to be true of his coronation in Germany later on. He was a wise psychologist: men might mutter about his extravagance, but they would remember his good food. As to his remark about

Wallingford, his critics would say that it was arrant hypocrisy, that he thoroughly enjoyed squandering vast sums on his Thames-side castle; but they would not be entirely right. He was no doubt quite sincere when he spoke to Matthew, flushed with pleasure and satisfaction at the fulfilment of his vow. The Saracen soothsayer had said he never left unfinished any task to which he set his hand: of this perseverance Hayles was an example, and Richard – in the medieval manner – was a pious man.

Hayles as then constructed was indeed a magnificent building. Its design followed closely that of the mother house at Beaulieu, with a great tower over the crossing of the transepts, and a square east end to the sanctuary. The thirteen altars were ranged round the High Altar in chapels of the ambulatory. The whole was built in the mellow Cotswold stone, golden and beautiful, blending with the green well-watered valley beneath the swelling breasts of the wolds, and designed in the loveliest style of English Gothic, more delicate than the austerer Early English style of a few decades before. For three centuries it was to become one of the chief shrines of England. It was to make a great impression on Richard's two young sons, Henry, now a squire and sixteen years of age, and Edmund, still a baby, but destined to bring to it the precious relic which would make men say 'God's in Gloucestershire' – the phial of the Precious Blood.

Early in 1252 the Pope, clutching at a straw, sent his notary Albert of Parma to England to negotiate with Richard about the crown of Sicily. Matthew Paris devotes one of his wittily sardonic passages to the episode. Richard procrastinated; but when Albert's demands became more pressing, so that – as he put it – he might advise his master of the Earl's wishes, Richard replied curtly: 'The Pope behaves towards me as if he meant to say – I will sell you or give you the moon. Climb up and take it.'[14]

This was pointed enough to make even the Pope desist from offering the crown to Richard again; but he was not to be deflected from his purpose, despite the danger inherent in a new wave of Guelf–Ghibelline fighting which engulfed the cities of Italy. Richard's prudence had told him that to accept the crown of

Sicily, truncated limb of the Hohenstaufen domain and virtual pawn of the Pope, was courting disaster. His unrealistic brother, on the other hand – hampered by no such caution – seized the opportunity of asking the Pope for it on behalf of his son Edmund Crouchback. The Pope was naturally delighted that the King of England had swallowed the bait; but the English people were disgusted, especially when Henry dressed the boy in Sicilian costume and paraded him before the unimpressed Londoners. While the King became ever deeper involved in this extravagant and foolish enterprise, Konrad IV continued his successful campaign in Italy. Indeed, he sent Richard a message regretting that King Henry had yielded to the policies of the Roman Curia, and congratulating Richard himself on his good sense. By October, 1253, Konrad had captured Naples, and soon afterwards the Pope was forced to play his trump card of excommunication against him.

Shortly before, Richard had again mitigated Henry's wrath – this time against Simon de Montfort. Simon had gone to the seething province of Gascony in 1248 as the King's lieutenant. He had made his headquarters with his Countess at La Réole, the fortress which Richard of Cornwall had reduced with such difficulty during his Gascon campaign twenty years before. Standing high above the Garonne, it was called the Castle of the Four Sisters – not from any connection with the family of Provence, but because of the great symmetrical round towers at each corner. Here de Montfort wielded almost regal power, so that 'all obey him and dare undertake naught against him'. His rule there was most successful; he had reduced the rebellious elements and sent their leaders – amongst whom was Gaston de Béarn – to London as prisoners, saying there would never be peace in Gascony if they stayed there. Henry did not have the sense to support him; and, after requiring the prisoners to swear an oath of eternal loyalty, he released them. No sooner were they back in Gascony than they started to rebel afresh, and Simon fell upon them with a heavy hand. Unable to defeat him militarily, they chose another weapon – slander – which they knew would be more effective with the

King.[15] Simon was accused of misappropriation of funds, and Henry required him to return to England to answer the charges.

Simon hoped Richard of Cornwall would support him, and he was not disappointed. The famous trial – almost a trial for high treason – in the refectory of Westminster Abbey is the subject of one of Matthew Paris's most colourfully descriptive passages. The air was thick with accusations thrown back and forth. Simon's defence was that he had simply been doing what he was sent out to do, namely to keep the King's dominions safe and at peace, and in this defence he was strongly backed up by some of the foremost magnates, including Richard, who remembered his own experiences of Gascon trickery and tergiversation. Eventually, the King and the magnates gave their verdict; they declared their full confidence in the Earl of Leicester and his subordinates. It might have been supposed that the matter would rest there; but the following day the fickle King changed his tune. Before all the nobles assembled in Westminster Hall he screamed abuse at de Montfort, calling him a traitor. 'If you had not had your royal authority above you like an umbrella,' shouted back Simon, 'this would have been an evil day for you. Do you call yourself a Christian? Have you been to Confession? You cannot have, for you do not repent you of your sins.' Simon, too, was hot tempered; he had had a great deal of provocation from Henry over the years, and had not forgotten the Abbey incident. But it was not politic to address an Angevin monarch in such a style. Henry shouted back furiously: 'Never have I regretted so much any act of mine as I do letting you land in England and permitting you to possess honour and anything else in my realm!' Richard of Cornwall, again sensing danger and the shadow of the Tower over his friend, once more stepped between them.

Simon made a final proposal to the King; either he would give up his seneschalship of Gascony, on condition that the King would protect him from disgrace, or he would return to that rebellious province and pacify it. Henry snapped back at him: 'Return to Gascony, then, inciter and lover of war, so that you may find your fill of battle and bring back its spoils like your father.' This allusion to the brutal Albigensian Crusade was not lost on Simon, but he seized the opportunity to take the King at his word and, leaving Eleanor at Sutton Valence Castle in Kent, set off with his eldest son Henry for Gascony. He met immediate opposition and found his own men imprisoned in the castle of La Réole. To teach the Gascons a lesson he destroyed a large number of vineyards; then the King's commissioners again arrived with a warning from Henry that Simon must keep the truce with the Gascons. De Montfort replied that he would not do so if they attacked him. The commissioners tried to confiscate his powers, but Simon refused to surrender them. Eventually Henry himself arranged for him to surrender his claims in the province to the Lord Edward against monetary compensation, and promised that either he or his son would go to Gascony in person to investigate matters on the spot. Money would be needed for their journey, and on 8th May Richard was granted authority to make new money in Ireland. Two months later the King acknowledged a loan of 2,000 marks from him to make the new money.

Five days later Henry took the precaution, before leaving for Gascony, of confirming Magna Carta in the presence of Richard and the barons. In a ceremony of great solemnity, he threatened anyone who disturbed the rights enshrined in it with excommunication. He then made provision for the government of the Kingdom in his absence. On 3rd July, at Sandwich, he made a proclamation regarding those bishoprics which should fall vacant, which began: 'Whereas the King has committed the governance of the realm of England and the lands of Wales and Ireland to Queen Eleanor with the counsel of his brother, Richard, Earl of Cornwall, until his return from Gascony . . .' On 7th July he was more precise: 'Appointment of Queen Eleanor to keep and govern the realm of England and the lands of Wales and Ireland with the counsel of Richard, Earl of Cornwall, the King's brother, until the King's return from Gascony, and mandate to all to be intendant unto her.'[16]

Some last-minute letters patent were granted to Richard and his family; on 5th July to 'the King's sister Senchia, Countess of

Cornwall, that out of the King's wards that first fall in, she shall have to the amount of 80.l a year, to hold during the minority of the heirs to such wards, with mandate to the Queen and the Earl of Cornwall to give her full seisin as they fall in'. The following day it was Richard's own turn: 'Grant to Richard, Earl of Cornwall, that on the hill above his manor of Mere he may build and fortify a castle of stone and lime, with reversion to the male issue of himself and Senchia his wife'; and he notified the justices of the Forest on this side of Trent that 'he had granted to the Earl of Cornwall that in his own wood of the forest of Blakemore he may take timber to fortify a castle at his manor of Mere and to do the works of the said castle'.[17] There is no castle now on the summit of the steep hill above the little town of Mere; but in Richard's day it was of great strategic importance to a magnate with holdings in the West Country, protecting as it did the approaches from the downs of Wiltshire into the Somerset plain.

On 6th August the King set sail from Portsmouth for Bordeaux, leaving his brother for the first time virtually joint master of the Kingdom, and soon to enjoy the supreme power alone.

CHAPTER SEVEN

A FATEFUL FAMILY PARTY

THE SUCCEEDING TWO YEARS, though it was not evident at the time, were probably the most important in Richard's life, when events led him inexorably to the summit of his ambition – first to the Regency of England, and then to a foreign crown. At the end of 1253 King Henry sent home an urgent appeal for financial support; whereupon Eleanor and Richard, on 27th January, 1254, summoned a parliament of magnates to assemble in London after Easter to raise funds. Ships were ordered to stand by to transport reinforcements to Gascony; and on 11th February two knights from each shire were also summoned to attend the assembly. Henry obviously hoped that Richard would go out to Gascony to help him, for, on 30th January, a writ was issued at Westminster to the barons and bailiffs of the Cinque Ports:

> The King, while making stay in Gascony with his expedition, is in great need of his magnates of England, and is therefore sending to the said ports Gilbert de London, the King's clerk, to arrest all ships of the ports able to carry sixteen horses, and all like other ships found there of whoseoever power they be, to be at Portsmouth on the octave of Easter next, ready for the crossing of the Queen, Edward, the King's son, Richard, Earl of Cornwall, the King's brother, and other magnates coming to him in Gascony, commanding them to be aiding and counselling to the said clerk in such arrest.
>
> By like letters the King sends Roger de Evesham to the barons and bailiffs of Southampton, Portsmouth, Poole, Lyme, Weymouth, Teignmouth, Dartmouth and Plymouth, in favour of Roger de Evesham; and John Blundel to the bailiffs of Newcastle on Tyne; and Richard Oysel to the barons and bailiffs of the ports of Dover, Sandwich, Faversham, Orford, Ipswich, Dunwich, Harwich, Yarmouth, Lynn and Boston. In like manner it is commanded to the sheriff of Devon to arrest ships in the ports of Topsham and Exeter.[1]

Eleanor and Richard agreed, however, that she should go and he should remain. Hitherto patents had been issued either by her alone or by them jointly, with Richard figuring alone only very occasionally: now, as the time for the Queen's departure drew closer, Richard figures more frequently by himself in the Patent Rolls. On 17th February he gave a mandate to the barons and bailiffs of the ports 'to let the ship called "La Helop of Winchelsea", which Stephen de Chelmersford caused to be laden with oats for Gascony, to go to Bordeaux, after taking security from him that with the first favourable wind he will return to Portsmouth; the like to the same to let the smaller ship of the Abbot of Quarr come and go where the Abbot will until St. Peter's Chains, keeping his greater ship for the Queen's crossing.'[2] This assembling of ships went on steadily, though the men of neighbouring ports were frequently at loggerheads. On 30th April the Queen issued a patent to 'the barons and bailiffs of the Cinque Ports and all others by the sea coast that the King wills that the good men of Yarmouth and Dunwich shall go with the fleet to Gascony with the Queen, and forbids them on pain of their lands, life and limbs from causing any damage or impediment to them by reason of any contentions between them'.[3]

On 17th May she was still at Windsor with Richard, but by the end of the month she had sailed, leaving him undisputed master of England. In July he sent a mandate to all sheriffs 'to distrain all debtors and persons detaining the money of the old Crusade which by grant of the apostolic see is due to Richard, Earl of Cornwall'; in October he obtained a 'grant to Richard, Earl of Cornwall, who has respited to the King until the quinzaine of Hilary the payment of six thousand marks which he borrowed of him before his last crossing to Gascony and of four thousand marks since that crossing, that he will pay him then, and if not, he may make his profit of the gold which he had pledged to him for the same'.[4] Richard was making sure, as Henry's credit was notoriously bad.

Henry had meanwhile received formal bestowal of the Kingdom of Sicily on his son at the hands of the Papal Legate. He sent Thomas of Savoy to the Pope to suggest commuting his crusading vow to an attack on the Hohenstaufen power in Sicily; but at the very moment that this suggestion reached Rome, news came of the death of Konrad IV on 21st May, 1254. The Pope realized that this might change the balance of power, and sent Henry an equivocal answer. The old Pope had excommunicated Konrad early that same year, and the King of the Romans – mortified by this on his deathbed – had given a dying mandate recommending his infant son, Konradin, to the Pope's protection.[5] Frederick's bastard son Manfred felt himself too weak militarily to withstand the Pope's demands, and agreed to surrender Sicily on Innocent's terms. For the moment it looked as if Rome held all the cards. But the Pope played them too greedily. Seeing his chance to seize Sicily completely, he ignored the claims of Henry, Edmund or Konradin, and sent his army towards the rich island. This stiffened Manfred to resist: he routed the Papal forces, and Innocent saw his hopes shattered. This last bitter blow proved mortal and he died on 7th December.

Henry III meanwhile decided to return home from Gascony through France. He was unwell and did not fancy the long sea crossing; moreover he wanted particularly to meet Louis, see the sights of Paris, and visit the holy relics which the French King had recently brought to Notre Dame. Matthew Paris gives a detailed and wholly fascinating account of Henry's pilgrimage 'through the kingdom of France and the cities which hitherto he knew only by name'.[6]

Moving up from Gascony through Poitou to the Loire he came on 15th November to the Abbey of Fontevrault, to visit the tombs of his illustrious forebears, Henry II and Eleanor of Aquitaine, and Richard Cœur-de-Lion, and also – as he fondly supposed – that of his mother. He was extremely shaken to find that the famous Isabella of Angoulême lay not in a sumptuous tomb in the Abbey but in the common grave of Fontevrault.[7] The Abbot explained how she had died distracted and wished to be buried simply, to atone for her sins; but Henry gave orders for her body to be exhumed and for a splendid tomb and effigy to be built for her in the Abbey, for which – as he wisely said, having an eye to his empty treasury – he would pay presently, presumably with money borrowed from Richard. Her painted effigy stands there today, in crown and wimple, mantle and belted gown, edged with a passement at the wrists and neck.

News of the intended royal visit to Paris came through to England. The Countess Beatrice of Provence was also going there, as was her youngest daughter, Beatrice, wife of Charles of Anjou. Three of the daughters of Raymond Bérenger would therefore meet again for the first time for years, and the fourth was not going to be left out of it. 'The Countess of Cornwall, hearing that the King of the English together with the Queen her sister was passing through the Kingdom of the French, and that the Queen of the French her elder sister, was coming to meet the travellers, obtained permission from her husband, Earl Richard, to visit her sisters; she crossed over with a great and noble retinue, lest her condition should appear inferior to that of her sisters.'[8] There were so many valiant knights, so gaily caparizoned, so nobly attired, wrote Matthew Paris, that the French marvelled at the spectacle.

'The King of the French, learning of the approach of the King of the English, went to meet him at Chartres, and when they saw each other, they rushed to embrace.' Sanchia had joined Henry and Eleanor already, and the whole party now made their way towards Paris: 'The Queen of the French with her sister the Countess of Anjou came to meet them, so that they might encounter their sisters, the Queen of England and the Countess of Cornwall, at the same time as the King of England, and they joined forces with mutual greetings, familiar conversation, congratulating and consoling each other. Their mother, the Countess Beatrice of Provence, was also present, an older Niobe but extremely beautiful; there was no mother in the world in all the female sex who had such a fruitful womb and could boast such beautiful daughters.'[9]

The chronicler of St. Albans gives a colourful picture of the vivacious meeting of five of the most beautiful women in Europe, two Queens and three Countesses. It probably took place at St. Germain-en-Laye, for by 9th December the royal party was in the French capital. They now indulged in a round of banquets and sight-seeing like any modern tourists, and Louis IX and Henry III discussed their problems frankly and fraternally.[10]

There was so much to see. Henry, a keen and able architect, particularly wanted to visit the Sainte-Chapelle recently erected by Louis. This had been begun in 1244 and was consecrated on 25th April, 1248, the upper Chapel being dedicated to the Holy Crown of Thorns and the lower Chapel to Our Lady. The beautiful proportions of this astonishing, soaring building, entranced Henry; and the royal visitors were privileged to be shown the Crown of Thorns and the section of the True Cross, transferred from Syria in 1241. It had arrived 'on Good Friday, the day on which our Lord Jesus Christ had died to redeem the world'. Louis had brought it first to the Church of Saint-Antoine-aux-Champs; and there, 'in the presence of Queen Margaret his wife, his mother Queen Blanche, his brothers, the archbishops, bishops, abbots and other religious leaders, as well as many of the magnates of France and vast numbers of the populace standing by, rejoicing at the glorious spectacle, the King, dissolved in tears, raised the Cross above his head as the churchmen intoned with a loud voice "Ecce Crucem Domini". And when all had adored it in reverence and devotion the King, barefoot, bare-headed and fasting, had led the way through the city of Paris to the cathedral church of Notre Dame'.[11] Matthew Paris provides a marginal sketch of this famous event, showing Louis crowned but in a simple *cotte*, holding aloft the double-headed Cross, on the pattern of the Cross of Lorraine, while beside him a churchman holds the Crown of Thorns.[12]

In the course of the family reunion the four sisters had much to say to one another and their mother was not behindhand in firing the ambitions of the two who had not yet reached royal estate. Sanchia doubtless mentioned Richard's visit to the Pope at Lyons in 1250; and if the project of the Imperial Crown had been mooted then, she would obviously have discussed it with her sisters. They were intelligent women who enjoyed the game of politics: indeed, King Louis had to keep Marguerite at arm's length in political matters. It was now evident that the Hohenstaufen power was collapsing, and that something would be needed to take its place not only in Germany but also in Sicily. Eleanor was glad that Richard had renounced Sicily in favour of her son Edmund; Marguerite knew that there was little likelihood of King Louis ever becoming Emperor; young Beatrice would also be grateful later on for Richard's renunciation, for it left the way open to her husband to become King of Sicily himself. Everything points to the probability that they all encouraged Sanchia to put pressure on Richard to seek the crown of Germany.

The royal visit to France lasted till Christmas, and the party then set out for the coast. 'On the Sunday following, wind and sea being favourable, the King duly embarked and came safely into Dover. Earl Richard his brother and other nobles hastened to meet him, having waited a long time in vain for him on the English coast, and received him and his party with rejoicing.'[13] One of the results of the visit was a broadening of Henry's viewpoint; 'henceforth his was less of an Angevin, more of a Continental outlook'.[14] Another result was a growth of a still closer friendship between him and Marguerite of France: their correspondence henceforth became very regular, and lasted till Henry's death, after which the French Queen continued it with Edward I.[15] She also took a great liking to young Henry – Richard and Isabella's son – and he came to enjoy thoroughly a holiday or a convalescence in her care.

Soon after the King's return to England came the news of the death of Pope Innocent. Within five days the Cardinals had chosen a very different successor in the shape of Alexander IV, a pious, pacific man. He confirmed the investiture of young Edmund Crouchback to the Sicilian Crown in April, 1255, and Henry promised in return to send an army against Manfred in eighteen months' time. Manfred, however, had other ideas: ignoring the English puppet of the Pope and, worse still, ignoring the rightful claims of Konradin, he proclaimed himself King of Sicily. This had the effect of infuriating Konradin's guardian, the Pfalzgraf or Count Palatine of the Rhine, and thereby influenced him to vote for Richard of Cornwall as Emperor rather than any member of the Hohenstaufen clan.[16] Thus by an irony of fate the downfall of

Henry III's hopes of the Sicilian throne for his son had a direct effect in improving his brother's chances of the crown of Germany.

Henry, hopelessly in debt, sold all the Jews in England to his brother Richard, who was indeed always regarded as the Jews' benefactor. Once again he was called on to lend money to the King, and not only to the King. 'At the same time the Pope sought money from Earl Richard to the tune of four thousand marks, for promoting the candidature of his [Richard's] nephew Edmund. To which the Earl replied; "I do not wish to oblige a superior, whom I cannot criticize, with my treasure."'[17] So, adroitly avoiding this problem, Richard conserved his treasure; he might soon need a great deal more of it than ever before.

Sanchia kept up her gentle, relentless female pressure, and Richard began to put out feelers about the imperial crown. He needed agents and spokesmen if he was going to risk another decisive throw on so great a venture, and he found one ready to hand in the person of Jean d'Avesnes, Count of Hainault. Hainault, covering what is today south-west Belgium and part of north-eastern France from the area of the old town of Avesnes west to Cambrai and north nearly to Brussels, formed one of the most westerly fiefs of the Empire and was traditionally well-disposed towards England. Jean d'Avesnes would make a good go-between, and Richard carefully sent him two hundred pounds.[18]

The next move was to get his brother's ear. Henry was still smarting from the failure of the Sicilian episode, but another facet of his Continental policy had borne better fruit. Since the accession of Alfonso to the throne of Castile in 1252, Henry had been wooing him with the object of securing an alliance. He arranged a marriage between his son, the Lord Edward, and Alfonso's sister Eleanor, which – though initially simply a political match – turned out to be one of the greatest love-marriages of English history. The couple were married in Spain, and 'when the King returned from the north of England about the feast of Saint Dionysius so that he might be present at the celebrations of Saint Edward's Day, Eleanor, sister of the King of Spain, wife of Edward, arrived at Dover with great pomp and circumstance, so that the arrival of so many Spaniards was suspect in England, where it was thought that they would be violently occupied by them'.[19]

Henry, pleased with the success of this latest political move abroad, was prepared to lend a willing ear to Richard's plans. He was, moreover, still very susceptible to the charms of his beautiful sister-in-law, and Sanchia needed no second bidding. While this remarkable Frenchwoman worked on the King in England, a strong Continental influence was planning along similar lines, in the shape of a remarkable German, the Archbishop of Cologne.

Beatrix von Falkenburg, third wife of Richard of Cornwall

The cloisters, Hayles Abbey

The dorter range, entrance to the modern Chapel, Burnham Abbey, Buckinghamshire

CHAPTER EIGHT

THE LONG ROAD TO AACHEN

IN THE RHINELAND, that country of spectacular castles, Burg Are crowns one of the most impregnable sites of all, perched on the narrow summit of a towering fang of rock round which the River Ahr cowers and curls like a silver snake on its way to join the Rhine. In a room whose shell now overhangs the precipice, Mathilde von Vianden gave birth to her son Konrad in 1205, third child of the Graf Lothar von Are. Small wonder that such a birthplace should produce a tough man, an example of 'that very mundane church of fighting archbishops which suited the German king and was indeed the chief pillar upon which his government was based'.[1]*

Given a country living in his brother's gift while still in his teens, Konrad von Hochstaden became a Canon of Cologne Cathedral at the early age of twenty-one. His appointment fell within a year of the murder of Archbishop Engelbert; but the great politician and administrator's influence was still very strong, and young Konrad was fired by Engelbert's idea of building a new Cathedral to replace the Romanesque structure. He needed power, and power steadily accrued to him: Provost in 1234, Archdeacon in 1236, he was unanimously elected Archbishop in 1238 on the death of Engelbert's successor Heinrich von Mullenark.

Initially Konrad's relations with his city were cordial, but they deteriorated as mounting Papal pressure caused him to turn against the Emperor Frederick while Cologne remained staunchly

* The mother's birthplace, Vianden Castle, was as spectacular as the son's. Perched on a mighty rock, it dominates the narrow valley of the Our and the little town, now in the Grand Duchy of Luxembourg. The Counts of Vianden were the ancestors both of the House of Orange and the present ruling house of Luxembourg.

pro-Hohenstaufen. The Kölner were and are an independent people, jealously cherishing hard-won privileges. The astonishing wealth of their city is illustrated by the fact that its walls enclosed so vast an area that no extension was needed till the 1880's. In Konrad's time there were already twelve gates on the landward side, eighteen on the Rhine side, and no less than fifty-two intermediate towers in the circle of the walls.[2]

The decision to fulfil Archbishop Engelbert's plan was hastened by a disastrous fire which swept the old Romanesque Cathedral. Konrad, presiding over a meeting of the Chapter early in 1247, brought them to a resolution – that they would build in the new soaring Gothic style already current in France for half a century. They summoned Meister Gerhard to be their master-architect and overseer of works. Gerhard had been trained in the construction of the tremendous vault of Beauvais, but above all in Amiens; and it was Amiens Cathedral that he followed most closely in his design for Cologne. Most German architects still clung to the heavier Romanesque style – indeed Konrad had consecrated just such a church in Cologne only that year – and his determination now was to build a cathedral that by its gigantic strength would put even the best of French architecture in the shade and ignite the Gothic torch in Germany.

On 7th June he had put his citizens in a good frame of mind by granting them freedom from tolls on the land and water routes below Cologne as far as Neuss. Then on 15th August, 1248, Maria Himmelfahrtstag (or as the contemporary documents puts it, 'up unswer Vrauwen dach, da sie zur Hemel vur' – on Our Lady's Day, when she went up to Heaven), he laid the foundation stone of Meister Gerhard's plan, 'declaring in the name of the Pope, himself, and the Papal Legate, hitherto unequalled indulgences for all who would give their alms'.[3]

For all his unscrupulousness and ruthlessness, Konrad was a man of considerable vision. It is not surprising that his splendid bronze effigy, with mitre, crozier and bible, in the Johanneskapelle in the ambulatory of his Cathedral, shows a strikingly youthful face. He was then only forty-three, a man of wide-ranging ideas for the secular world as well, who saw himself as a 'Kingmaker' on the grand pattern, the man who would really lead the search for a successor to the Hohenstaufen. William of Holland, the Pope's puppet King, whom he had had with him at the founding of the new Cathedral, he discounted as too mean a spirit; so with typical drastic impetuousity he set fire to the house in Neuss where William was staying. The King escaped with his life, but Konrad received a stern rebuke from the Pope and the threat of excommunication, coupled with a warning to cease his overtures to Ottokar of Bohemia, whom he hoped to elect in William's stead. Had he succeeded, a very strong and acquisitive hand would have taken Germany in its grasp. Konrad must have been grimly satisfied when William of Holland's horse killed him by throwing him on the ice-covered marshes of Friesland in January, 1256. As principal Elector he was now free to choose a successor but, chastened by his recent experiences, he would choose someone not too closely identifiable with Papal interests, and he bided his time. Two meetings with his fellow Electors proved abortive.[4]

Meanwhile the death of William had brought home to the principal powers of Europe the importance of who should sit on the German throne. Henry III, spurred on by Sanchia, was first off the mark with a letter to Sir William Bonquer, his representative in Rome, telling him to inform the Pope of his wish that a King of Germany should be chosen 'who would be well disposed to the Roman Church and acceptable to us'.[5] He still cherished his Sicilian dream, and also the hope that he would be able, with Richard as Emperor, to emulate his father's encircling tactics on the King of the French and so recover Normandy and Poitou. King Louis's interests were of course the direct opposite: the hardly-won French ascendancy over the Empire must not be thrown away. The Papacy wanted no ruler as powerful as itself in Central Europe, and did not fancy the kingdom of Sicily being in the hands of the same family as the Empire, even if that family were not the Hohenstaufens. As a result, for the whole of Richard's reign the Pope was to play a crafty game to preserve the balance of power.

Bonquer must have done his task well, for in November, 1256, Henry III rewarded him with exemption from jury or assize service for life. But the King did not wait for the Pope to reply to the letter Bonquer had transmitted to him. On 12th June he sent Richard de Clare – Richard of Cornwall's stepson – and Robert Walerand, as his emissaries to the German princes. John Mansel, the Provost of Beverley, Richard's friend and a crafty diplomat, went with them probably at Richard's instigation.[6] It was to Konrad von Hochstaden that the English ambassadors turned, and they found a ready ear.[7] No sooner had he decided that Richard was the desirable candidate than he flung himself with his innate energy into obtaining at least a majority vote in his favour, inspired by a declaration of the Rhenish League towns that they would not admit any King not unanimously chosen, and by a threat from the Pope that he would excommunicate the ecclesiastical electors should they choose another Hohenstaufen.

Konrad sent his friend Philip von Falkenstein – a leading member of a family of 'ministeriales', or Imperial officers* – to sound out the Pfalzgraf Ludwig, who might well have been chosen himself had he not been under a cloud for having beheaded his wife that January on a trumped-up charge of adultery. He, too, was a man with an eye to the main chance, and secured his agreement to vote for Richard with all kinds of stipulations. He was to marry a daughter or niece of Henry III before Whitsun the following year; and she was to bring a dowry of 12,000 marks, 4,000 payable three weeks after Christmas and the rest by Easter at the latest.[8] In return he would give her all his holdings along the Rhine and Nahe. Everything pointed to Beatrix, daughter of Henry III as the bride; but luckily for her the marriage did not materialize.

Konrad called on his fellow Archbishop Gerhard of Mainz (at the time in a prison of the Duke of Brunswick), obtained his agreement to Richard's election, and went on to Prague to see Ottokar of Bohemia. He reached the capital on 17th July but had

* The 'ministeriales' were not of as noble birth as the old landed families. They were virtually civil servants *de carrière*, dedicated to the service of the Empire.

to wait there till Ottokar returned from Austria on 9th August. When the King arrived he sent Konrad away loaded with gifts but with an equivocal answer.

On Konrad's return to Cologne he clinched the matter with the English envoys, including Richard's own plenipotentiaries, Bishop Nicholas of Cambrai and the Count of Hainault, Jean d'Avesnes. At Zundorf on 15th December these two 'promised the Archbishop that (should Richard be chosen King of the Romans with his help) Richard would protect the Cathedral Church of Cologne in all her possessions, and would change the hostile attitude which Cardinal Petrus Capucius, the Papal Legate, and the Roman Curia adopted towards Konrad, before Whitsun, or else pay 2,000 marks sterling'. For his trouble and expenses in procuring the election Konrad would receive 8,000 marks before 13th January, 1257 – the day fixed for the election. Officials and judges in the city of Cologne were only to be appointed with the Archbishop's approval; while nobles, knights and burghers recruited in the city for the imperial cause were also only to be chosen with his consent. The status of Cologne and the finances of the Cathedral for some time were thereby safely assured.

On 13th January the Pfalzgraf and Konrad – voting for himself and the absent Gerhard of Mainz – elected Richard King of the Romans outside the walls of Frankfurt, which declined to admit them. The news that Ottokar had also cast his vote for Richard did not reach Wallingford Castle until 30th January.[9]

The genesis of the College of Electors is obscure; their numbers had varied over the centuries since the death of Charlemagne, but had now been fixed at seven: three ecclesiastics – the Archbishops of Cologne, Mainz and Trier; and four laymen – the Pfalzgraf, the King of Bohemia, the Duke of Saxony and the Markgraf of Brandenburg. Four of these, two churchmen and two of the laity, had now cast their vote for Richard; but the other three, headed by Arnold von Isenburg, Archbishop of Trier, had chosen Alfonso of Castile, the brother-in-law of the Lord Edward. This was the candidate most favoured by the Papacy, although Sir William Bonquer seems to have conditioned the Holy See satisfactorily to the choice of Richard. In the event, the Spanish prince never went to Germany, contenting himself with issuing desultory charters from his palace in Toledo; but in 1257, gloomy prognostications of strong opposition to Richard on Alfonso's behalf were rife. Although opposition certainly existed, it is surprising how little there was, and how successful Richard immediately became in the Rhineland.

Just before Easter Konrad arrived in England at the head of an influential German delegation, and formally offered Richard the crown. The Archbishop took care to see that his Cathedral was not forgotten, for on 30th March the following entry in the Patent Rolls was made at Westminster: 'Whereas the Church of Cologne, wherein the bodies of the three blessed Kings rest, has been consumed by fire, the King, at the petition of Konrad, Archbishop of Cologne, has written to the Archbishop of Canterbury and other prelates in England to receive the messengers of the said fabric when they come to them for aid, and to give them their protection.'[10]

Richard hesitated for some time about the offer of the crown; but Henry, Sanchia and some of the magnates, who believed the election to have been unanimous,[11] used the most persuasive language to convince him, telling him that the whole English nation would be honoured by his acceptance.[12] Eventually, 'speaking clearly and quickly', the Earl agreed, confiding himself – though altogether insufficient and unworthy – to God's mercy in shouldering this honourable burden. The German emissaries wept with emotion. Richard now presented Konrad with a richly jewelled mitre, and the Archbishop, in accepting the gift, remarked significantly: 'Earl Richard has done so much for me and my Church; he has mitred me, and I will crown him.'[13]

'Thus,' said Matthew Paris scornfully, 'were the English tricked by the wiles of the aliens.' The chronicler of St. Albans viewed the proceedings with a wintry eye; for the election of Richard had made considerable inroads into the Abbey's treasury. He observed that the cynics said: 'The money cries, for my sake Cornwall is married to Rome.'[14] But he gave a very fair assessment of why the

German electors had chosen Richard. It was partly, he said, because of his abundant wealth, but also because 'they hated French pride and did not wish to see any Frenchman lord in Germany, nor any Italian who would make the Empire too Roman. After diligent deliberation they therefore chose Earl Richard, partly because the English language which he spoke was so similar to the German, having a common root; partly because they had not forgotten that the Emperor Otto IV had been the son of an Englishwoman; but also because of Richard's faithfulness, constancy and wisdom'.[15]

This is doubtless the best synopsis of the reasons of the Electors in their choice, a riddle which has fascinated historians for centuries. Professor C. W. Bayley wrote that 'the initial impetus to Richard's candidature came from the Low Countries, for Flanders and Hainault tended increasingly to fall within the French sphere of influence after Bouvines. . . . The English embassy's initial advances were made to Konrad of Hochstaden, Archbishop of Cologne, a warlike and unscrupulous prelate indurated by long participation in the rough and tumble of German politics'.[16] Bappert, writing in nineteenth-century Germany, observed that 'Richard had powerful support in Germany from the outset in the shape of the North-west German party which had grown even stronger since the days of Otto IV; it was tied to England by the most vital trade interests and had stood at her side throughout. Its leader, the Archbishop of Cologne, was one of the most important and influential personalities of the time'.[17] Trautz, writing in 1961, has this to say: 'At the cardinal point in relation to the Netherlands, in Cologne, the Archbishop Konrad von Hochstaden resumed an already well-tried tradition in placing himself firmly on the English side; this Cologne partisanship is one of the few constants in German foreign policy of the high and late Middle Ages.'[18] Whatever the divergence of view of Konrad's character, this cross-section of historical opinion agreed that he was the focal point of the negotiations.

Soon after Easter he sailed away down the Thames in a royal galley to return to Germany to make final preparations for the coronation.[19] Arriving back in Cologne he was immediately embroiled again in local skirmishes and had to pacify his own city before he could go to Aachen and obtain its agreement to admit the new King. A peculiar incident had occurred during his stay in London: it would seem that one of his entourage had been killed in suspicious circumstances, but that Konrad did not wish to penalize the owner of the house where it happened. The Patent Rolls include the following entry, dated at Westminster on 8th April: 'Pardon, at the instance of Konrad, Archbishop of Cologne, to Master Adam de Lynton for the death of William Assebuf, merchant, lately killed in the house of the said Adam in London.'[20]

Having placed his castles and lands in the care of the Bishop of London, Richard, with Sanchia, his sons Henry and Edmund, and an enormous company, left London on 10th April. Among this household were two Cornish clerks, Roger de Constantine and Ralph de Arundell; but, as was Richard's wont from then onwards, he was to send them back to England when the journey was over and retain only German household members in Germany. Two other English servants of his fell foul of the laws, however, during a long wait at Yarmouth, due to bad weather. 'Whereas Richard, Earl of Cornwall, elected King of the Romans, being lately at Yarmouth and ready to go on board his ships and embark to cross to Almayne, caused to be taken in the King's forest at Colchester because of the shortness of time for his passage, to wit in the wood of Kingeswude, sixteen oaks; in the wood of John de Boxstede, twenty oaks, and in the woods of Langeho small oaks and rods to make bridges and hurdles to equip his ships, because the bridges and hurdles which the King had ordered the Sheriff of Essex to have prepared against his passage were not ready; John de Kayley and John la Enveyse, servants of the said Richard, entered without warrant and cut down and took the same; the King accepts this and grants that the said John and John and others taken by them for this to be quit and harmless touching such felling and taking.'[21]

Eventually the storms abated somewhat, and they set sail from Yarmouth on 29th April in a fleet of fifty ships; but it was still rough, and they reached Dordrecht at the mouth of the Rhine in Holland on 1st May, after a distinctly unpleasant crossing. A large party of magnates including the new Count of Holland and the Bishops of Liège and Utrecht were there to meet them. A slow and triumphal progress followed. Sanchia, shrugging off the rough sea as of no consequence, described it all succinctly in her letter to the Prior of Wallingford: 'Know then that our Lord the King, ourselves, Edmund and all our household arrived safe and sound without hindrance or peril at the most suitable port for us in the territory of the Count of Holland, where we were received honourably by the magnates of those parts. After a few days we continued on our journey, passing through the territories of numerous nobles who received us kindly enough. At Rogationtide we came to Aachen where we were received with the greatest honour and rejoicing as well as by the citizens of that town as by the magnates.'[22]

Aachen indeed, far from closing her gates as she and the other Rhenish League towns had sworn to do to any King not unanimously chosen, opened hers wide to Richard and received them all with a magnificence which took the Germans' breath away – a fact no doubt connected with the city's widely-developed weaving industry, which found its readiest market in England; and also with Konrad's work in preparing the ground for Richard's arrival. Aachen had already had cause to be grateful to Richard, who had realized that some granting of privileges in advance might tip the scales in his favour. On 9th April he had prevailed upon King Henry to grant 'exemption, at the instance of Richard, the King's brother, elected King of the Romans, of the citizens of Aachen from toll and pledge for the life of the said Richard'.[23] Among those who now came to meet him at the gates of the old imperial city was Gerhard, Archbishop of Mainz, released from captivity, and – to quote Richard himself – a glittering company of 'bishops, dukes, counts, barons, marquesses and nobles of our realm'.[24]

The great day dawned – Ascension Day, 17th May – the same date as Henry III's coronation thirty-four years earlier. Seated beneath the mighty cupola of the polygonal Minster of Aachen,

Richard was anointed by Konrad von Hochstaden and received at his hands the silver crown of Germany and the title of King of the Romans.* Philip von Falkenstein placed in his hands the eagle-crowned sceptre and orb, and then Richard withdrew to the marble throne of Charlemagne, commanding the whole interior of the Cathedral, where all the magnates of Germany came and knelt on the steps to do him homage. 'Our dearest consort was similarly crowned with us that day', he wrote to his seneschal afterwards; and according to Thomas Wykes it was Sanchia who stole the show: 'With him was crowned his most serene lady Sanchia, whose inestimable beauty illuminated in no small way the solemnity of the occasion.'[25] The long road to Aachen was behind Richard, and another daughter of Provence had realized her life's ambition.

* The title of 'King of the Romans' was borne by the prince elected by the seven German Electors, and crowned at Aachen, until such time as he achieved the full imperial dignity by being crowned in Rome by the Pope. Protocol demanded that the King of the Romans awaited a formal papal summons before proceeding to this last stage, and becoming Holy Roman Emperor.

CHAPTER NINE

LORD OF THE RHINELAND

THE DAY after the coronation another family ceremony took place. Kneeling before his father in the great hall of the Imperial 'Pfalz', or palace, at Aachen, the twenty-two-year-old Henry received the coveted order of knighthood with the title of 'Henry of Almayne' (d'Allemagne), and his beloved step-mother fastened the belt round her whilom page. Henry's rather belated elevation to knightly estate was no doubt deliberately planned so that the ceremony might be a direct sequel to the coronation; while the choice of his title shows equally that it was intended that he should succeed Richard on the throne. The feasting which followed the double ceremony was unique in the century for magnificence, and the Germans were amazed.[1] Robert of Gloucester wrote:

> The erl of Cornwaile
> Made so noble feste
> That of all that me wuste
> It was the richoste and the meste.[2]

Richard himself, describing the occasion in a letter home, writes that besides the two archbishops there were present ten bishops, thirty dukes and counts, and 3,000 knights. Among these were the Count Floris of Holland; the two Counts of Jülich, the Comte de Bar and the Count of Hainault, as well as Philipp von Falken-stein and Dieter or Dirk van Falkenburg.

Gerhard, Archbishop of Mainz, had distinguished himself a few days previously by defeating the forces of Archbishop Arnold of Trier, who had emerged from his castle of Koblenz and tried to bar Gerhard's passage down the Rhine from Mainz to Cologne *en route* for the coronation.[3] It was clear to Richard that no parley or mediation would have any effect on the bellicose Trierer. He wrote home to England on 18th May that he had assembled all possible forces and intended 'to break the Archbishop's horns'.

From Aachen he and Sanchia went on to Cologne, where Konrad showed them with pride the choir of his new Cathedral, steadily rising under the expert eye of Meister Gerhard.

Colonia Agrippina, the cross-roads of Western Europe, was the meeting-place of the nations where ancient Rome's civilization rubbed shoulders with that of the modern Holy Roman Empire. The narrow streets were thronged with the jostling merchants whose laden ships moved off up and down the Rhine continuously, many bearing the wines of the province across the sea to England. English ships came alongside to load, so that English seamen were a common sight in the city. Now Cologne was to become the seat of an English King, who felt himself immediately at home there. He wisely saw that, as peace could not be restored until he had personally cleared the Rhineland of opposition, he must leave his Queen behind to hold Court there in his stead. Although the Germans, as Matthew Paris said, loathed French pride and did not want to see any Frenchman lord in Germany, they were by no means averse to a beautiful, vivacious and intelligent Frenchwoman holding Court in her husband's absence. She was a tremendous magnet, and even Archbishop Konrad decided – when Richard moved off southwards – that his rightful place was in his own see.[4]

Richard left Cologne in the middle of June, a month after his coronation, at the head of all the forces he could muster, and rode up the Rhine at what for a medieval monarch was a cracking pace. Everything pointed to a trial of strength with the Archbishop of Trier, whose lands barred his path a little south of Linz-am-Rhein. When Gerhard of Mainz had defeated the forces of Arnold of Trier on 9th May he had also freed the important island castle of Pfalzgrafenstein at the entrance to the Rhine Gorge, some fifteen miles south of Koblenz; but Arnold, though he had been forced to retire up the Moselle to Trier, was still able to emerge, if he were so minded, and obstruct the King's path through the northern Rhine-narrows between Koblenz and Breisig.

Richard halted briefly at Bonn on 21st June. On the opposite bank, a short way inland amongst the steep valleys of the Siebengebirge, lay the Cistercian Abbey of Heisterbach, which now hoped to obtain from Richard a re-grant of the privileges accorded to it by the Emperor Henry VII. The natural place to have done so was Bonn, but Richard's stay there was so brief that the Cistercians' representatives had to hurry after him and only caught him up at Andernach, thirty miles farther south on the opposite bank, where he duly acceded to their wishes on 24th June.[5] Andernach was a town of the Archbishop of Trier, but the castle was a last outpost of Cologne, put there deliberately to defy the adjacent see and protect an important Rhine toll.

As yet there was no sign of Archbishop Arnold. If he wanted to attack Richard, now was his chance to come out of the valley of the Moselle and block that of the Rhine. He was strongly backed in his opposition to Richard, first and foremost by King Louis himself, and also by the Duke of Brabant, and the cities of Worms and Speier and their respective bishops. For some reason he hesitated to attack and Richard refrained from turning aside to provoke a clash. The cause of this procrastination lay in the relations between England and France, and was probably the first of those incidents which were to interfere with the planned evolution of his kingship throughout his reign.

Henry III wrote on 22nd June that he had begun negotiations with France for a resumption of the truce between the two countries. He had sent Walter de Canteloup, Bishop of Worcester, Hugh Bigod, Earl of Norfolk, and Brother Adam Marsh to King Louis as his ambassadors. The Bishop, when he had learned the wishes and intentions of the French King, was to come on to Germany to consult Richard. Henry wrote that he did not wish to enter into any firm commitments without first knowing Richard's opinion,[6] but meanwhile he besought his brother to do nothing which might jeopardize his own relations with Louis.

Clearly a frontal attack on the Archbishop of Trier would come within this category, and the trial of strength therefore never occurred;[7] but there were some obstinate castles in Arnold's territory along the Rhine – Rheineck,* Koblenz and Stolzenfels – and each of these Richard invested with a garrison of his own. Then he pushed on round the great bend of the Rhine, intending to hurry on to Mainz, whither Archbishop Gerhard had preceded him. It was in Richard's view essential to win over quickly those Rhenish towns which still sided with Arnold – particularly Worms, Speier and Oppenheim; but long before he could get there he was brought up short by the obdurate little walled town of Boppard.

Boppard lies below a towering hillside, where the Rhine Gorge begins in earnest. It was the Roman city of Bodobriga, and ever since the days of Charlemagne it had been a free imperial town. Within its walls stood a Preceptory of the Templars; and Richard was well aware that it was the Templars of Boppard who had particularly distinguished themselves in the Holy Land in the Third Crusade led by his uncle, Richard Cœur-de-Lion. Near by stood the newly consecrated Severinskirche. There were therefore cogent reasons why he should not destroy Boppard; yet, unlike Aachen, the little place stood firmly by the declaration of the Rhenish League not to admit a King who had not been chosen unanimously, and it had deliberately made a treaty of offence and defence for this special purpose with the town of Oberwesel, some miles farther upstream.[8] Between the two places stood the island castle of 'die Pfalz', on the Pfalzgrafenstein, and this Richard made his headquarters while the siege of Boppard proceeded; for it could be reached from downstream by barge conveniently without worrying about Oberwesel.

The siege was entrusted to Walram von Jülich, Richard's Marshal. As we have seen, it was Richard's policy to keep his English and German affairs, policies and households strictly apart. Lemcke takes the view that this was unintentional, as the Germans forced him to send his English henchmen home. But Richard's

* Actually a fief of Cologne, held of the Archbishop by the lords of Rheineck, but at the time occupied by a Trier garrison. It stands on a prominent rock just south of Niederbreisig.

policy in Cornwall gives this the lie; he used only Cornishmen to deal with Cornish matters, a wise and popular move. So it was now with Germany: Walram, one of the two Counts of Jülich, was appointed Marshal, Bishop Nicholas of Cambrai Chancellor, Konrad von Bolanden-Hohenfels Butler, Philipp von Falkenstein Chamberlain, and Monseigneur Arnold, Provost of Wetzlar, his Prothonotary. The appointments were made while he was still at Aachen, and the Marshal did not have to wait long for his abilities to be put to the test.

The siege dragged on for a month. Boppard was not in alliance with the Archbishop of Trier, but simply stood by its pledges. The castle of the Archbishops at the town's northern perimeter was then not of much account and was destined to be strengthened heavily for this reason by Arnold's successor. Konrad von Hochstaden, hearing of Richard's predicament, hurried south from Cologne to help him; while Gerhard hurried back north from Mainz. The Pfalzgraf was already with Richard: he had been hoping for a fight with Trier but Boppard would do. Faced with this formidable combination of the best fighters in the Rhineland, Boppard's ally Oberwesel took fright and made a private peace with Richard, obtaining from him a re-grant of the imperial independence and freedom from overlordship which Frederick II had bestowed on the town. The lords of the neighbouring castle of Schönberg had enforced their overlordship on the town since Frederick's death, and it was obviously politic to seize the opportunity of Richard being at the Pfalz to bargain with him at a time when the lords of Schönberg would know it was unwise to interfere.[9]

To Boppard, the defection of Oberwesel was a serious blow. Towards the end of August, after Walram von Jülich had been battering away with his siege engines for over a month, the little town surrendered on the verge of starvation, and Richard gave the garrison magnanimous terms. Boppard's important Rhine toll fell into his hands, as did that of Oberwesel, strategically straddling the narrow gorge at the Lorelei Rock. Well-pleased, he paid Oberwesel a brief visit and moved on towards Bingen, while Konrad von Hochstaden returned to Cologne to bear the good news to Sanchia.

Bingen was in the archdiocese of Mainz, and Richard's fame had gone before him by the mouth of Archbishop Gerhard. He received an enthusiastic reception from Bingen; and, after a day there, moved on to the vicinity of Mainz, where he spent Saturday, 25th August, preparing for his formal entry into the 'Golden City'. The following day, Sunday the twenty-sixth, was the occasion to which he had looked forward ever since his coronation; he could now reckon that the whole of the Middle and Lower Rhineland acknowledged his sway. At Gerhard's episcopal palace the Bishop of Strasbourg was waiting to pay him homage. In due course this support was to be very useful to him, and it already gave him an earnest of success in Alsace and the Upper Rhine Valley.

Richard spent three weeks in Mainz, exactly the same time as he had spent in Cologne, so as to be scrupulously fair to both Archbishops. He was at pains to use the time granting lavish privileges to the towns which had hitherto been his principal opponents. The Bishop of Strasbourg used his good offices energetically on Richard's behalf, and the apogee of his Rhineland journey was reached on 8th September. On that day he held formal Court in Mainz, having got Sanchia to come up from Cologne to join him; and they received the homage of Frankfurt, Oppenheim, Nuremburg, Friedberg, Wetzlar and Gelnhausen, all of which received extensive privileges in return.

When the great occasion was over most of his English knights had to return to England, because the leave granted them by Henry III up to Michaelmas, 1257, had expired. With them went Henry of Almayne,[10] leaving only ten English knights behind. In the middle of September Richard rode into Oppenheim, which had submitted to him on condition only of liberal privileges, one of them being the humiliating clause that he would release it from its homage if another king should be imposed by Papal decree. Nevertheless Richard knew that any concession was worthwhile if he could buy the Rhenish towns over to his side. Though one of the last towns to join him, Oppenheim was to become one of his favourites, a great beneficiary of his generosity, and the imperial castle of Landskron which rose immediately above it was to become his favourite German residence.

Seeing this, more and more towns sent their representatives to do homage, even Berne and Murten in what is now Switzerland;[11] but Worms and Speyer still held out. Richard, having reached Weissenburg in Alsace, sent his agents to them, but to no avail. It was too late in the year to conduct a campaign against them; and, moreover, disquieting intelligence had reached him – that his supplies of treasure, which came to him regularly from England, were in jeopardy by his remaining south of the territories of the Archbishop of Trier. It would not do for the Emperor-elect to run out of money in an area which he had only recently won over, and by 22nd September he had made up his mind. On the twenty-sixth he started northwards again, and by 22nd October was esconced in his winter quarters at Neuss, near Düsseldorf.

Thence he wrote to the Bishop of London, trustee of his lands, describing his great success, and pointing out that the whole Rhineland with the sole exceptions of Worms and Speyer, as well as Alsace, Swabia, Saxony and Upper Bavaria now recognized him. The Bishop of Lübeck, writing at the same time, calls him 'Lord from Basle to the sea'; and Powicke in the twentieth century describes him as 'astonishingly successful'. Six months earlier anything might have happened: Richard had been totally unsure of his reception. Now that he was undisputed lord of the Rhineland, Sanchia and he spent a joyful and sumptuous Christmas in his imperial palace of Kaiserswerth on an island in the Rhine.

CHAPTER TEN

AN URGENT SUMMONS HOME

WHILE in his winter quarters, Richard received some heartening news from Rome. The Papacy, originally favourable to his rival Alfonso, sent its representative Master Arlotus to Richard 'with very affectionate and favourable letters'. In return he wrote a letter to the Senate and people of Rome to the effect that the vote of the electors had been given unanimously for him, and that he was ready to accept the burden of the Empire – not out of avarice for the honour of rulership, or avarice of riches, but to the honour of God, from gratitude to the holy Church of Christ, to the honour of the Holy City, and to the security of the true faith. He regarded it as his chief duty to increase the splendour of the city of Rome, to maintain peace in her, and to regain all her own former rights.[1]

The reason for the Pope's change of heart was rather obscure. The cities of Lombardy were completely divided by the Guelf-Ghibelline feud and were looking for any outside allies they could find. In the autumn of 1257 one party, under Ezzelino da Romano, turned to seek alliance with Alfonso of Castile; and as Ezzelino was the Pope's sworn enemy it was a simple equation that the Pope should now turn to Richard.

By February, 1258, some of the Italian cities had already recognized him as Emperor, and later on messages reached him saying that they most earnestly desired him to come to Rome to receive the Imperial Crown. Principal among these cities was Milan.[2] As for Pope Alexander, he was convinced by Richard's prudent practice of scrupulously keeping his German and English affairs separate, that he would do the same if he became Emperor, and that the Papacy would have nothing to fear from him in the way of Italian aggrandizement on the Hohenstaufen pattern. Arlotus, the Pope's representative, was at Kaiserswerth for Easter, 1258, and informed the Bishop of Lübeck of Richard's successes in the eyes of Rome.[3] Everything therefore now seemed propitious for Richard's journey to the Holy City: protocol required that he should await an official summons from the Pope first, but meanwhile he used the Patriarch of Aquilegia, Gregory de Montelengo, as his intermediary. Gregory wrote glowingly about Richard to the Pope, and congratulated him on having now decided in Richard's favour.

From Aachen Richard sent promises of military and financial help to Sanchia's uncle, Thomas of Savoy, who would be very usefully placed *en route* to ensure a safe course to Rome. This was on 14th April. For his own financial requirements he turned to Henry III, who declared himself very ready to assist. Richard therefore sat back and waited for the Papal summons. He was probably never again so near the full Imperial dignity as in the spring of 1258.

While waiting he occupied his time in his favourite mission, peacemaking, this time between Archbishop Konrad and the city of Cologne, who had again fallen foul of one another. He had seen a good deal of Konrad in the winter of 1257–8, both at his palace at Neuss and at his other winter residence, the castle of Siegburg, crowning a little hill-top above the River Sieg a few miles east of the Rhine. The Archbishop had cause to be grateful to Richard, who had arranged a settlement between him and the city in March.[4] In return, Richard was content to be Konrad's guest for a while; he was short of money and did not want to overspend in view of his projected Italian adventure. Apart from a brief journey to Huy, on the Meuse, for the funeral of his old friend Jean d'Avesnes, on 26th March, he lay low in the neighbourhood of Cologne, waiting, but he waited in vain.

Once again the trouble was Alfonso of Castile, but this time he did not go to Italy.[5] As soon as the wily Pope learned that Alfonso had his hands full in Spain – where the Moors had besieged Cordoba – and that he could not come to Italy to interfere in

Lombardy's affairs, he cooled off towards Richard, because he was no longer in danger at home. He therefore sent no summons to Richard, forcing him thereby to cancel all his preparations for his Roman journey – despite advice from the Cardinal of Toledo that he should ignore the official summons and go without it. Since this advice came from a Spanish Cardinal, it may well have been designed to embroil Richard with the Pope and so play into the hands of Alfonso. Richard was, however, too shrewd for all this, and instead devoted his energies to securing peace between England and France with the object of drawing off the most formidable of Alfonso's supporters, King Louis.

While these political moves were taking place, Richard made another journey up the Rhine with the intention of bringing Worms and Speyer to heel. He was at Mainz for Whitsun, and pushed on to Oppenheim directly after the festival, fully expecting to be able to make a triumphal entry into Worms right away. But the city still obstinately refused to accept him, until it learned that he was gathering an army at Oppenheim with the intention of attacking. Then at last, on 24th July, 1258, it agreed to accept Richard as King in response to the grant of numerous privileges. Worms was to become his favourite among Imperial cities, as Oppenheim was among towns.

This stage accomplished, Johann, Bishop of Lübeck, an active partisan of Richard's, turned his energies to cracking the hardest nut of all – Trier. Johann agreed to meet its Archbishop, Arnold von Isenburg, at Koblenz early in August. Richard had commissioned him to offer Arnold twelve thousand marks for his adherence; and the Trierer Archbishop was known to be vacillating already. He had in fact written to Alfonso of Castile saying that if he did not come to Germany quickly he would withdraw his support. There now occurs one of those infuriating gaps in the chronicles, so that we do not know exactly what transpired at the meeting at Koblenz; but Arnold's opposition to Richard certainly cooled thereafter.

News from England earlier in the year had been bad. The harvest of 1257 had been disastrous, and that winter famine threatened the country. Henry realized the advantage of having a brother as a Continental monarch, and in the early months of 1258 sent off an urgent appeal to Richard, who responded promptly by dispatching fifty ships laden with corn to alleviate the English distress.[6] Floods followed famine, and throughout England there was an undercurrent of misery and discontent. The great magnates, though not immediate sufferers like their serfs, were in an irritable mood.

Politically, Henry went on trying to secure a truce with Louis. On 20th May a treaty was signed in Paris at a ceremony attended among others by Richard's prothonotary, Arnold von Wetzlar. Soon after his return from France, Monseigneur Arnold was dispatched to Rome in a new attempt to obtain the Pope's recognition.[7] He was bidden to say that Richard had now extended his rule to practically the whole of Germany – indeed, the only great magnate who still stood out for Alfonso of Castile was the Duke of Brabant, though he was unable to offer any serious resistance to Richard. To cap his success, Speyer and its Bishop acknowledged Richard in October. Monseigneur Arnold wrote back from Rome that support for Richard was forthcoming from the majority of the College of Cardinals. All seemed set fair – if only it had not been for Henry III.

'Wax heart' was the sobriquet which Matthew Paris once gave him, very deservedly. Henry fancied himself as the supreme ruler, riding roughshod over the wishes of the baronage; but when it came to a collision his nerve invariably failed him. While Richard was at his side, his moderate counsels prevented disaster;[8] but when Richard was away in Germany, Henry was helpless under the influence of Queen Eleanor and her swarm of Provençal relatives, whom he loaded with privileges. The baronial party, led by Simon de Montfort – now back from Gascony – was the spearhead of the national wave of disgust and xenophobia, exacerbated by Henry's Sicilian venture and consequent indebtedness to the Pope. To put it bluntly, 'Henry had got his kingdom in a dreadful mess.'[9] The Papal Nuncio Arlotus had come to England from Germany at Easter, 1258, with a mandate to squeeze out of the

English the taxes due for the 'Sicilian business'. This was more than the barons could stomach. As Denholm Young observes: 'Richard's departure for Germany in 1257 had been a momentous event, a prime factor in letting loose the biggest political storm since Magna Carta.'[10]

Simon de Montfort came back to England for the Hoke-tide Parliament of 1258, and this assembly was the signal for an outburst of discontent. Simon's leadership of the baronage was not as yet undisputed – rather did that honour fall to Richard de Clare, Earl of Gloucester; and on 12th April he formed a confederation of nobles, including Simon and Roger Bigod, the Marshal, swearing to stand together in all things. Henry's financial demands were stubbornly refused. On 1st May they all turned up at Westminster early in the morning in full armour. Henry was terrified. 'What is this, my lords? Am I your prisoner?' he cried. The Marshal replied that this was not so, but that the intolerable Poitevins and other aliens must be banished; moreover, the King must promise that he and the Lord Edward would not act without the advice of 'twenty-four good men of England'. To this the trembling King agreed, and the twenty-four – half royalists, half baronial nominees – were appointed a few days later. A further Parliament was called for June at Oxford.

At it the barons drew up their famous Provisions, a series of memoranda, and from the twenty-four they chose a steering committee or inner council of fifteen designed to control the King's activities. These fifteen were to report three times annually to Parliament.[11] Orders enacted at Oxford included a requirement for all aliens to give up whatever lands, revenues and castles they held. The Poitevins were furious, and, determined to resist, escaped from Oxford and galloped full-tilt to the protection of Wolvesey Castle at Winchester, the stronghold of one of their number, the Bishop Aymer de Valence. The barons understood their intentions, besieged Wolvesey, and, when it surrendered, insisted that the Poitevins, including the Bishop, should be banished. As a final fling the Poitevins plotted to poison the magnates in the royal castle of Winchester, and succeeded as far as some of the lesser lights were concerned. Young Henry de Montfort was the leader of a band of infuriated young noblemen who pursued them across the Channel. The other barons, once restored to health, set out for London in the hopes of rallying the citizens to their cause. Prominent amongst them was Simon de Montfort, who took up his abode in the palace of the Bishop of Durham by the Strand.

The atmosphere in the capital was tense, matching the oppressive thundery weather. King Henry had gone down-river in his barge for an *al fresco* meal away from the noisome city, when suddenly a violent thunderstorm broke out. 'Wax heart' was terribly afraid of thunder, and ordered his oarsmen to row for the near-by town house of the Bishop. As the royal barge came alongside the watergate, the Bishop and Simon de Montfort hurried to meet it. Simon asked the King quite solicitously why he was afraid: 'See, my lord, the storm is over.' Shaken by having unexpectedly encountered his formidable brother-in-law, Henry replied: 'By the head of God, I fear thee more than all the thunder and lightning in the world.' This chance encounter, though Simon was completely innocent of any fell intent, added one more link to the chain of mutual dislike and distrust which had been steadily forged between the two men since the incident in the Abbey twenty years before. Coming just when it did, it served to underline the hatefulness of the Provisions to the King. He saw his authority frittered away by them; his judiciary decentralized; the extension of governmental responsibility by the appointment of temporary sheriffs; and the widening of the base of the pyramid by the election of four knights from every shire, who were to attend the shire court and make a record of complaints, injuries and trespasses.[12]

In addition to Henry III, neither the Lord Edward nor Henry of Almayne – who since his return from Germany had been drawn into ever closer friendship with his cousin – would at first subscribe to the Provisions; but the barons were determined to get their way. They informed Henry of Almayne that if he did not agree within forty days they would confiscate Richard of Cornwall's entire holdings in England.[13] Richard had attempted to make his eldest son more independent of the barons by making over to him the castle and honour of Knaresborough, but with little success.

To avoid such a disaster as the confiscation of his father's lands, Henry of Almayne gave in, but sent off an urgent message to Richard. Henry III also directed a *cri de cœur* to his brother to come home, the one thing the barons really feared.[14] As Bappert observed: 'Richard had been brought into close union with the barons through his first wife, Isabella; as a result of his marriage with his second wife, Sanchia, he had turned closer to the King, though he did not lack understanding of the English national movement.' Richard was at Worms when Henry's appeal reached him, and he was prudent enough to see that if his vast possessions in England were endangered, so was his German crown, which relied on them for its financial foundation. He turned about and headed down the Rhine.

This was one of the most momentous decisions of the many which Richard had to take. It vitally affected for the worse his future career in Germany, for, having made such progress, he now had to leave the country at a critical time. It is difficult to see what other decision he could have made, but he must have made it with anguish of heart.

In his dispositions for the care of his kingdom in his absence he betrayed his Englishness, appointing temporary regents in the most important territories, a practice almost unknown in Germany.[15] The lower basin of the Upper Rhine and the whole of Alsace were entrusted to Bishop Heinrich of Strasbourg, who had served him so well; the Wetterau, lying north-west of Frankfurt, he delivered to his trusted Chamberlain, Philipp von Falkenstein; while the Rhine tolls of Boppard and Oberwesel, which were so important and must remain in friendly hands, were placed in the care of Philipp von Bolanden–Hohenfels. The Lords of Bolanden were one of the most powerful families in the Middle Rhine area, with their castle on the edge of the Donnersberg mountain east of Kaiserslautern; and to Philipp was to be entrusted in years to come the safe-keeping of Richard's third wife. The obvious choice for Vicar-General of the whole Kingdom was Konrad von Hochstaden, who was also specifically charged with ensuring the peace of north-western Germany up to the River Weser. On the strength of this, the see of Cologne was in future years to lay claim to the northern part of Westphalia.[16]

Richard set off westwards from Cologne directly after Christmas. It had been his intention, as envisaged in the treaty with France, to meet his brother and King Louis at Cambrai.[17] He hoped to get them to join forces with him for a three-pronged attack on the barons; but as it was, the latter suspected such a plan, and refused to let Henry III leave England. Louis IX, hearing of this, decided to stay in Paris, so the projected meeting came to nought. On 14th January Richard reached Arras, and turned north thence to St. Omer, making for the coast – having previously sent messengers to the Parliament of barons assembled at Westminster, to announce his intended return. This announcement threw them into considerable confusion. Their leader, Simon de Montfort, was in Paris, negotiating with Louis IX; in his absence, something had to be done quickly, and they decided to send an embassy to waylay Richard at St. Omer and use all possible pressure to make him subscribe to the Provisions of Oxford before he crossed the Channel. They issued a warning to the Cinque Ports that anyone who ferried him across would be executed.[18]

The embassy which met him at St. Omer was headed by young Guy and Simon de Montfort, his former pages – not a very diplomatic choice; for Guy, spiteful and aggressive, took pleasure in humiliating his former master and mistress. He now informed them that unless Richard subscribed to the Provisions he would not be allowed to land at Dover. The King of the Romans had with him only Sanchia, Edmund, the ten English knights who had stayed with him, and a handful of German ones. Resistance was useless and he formally promised to comply. On 28th January they landed at Dover, to be greeted effusively by Henry, but the baronial castellan of Dover Castle refused to admit them. Humiliated now in the eyes of his German knights, Richard rode on to Canterbury in whose Cathedral, in the presence of the King and barons, he swore on the four Gospels in accordance with the undertaking he had given at St. Omer, that he would work with the magnates for the reform of the realm and would do nothing to obstruct them on pain of confiscation of his estates. The oath was dictated by his stepson, Richard de Clare, Earl of Gloucester, who treated him with scant courtesy, never once using his royal title but referring to him as 'Earl of Cornwall', and declaring himself barely satisfied with the undertakings given.[19]

The whole degrading affair made a most unfavourable impression on the German knights, who wrote back home asking how they could be expected to have respect for a King who was treated with such contempt by his fellow-countrymen. The English in their turn wondered why the Germans allowed their King to return to England with such a paltry escort, and concluded that they were more interested in Richard's money than in Richard himself.[20]

CHAPTER ELEVEN

TO ROME OR NOT?

THE COLOURFUL WELCOME which awaited Richard in London compensated him somewhat for his chilly reception at Dover. A week later he was present at the Parliament of magnates held at Westminster, also attended by Simon de Montfort, who had just returned from France. The principal business was the final preparation of the peace treaty with Louis, but the assembly also saw the first open breach between Simon and Richard de Clare.

They were discussing an ordinance for the shire courts which greatly enhanced the rights of the lesser men *vis-à-vis* the baronage.[1] Simon had always been inclined to champion the rights of the underdog – indeed, foreigner though he was, the common people regarded him as their hero. Richard de Clare, however, did not like it and played for time. Simon saw through this manœuvre, and, his impatient nature getting the better of him, burst out furiously: 'I hate to live with such changeable and treacherous men. We took our oath to do these things!' Ironically enough in the light of subsequent events, it was Richard of Cornwall who patched up the quarrel between them. Simon returned to France to continue his diplomatic mission, but de Clare, still smouldering, followed him to Paris and poured scorn on him before Louis's Court for delaying the ratification of the treaty in order to serve the private interests of his wife. Simon replied with fury, and the spectacle of two English magnates indulging in verbal thunderbolts vastly amused the French onlookers.

Richard of Cornwall meanwhile was touring his estates with Sanchia, collecting money for a journey to Rome. By an unhappy mischance Pope Alexander IV, who had decided to summon

Richard to his Imperial Coronation,[2] had assumed he was still in Germany and had sent an English monk, Walter de Rogate, to Worms to look for him. When Walter eventually caught up with Richard in England he was five hundred miles farther from Rome than he would have been at Worms, and he had not yet amassed sufficient treasure to attempt the journey. His reply to the Pope was therefore courteously evasive.

None the less, he resumed his preparations with zest, intending to go first to France with his brother in the autumn, to fulfil the tryst Henry had with Louis at Abbeville.[3] Even this appeared on reflection to be too soon for him, and he decided to postpone going to Rome till the following year. A journey to the West Country would provide the needed resources, and he had neglected Devon and Cornwall too long. As if by way of expiation he granted a charter to the city of Exeter in London on 7th December, and rode out westwards with Sanchia the following day. They were at their new castle of Mere on the eleventh, and on the twenty-third crossed the Tamar into Launceston, in whose castle they celebrated Christmas and remained till Richard's fifty-first birthday on 5th January.

On 29th October Henry had granted a 'licence for Richard, Earl of Cornwall, going to the court of Rome on his own affairs, to tallage* his boroughs and manors which were the King's demesnes.'[4] His coffers were thus steadily filling. While still at Launceston he was engaged in intense diplomatic activity with the Pope through his English and Imperial emissaries, among whom was the Bishop of Liège, who was dispatched to Rome from Launceston on 28th December, directly the Christmas festivities were over. With his usual attention to detail, Richard wrote from Cornwall to the German princes requiring them to repair the roads in their territories so that he could make a rapid transit of of the country *en route* to Rome.

By the time he got back to London he considered he had amassed sufficient treasure to start on his journey. But again the contrariness

* *Tallage:* A special tax levied with royal approval only. The name originates from the French word 'tailler', to cut or trim.

of fate intervened, in the shape of a violent quarrel between Richard de Clare and the Lord Edward, an extension of the already irreparable breach between the former and Simon de Montfort. While King Henry was absent in France this grew worse, and Gloucester put about the rumour that the Lord Edward intended to seize the opportunity of his father's absence to usurp the throne with the help of Simon de Montfort. Credence was added to this scandal when Simon came back to England secretly in February, 1260, bringing a good deal of war material with him. Civil strife appeared inevitable.

Henry made a feeble attempt to avert disaster by writing from France to forbid the holding of the spring Parliament provided for by the Provisions of Oxford. His son and the barons of both factions decided to ignore this ban and to hold it none the less. It was obvious that London would become the battleground. Richard decided that now was another moment for immediate and decisive action on the Taillebourg pattern. He rode hurriedly from Wallingford to London, where he met his friends Hugh Bigod and Philip Basset and together they prevailed upon the Mayor and citizens to close the city's gates and keep Gloucester and Edward out. Then he set to work to obtain a reconciliation between them, and eventually brought about a compromise on 18th April.[5] An urgent summons to King Henry to return was then sent to France. Henry could now come back without danger; but just to be on the safe side he brought a large number of mercenaries with him and landed at Dover on 23rd April.[6]

His son, Simon de Montfort, and their followers hastened to meet him, but he refused to have anything to do with them. On arrival in London he admitted Gloucester to the city but left Edward and Simon outside. He took up his residence inside London instead of at his usual palace of Westminster. It took Richard a week's steady persuasion to effect a reconciliation between father and son, which eventually took place at St. Paul's Cathedral on the thirtieth. Henry was at last convinced that Edward had not intended to supplant him. He was not so sure about Simon; and at a Parliament held in May, the King seized the opportunity to put him on trial again. De Montfort declared that he was entirely willing to answer anything, and at this bold reply the King hesitated. Meanwhile news of Henry's intention reached the ears of Louis IX; the French King's strong sense of justice was outraged, and he was most unwilling that Henry III should take any action against Simon. He accordingly sent the Archbishop Odo of Rouen, one of the most respected of French churchmen, as a secret emissary to Henry to intercede on de Montfort's behalf. Odo succeeded in getting the King and Simon to submit their quarrel to a commission of bishops. There was insufficient evidence to convict Simon at his trial, despite Henry's impressive list of charges, and the case was dropped. But though Simon was free, the inquiry had stirred up yet more resentment within him against the King, albeit they were nominally reconciled in June. Henry emerged from the city on the sixteenth and resumed his normal residence at Westminster.

Complete reconciliation between Edward and Gloucester took place on 11th June.[7] On the Tuesday before St. Botolph's the following judgement was given by Henry and Richard; 'Whereas divers contentions were moved between Edward the King's son and Richard de Clare, Earl of Gloucester and Hertford, and they have submitted themselves to the decision and ordinance of the King and Richard, King of Almayne, the Kings pronounce as follows to wit that all contentions up to the feast of St. Botolph, 1260, be remitted on condition that all covenants and instruments between them before this date be firmly kept and if any further discords arise between them and their men, these shall be amended by the dictators nominated in the said instruments.'[8]

This document bears Richard's stamp very clearly. By the time it was issued he was free to attend to his own interests, but the two months' extra delay had been fatal. He had completely regained his political influence in England, but he could not wait any longer to enjoy it. On 17th June he embarked in London and sailed down the Thames to Gravesend, where Sanchia and a huge retinue met him; thence he continued his journey overland through Canterbury to Dover, embarking there on 20th June. On the twenty-second King Henry issued a 'request to the King's brother, Richard, King of the Romans, who before leaving the King, pronounced his award in the matter of the Lord Edward and the Earl of Gloucester, to cause his seal to be put on the above letters patent. And the King desires him to let him know by the bearer his state and good pleasure and how he crossed the sea, and how the affairs of his realm are'.[9]

Henry might well ask, seeing that his misgovernment was the root cause of Richard's affairs not going well. Though he had re-established his old political ascendancy in England, his German companions had gone away with a different impression which had been widely bruited abroad in Germany with the most unfortunate effect. Though his Vicar-General had done his best and had effected a nation-wide peace treaty in November, 1259, and though even more German towns had recognized him and were awaiting privileges at his hands, the barons had become very obstreperous. New castles, little better than robbers' nests, were growing up at points where they could interfere with travellers and trade. There had been a falling off of some of his adherents, including – astonishingly enough – Archbishop Gerhard of Mainz, one of his own Electors, who shortly before his death had gone over to Alfonso of Castile. Frederick II's grandson Konradin had also made sporadic attempts to assert his rights in Germany.

Trouble in the archdiocese of Mainz was mirrored even in Cologne. The long struggle between Konrad von Hochstaden and his city had taken a turn in his favour: he had driven out all the principal noble families from Cologne, for while he might be busy ensuring 'Landsfrieden' on behalf of his master Richard, he was equally busy increasing his own temporal authority.[10] The previous year he had influenced the Gräfin Mechthild von Sayn to stop work on a castle at Alsnach, near Rossbach on the Wied River; and in January he had set up one Wigand von Medebach in the castle of Hallenberg as his own castellan. Thus steadily he extended his sway over the Rhineland.

An interesting extract from the 'Domstift' dated 7th May, 1259, throws some more light on his relations with the citizens:

'Archbishop Konrad, at the request of the citizens of Cologne, decrees that no merchant from Hungary, Bohemia, Poland, Bavaria, Swabia, Saxony, Thuringia or Hesse and other eastern lands may travel west of Cologne with his wares; no merchant from Flanders, Brabant or from beyond the Meuse or from the Netherlands may travel south of Rodenkirchen. Foreigners may only remain in the city six weeks, pay for certain goods only in merchants' marks and trade in other goods only *en gros*. The silver trade is granted to the citizens of Cologne in restricted measure, but foreign goldsmiths and dealers in precious stones do not submit to any restrictions. Citizens of Cologne may not accept any monetary loans from enemies of the Cathedral Church of Cologne. An alderman of Cologne may not be a coiner or moneychanger and is excluded from the guild of coiners.'[11] It was clear that if Konrad was to maintain his ascendancy over his neighbours and his flock he could not afford to leave Cologne to accompany the King to Rome. No sooner would the archiepiscopal cat be away than the Kölner mice would be playing the game of independence.

Richard's old enemy, Archbishop Arnold of Trier, was now dead, and neither his possible successor, nor Gerhard's at Mainz, had yet shown his hand. This could well be to Richard's advantage; and though elsewhere circumstances seemed unpropitious, he decided to proceed with his journey. He left Cologne at the end of July, after sealing a treaty between Konrad and the Duke of Brunswick,[12] and placing in Konrad's hands the authority to invest bishops in his absence. He paused briefly at Koblenz, where he secured the adherence of the favourite candidate for the see of Trier, Heinrich von Vinstingen. This time Boppard did not gainsay him; so he hastened on to Mainz, won over its new Archbishop, Werner von Eppstein, and on 4th August rode into Worms. He had had the city in his mind's eye as a jumping-off point, where he would take the final decision whether to proceed to Rome or not. What he needed most was what he could not be sure of – the loyalty of the German princes. Even the Pfalzgraf was known to have cooled towards him.

Nevertheless he sent one of his English knights ahead of him to seek still greater support in Italy. He had high hopes of the Guelph faction, and indeed they sent an emissary to him – Guilielmo Beroardi of Florence – to seek his help against the Ghibellines. The College of Cardinals also sent messengers, begging him to hurry before the Pope changed his mind.[13] If only Richard had had the courage to repeat his feat of Taillebourg and go virtually alone to Rome, he would probably have succeeded; but – to the exasperation of his admirers – his prudence and caution got the better of him. He would not stir without sufficient backing from his German vassals and this was simply not forthcoming. He decided to wait, disbursing money open-handedly to win the support of such magnates as the Count of Württemberg and the new Bishop of Strasbourg, Walter von Geroldseck. Thus in the late summer his chances hung in the balance; the year was wearing on, and a crossing of the Alps would not be possible very much longer.

Suddenly in early September came intelligence which dashed his hopes completely. The news of his projected journey to Rome had reached the ears of Alfonso of Castile who immediately sent his brother Manuel as Ambassador to the Pope and rapidly persuaded him to renounce his partiality to Richard and become once more strictly neutral. The Pope sent his notary to Richard with a polite note, making no further mention of his election to the imperial crown but saying that he could not decide between the two candidates.[14] Hard on the heels of this dismaying communication came the news of the complete defeat of the Guelphs by the Ghibellines at the battle of Montaperto on 4th September. Richard had counted on their support to bring him to the imperial dignity; and in this bitter moment he saw the frustration of all his ambitions. Whatever successes he had again achieved in Germany by his presence – and large tracts of formerly hostile territory were now his – they were as nothing compared to his overwhelming disappointment when success had seemed so near.

Sick at heart, Richard turned again towards England on 17th September. It is a measure of his disillusionment that he could not bear to stay in Germany, although he had only been there three months. What Sanchia felt may be imagined, and it is not impossible that the tremendous disappointment hastened her untimely death.

The day before his departure from Worms Richard held a Diet there, at which he made arrangements for the government of Germany in his absence. He granted the city all its former privileges, including the Rhine toll of Oppenheim; and adjudicated in a long-standing feud between Worms and the Ritter Jakob von Stein, paying the knight's expenses out of his own pocket. The same viceroys were again appointed to rule the kingdom, with some extension of privileges to the Bishop of Speyer and the Graf von Katzenelnbogen. Then he got under way, passed rapidly down the Rhine through Mainz and Boppard along the familiar route. At Cologne he confirmed Konrad's right to invest bishops, and hastened on – for his treasury was nearly exhausted – through Liège and Cambrai to the coast; and so, with Sanchia and his small English retinue, came into Dover on 24th October.

His German subjects had picked him clean so effectively that he had to borrow horses from the Prior of Dover to make the journey to Canterbury.[15] Thus the man who had left to obtain the imperial crown in Rome re-landed in England a virtual pauper. Poverty was a quality never before associated with Richard, and the country buzzed with rumour. Some said he had been robbed by Manfred's partisans; others that the Germans had dissuaded him from making the journey to Italy because of the approach of winter, others again that he had returned to supervise his estates and glean more money, yet others that the Pope had ordered him home.[16] There is a modicum of truth in some of these opinions, but the turning-point in Richard's career had come; henceforward he identified himself far more closely with his brother's English kingdom, and let his imperial dreams remain dreams. Instead of receiving a triumphal welcome, husband and wife came sadly and almost unnoticed into London on 29th October, 1260.[17]

CHAPTER TWELVE

THE QUEEN OF ALMAYNE

THE DAY after Richard and Sanchia's arrival in London King Alexander of Scotland also arrived, followed a few days later by his Queen, the former Princess Margaret of England, who was expecting a child and wished to have it in her parents' palace. The meeting of the three royal couples was a brilliant occasion and raised the flagging spirits of Richard and Sanchia. Alexander returned to Scotland in the middle of November, leaving Margaret behind – having obtained a sworn promise from Henry, Richard and the English magnates that they would allow her to return to Scotland unhindered after the birth of her baby.

Richard and Sanchia now withdrew to Berkhamsted. He had virtually to begin his English affairs again from scratch and much had happened during his absence in Germany. One of the most serious from his biographers' point of view, was the death in 1259 of the chronicler of St. Albans Abbey, Matthew Paris, the greatest of all the sources on his life. Richard had been on quite friendly terms with Matthew of later years; the monk had appreciated his coolness, level-headedness and deep religious sense, though in Richard's younger days he had been critical of his brashness and extravagance. Matthew clearly regarded the Earl as his most reliable source and contact in high places, and quoted him widely in his *Chronica Majora*. His mantle now fell upon Thomas Wykes, annalist of Oseney Abbey, Oxford, who was, however, much more Richard's man pure and simple than Paris had been.

From Berkhamsted Richard went to Wallingford and thence to his manor of Beckley, near Oxford, where he settled a dispute between Wykes's House of Oseney and one of his tenants. Richard was always addicted to Beckley and was instrumental in improving the cruciform church with its skew chancel, through which the rising sun shines upon the patron's day. It will be recalled that he had bitterly resented the sacking of his manor there by Richard Siward many years before.* Richard spent Christmas at Windsor with Henry, but Sanchia stayed behind at Berkhamsted. She was already ill, though none of the chroniclers appears to have known the exact nature of her malady.[1]

Meanwhile both Simon de Montfort and the royal family had striven towards greater reconciliation. The Lord Edward knighted Simon's two elder sons, Henry and Simon, at the feast of Saint Edward on 13th October, 1260, and then crossed to France with Henry of Almayne and the two new knights to take part in tournaments. Richard's son had acted as deputy at the feast for Simon the elder, who had gone into Wales at the head of a royal army – a deliberate move by Henry III to get him out of the way. When he returned the King persuaded him to submit his long-standing quarrel about Eleanor's estate to the arbitration of Louis IX. Again and again Eleanor had had to fight for her lands in Poitou which her mother, Isabella, had calmly annexed in favour of her Lusignan offspring. Henry III, considering that his sister had been unfairly treated, therefore recommended that she submit her claims to the one arbiter who was completely impartial.

Nevertheless, while professing concern for Simon and his wife, Henry tried to disentangle himself from his oath to keep the detested Provisions of Oxford.[2] He sent messengers secretly to the Pope seeking absolution from this oath, among them Richard's old friend John Mansel. This seasoned negotiator succeeded in persuading the Pope to grant a Bull revoking the Provisions of Oxford. Having protected Mansel by seizing Dover Castle from the barons, Henry returned to London and made a public announcement that in future he intended to disregard the Provisions. The ensuing uproar was sufficient to send him scuttling for the safety of the Tower, where Queen Eleanor was already ensconced. Henry immediately set about strengthening its defences,[3] and sent an

* See p. 48.

urgent appeal to Richard – who was temporarily at Wallingford – to come to London to use his influence with the citizens, as his stock with them stood much higher than the King's own. Richard succeeded in putting them in a good mood, which Henry promptly spoiled by requiring every Londoner over the age of twelve to swear fealty to him in a ceremony in St. Paul's on 12th February.[4] He contrived by this action to make himself almost as ridiculous as he had when he made young Edmund appear in Sicilian dress.

Richard, anxious to retain his influence with the barons, did not wish to bring his support for his brother out into the open; so, after a brief and furtive visit to London, he retired to Berkhamsted again to be with Sanchia who was growing steadily worse. Here he remained for most of the summer, taking little part in politics, but clandestinely supporting Henry from a distance. At Whitsun Henry was at Winchester, where he produced to the astonished barons a Papal Bull, received in reply to his letter of January, releasing him from all the terms of the Provisions of Oxford.[5] His duplicity naturally enraged them still further and sparked off many threats; the barons planned to meet him fully armed, but Mansel got wind of it and warned Henry in time for him to creep back to the safety of the Tower. Emboldened by the strength of those ancient walls, he removed the sheriffs and castellans appointed by the terms of the Provisions of Oxford and replaced them by his own nominees. The barons wrote to King Louis imploring him to arbitrate between them and the King. Simon de Montfort went over to France to reinforce their request; but Henry, hearing he had gone, took fright again and also wrote to Louis in order to ensure the French King's favour towards him.

In May came information that the city of Rome had elected Richard a Senator for life. An embassy from the Holy City brought him the news, assured him of their loyalty, and handed over a letter from the College of Cardinals advising him to come to Rome in haste in order to take up his senatorship and use the opportunity to obtain his imperial crown at the Pope's hands.[6] But Richard played safe: his experience of the previous year did not recommend the idea to him. Nevertheless his repute in Italy was now so great that his former enemies, the Ghibellines, wrote to him on 20th May asking him to lend them his support against the Guelphs.

Still he hesitated, and while he did so came news of another important event – the death of Pope Alexander IV. His successor was a French cardinal, who assumed the name of Urban IV and who – as might be expected – took a very different view of an Englishman becoming Emperor. He declined to recognize Richard's election as Senator of Rome and announced that he would personally deal with the problem of the rival imperial candidates. It was clear to Richard that there was practically no further hope of his becoming Emperor, and he decided to concentrate on his German kingdom.

Initially the Germans saw nothing strange in Richard's absence, since they were used to Frederick II spending long periods in Italy; but, as time wore on, there were signs of the settled pattern breaking up. A severe blow to Richard's prestige was the death, on 28th September, of Archbishop Konrad von Hochstaden after twenty-three years in the see of Cologne. The man who had always been Richard's chief supporter in Germany was thus suddenly removed from the scene; and though his successor, Engelbert von Falkenburg, immediately did homage to Richard by proxy, and excused his own absence from London, the withdrawal of Konrad's energetic personality was not so easily overcome. The appointment of one of the Falkenburgs to succeed him was to be of great significance to Richard, but in another sphere. He had already had friendly relations for some time with this noble family whose castle lay conveniently along the route from the coast to Aachen; and Engelbert was also a stepbrother of Richard's faithful henchman Philipp von Bolanden-Hohenfels.

Towards the end of October Richard was at Berkhamsted at Sanchia's bedside; but early in November emissaries from Germany, including Bishop Johann of Lübeck, arrived in London, urgently requiring Richard's presence, and he left his wife to go to the capital. Her imminent death was already a foregone conclusion, and she may already have been unconscious; for on 1st November the King issued a patent at the Tower of London to 'grant that the executors of the will of Sanchia, Queen of the Romans, for the good of her soul, may dispose of the manors of Eston and Beneby, late of William de Canteloup, which the King had granted to her'.[7] A week later Richard was immersed in German business; and on the eighth he issued a patent to Engelbert of Cologne entrusting him with the coronation regalia in his absence but requiring him to renew his oath of fealty directly Richard returned to Germany.[8]

Late the following day he was still sitting in Westminster Hall with the Bishop of Lübeck and Monseigneur Arnold beside him, when a messenger from Berkhamsted came hastily in. 'In the same year on the Wednesday next before the feast of Saint Martin there died at Berkhamsted Sanchia, Queen of Almayne, sister of Eleanor, Queen of England, and her body was conveyed in the care of the venerable father Boniface, Archbishop of Canterbury, and two other bishops and of the Lord Peter of Savoy and other magnates to the House of Hayles, where she was buried.'[9] Thus wrote the annalist of Oseney.

It has been fashionable to condemn Richard for not being present at her deathbed and for not attending her funeral. The former is explained by the illness having dragged on for a twelvemonth so that it was very uncertain exactly when the end would come; but the second is not so easily explained. It seems fantastic that Richard should have regarded any German business as being important enough to justify keeping him from his wife's funeral, when one remembers his break-neck ride from Devon to Berkhamsted at Isabella's death twenty years before.

Denholm-Young goes as far as to say that 'it would be wrong to assume any great depth of affection between them'. This is a very doubtful statement. We have seen that their courtship and marriage was one of the few love-matches of the time, that fifteen years later she was still described as of inestimable beauty – a characteristic to which Richard was always susceptible, and that he was with her most of the summer of 1261, and indeed was still there on 23rd October. He raised for her a magnificent tomb and effigy in the choir at Hayles, and on 7th December obtained from his brother a grant 'for the saving of the King's soul and the soul of Sanchia, Queen of Almayne, to the master and brethren of the hospital of St. Katherine without the Tower of London, of 50 shillings a year at the Exchequer for the maintenance of a chaplain celebrating divine service daily in the chapel of St. John within the Tower for her soul'.[10]

Did Richard have other interests? It is generally thought that he did have a mistress, though her identity is obscure. The *Flores historiarum** states that on 5th August of the same year an illegitimate son of Richard died at Winchelsea, but other authorities doubt the accuracy of this. Elsewhere there are hints about an illegitimate daughter. Richard was always a 'coveter of women', a '*Frauenlob*' on whose career the female sex had the profoundest influence. There is no positive ground for ascribing to him any cooling off towards the only wife of the three who lies buried beside him.

Thus died, much younger than her three sisters, the beauty of Provence who had been so instrumental in making Richard a king – leaving behind a son of eleven years, Edmund, who was later to bring to the Abbey where his mother lay one of the most precious holy relics of the Middle Ages. With her death, a period of Richard's life also reached its close. Before him lay lonely years of warfare, imprisonment, the disintegration of Germany, even of murder, redeemed but briefly by the presence of a German girl-wife nearly forty years his junior.

* Roger of Wendover's great history of mankind from the days of Genesis up to the contemporary period of the mid-thirteenth century, commonly known as *The Flowers of History*.

PART THREE

THE PRISONER OF MONTFORT AND BEATRIX VON FALKENBURG

1261–1272

CHAPTER ONE

THE UNCROSSED ALPS

SANCHIA was barely in her grave when news of trouble in Germany reached Richard. His neglect was having its effect, and the new Archbishop of Mainz, Werner, had started quarrelling with Philipp von Bolanden-Hohenfels. Doubtless encouraged by the cooler attitude of the Pope towards Richard, Werner entered into secret negotiations with some of the other Electors, and suddenly wrote to summon them to a fresh election. They were bidden to choose Konradin, Frederick II's grandson, who had succeeded in getting himself made Duke of Swabia and had held his first Court at Ulm.[1]

Fortunately Archbishop Engelbert von Falkenburg warned Richard of what was afoot. Ottokar of Bohemia sent him a similar warning – for although he had had practically nothing to do with Richard since his election, the prospect of a return of the Hohenstaufen was incomparably the greater evil in his eyes. Richard decided that he must go to Germany at all costs. He declined a proposal of Henry III to meet him at Cippenham, gathered together all the funds he could, and set off for the coast on 20th June, 1262,[2] accompanied by Henry of Almayne, who was bound for France with the Earl of Warenne. Richard embarked on the twenty-second, landed at the mouth of the Zwin, and on 2nd July was in Ghent settling a long-standing quarrel between the houses of Avesnes and Dampierre. On Alice, the widow of his old friend Jean d'Avesnes, he bestowed the guardianship of the young Floris of Holland; and then made his way on through Brabant. His route to Liège was continually delayed by contesting parties claiming his judgement; but eventually, on 13th July, he entered his faithful Aachen.

He presented the Cathedral with new coronation insignia, some of which are still to be seen in its treasury. They were ceremonially borne into the Lady Chapel in the presence of the Provost, Dean, Chapter and Jurats of the city, to be kept there for future use by all German kings. They consisted of a gold crown, sceptre, orb and robes with his arms of the red lion and silver bezants.[3] The ancient Frankish capital had cause to be grateful to Richard, and his memory is still green there after seven centuries. Into the later Rathaus is incorporated König Richard's Curia, which he added to the Carolingian palace of which the Granusturm at one end is still extant. His great gilded casket, or 'Wappentruhe', specially made for him by a smith of Limoges, is still in the Cathedral treasury, and his statue adorns the front of the Rathaus with those of the other Kings crowned in the Cathedral.

On 6th August he rewarded Ottokar of Bohemia for his loyalty in frustrating the election of Konradin and in enlisting the Pope's opposition to the Hohenstaufen. He confirmed the Bohemian King in the possession of Austria and Styria, to which he was not really entitled, as they were the holding of his divorced wife, Kunigunde von Babenburg. In return Ottokar, the most powerful of the German princes, could now be regarded as completely on Richard's side, and there ceased to be any question of holding a re-election.

Richard was now able to follow his usual route up the Rhine. The princes and nobles flocked to him, more than ever before; even Werner of Mainz, seeing all the others adhere to Richard, decided to drop his opposition, so that Richard was able to pass unhindered through his lands. On the twentieth he had reached Andernach, the last castle of the Electors of Cologne, where the newly elected Archbishop of Trier, Heinrich von Vinstingen, was awaiting him. A week later Richard reached Boppard, and here the Pfalzgraf came to do homage, concerned to clear his name from the rumour that he had been plotting to put Konradin on the throne. As an earnest of his good faith he renewed his treaty with Engelbert of Cologne, who had accompanied Richard on his journey southward.

This time the King spent a week in Boppard before he travelled on to pay his first visit to the growing imperial city of Frankfurt. Here he confirmed the privileges of several religious houses in the vicinity,[4] and proceeded thence to Oppenheim where, on the hill-top above the town, he laid the foundation stone of the Katharinenkirche, whose nave and choir were built to his plans in the succeeding years, and are noted today for their lightness and beauty. His favourite German castle, the Landskron, immediately above Oppenheim, provided him with a convenient base for some days before he went on into Alsace to settle a feud between the Bishop of Strasbourg and the town of Hagenau. The Bishop, Richard's regent in the province, was having a bad time as he had just been soundly defeated by his own city; but the King did not attempt to take sides at this stage. He rode on to Schlettstadt, the modern Sélestat, where Archbishop Werner of Mainz now came to meet him.[5]

The return to the fold of the great Elector was a major achievement. Indeed Richard, who but a few months before had been in danger of losing his throne, could afford to be well pleased with the results of his journey. He decided, as the climate of opinion was so favourable, to make his way still farther south. At Schlettstadt the Graf von Freiburg came to do him homage, and – more important still – the Graf Rudolf von Habsburg, one of the greatest men in the Swiss country. As Rudolf knelt to do homage to the King, no one could have foreseen that he, instead of Henry of Almayne, was to succeed Richard and usher in a line of Emperors which was to outlast the Empire itself.

No such thoughts could have presented themselves to Richard as he rode towards the Swiss mountains with Rudolf von Habsburg beside him. Early in November he entered Basle and, after a brief visit there, accompanied Rudolf to Zürich. Before him, beyond the great lake, rose the distant barrier of the still-uncrossed Alps, blocking the path to Rome. It was very late in the year – too late to consider crossing them; but even so he might have gone by way of Burgundy or Savoy, had there not been the usual interruption – bad news from England.

Henry had decided to go over to France and discredit Simon de

Montfort before King Louis. He arranged for some of Simon's chief opponents from Gascony to be present at the French Court at Valenciennes. Here another trial, or rather a series of acrimonious exchanges, took place, again inconclusively. To Henry, Simon's instransigence had become an obsession; to Simon, Henry was a feeble tyrant. He had forgotten that he owed his great standing in England to the King's sometime generosity, albeit under the influence of Richard's advocacy. Early in September, 1262, Henry and many of his knights fell dangerously ill, and while they so lay Simon – seizing his opportunity – rushed back to England, rallied the barons, and proclaimed again the Provisions of Oxford, claiming Papal authority for doing so.

Richard realized that he must again act swiftly and not let his regained English political influence wane if he was to save his brother. The imperial crown was, with a French Pope in Rome, too uncertain a goal to strive for, even though he was so close. He therefore turned northward from Zürich. At Hagenau he paused again, however, to adjudicate in disputes, order the city of Zürich to be taken into imperial protection, and declare Konradin's claim to it to be null and void.[6] By 3rd December he was again in Mainz, where he learned that King Henry was on his way back to England. Such precipitate haste was therefore no longer necessary, and he decided to spend Christmas with Archbishop Werner. It was very important to Richard that he should effect a reconciliation between the Archbishop and Philipp von Bolanden-Hohenfles, and on 7th January, 1263, he succeeded. Times had changed; and he gladly paused first in Boppard, then actually in Trier, visiting the new Archbishop. Both stops were an indication of the considerable success of this third visit to Germany, for he was now generally recognized by all the magnates of real importance. Fondly imagining that it would not be long before he again set foot in his continental kingdom, he landed at Dover on 10th February, 1263.

CHAPTER TWO

THE KING IN THE WINDMILL

RICHARD at once realized that conditions in England were far worse than he had imagined. Henry had alienated those who might have been his friends.[1] Richard de Clare, the fiery Earl of Gloucester, had died, and his son, Gilbert – full of good intentions – had gone over to Boulogne to offer Henry his homage and receive his family estates in return. Instead of receiving him reasonably, Henry had rebuffed him, and the young man – smarting with rage and mortification – returned to England and joined Simon de Montfort.[2] Henry of Almayne had been present at the interview at Boulogne and, disgusted with his uncle, had come back to England a staunch convert to the baronial cause.[3]

Richard was of course too late. He hurried up to London and met the King at Westminster, upbraiding him with his lack of statesmanship. In the Marches of Wales Llewellyn was again in revolt, and Simon de Montfort was in secret alliance with him. On 25th February the Lord Edward arrived at Dover with a large force of mercenaries, ostensibly for use against the Welsh,[4] but the barons saw through the manœuvre and let it be known that they would bar Edward's route westward. Richard and Queen Eleanor encouraged Henry to reassert his authority, urging that he should first require the renewal of a nation-wide oath of fealty and then seize the opportunity to repeal the Provisions of Oxford. The barons saw through this too, and Gilbert de Clare led a group of recalcitrant magnates who refused to take the oath and appealed for help to Simon de Montfort, who had again returned to France.[5] This was enough to bring him back to England in haste at the head of an army of mercenaries.

He landed on 25th April and the barons flocked to his standard. A general Parliament was held in London on Whit Sunday,[6] at the same time that the Chapter-General of the Dominican Order was meeting in the city. Richard and Henry dined with them at the Palace of Westminster. Despite the seriousness of the political situation, the King was much more concerned with planning a cycle of Old Testament paintings on the walls of his private chamber in the Palace, an idea he had harboured ever since his visit to the Sainte-Chapelle in 1254. But by the twenty-sixth even he had grasped the danger of the situation, and withdrew into the Tower with the Queen, the Lord Edward and Richard.[7]

Encouraged, the barons seized and imprisoned Pierre d'Aigueblanche, the Savoyard Bishop of Hereford, who was a favourite of Henry's and had carried Richard's marriage offer to Sanchia twenty years before. They then seized the cities of Gloucester and Worcester and as many of Eleanor's lands as possible.[8] Henry retaliated by seizing those baronial holdings within his grasp,[9] while the furious Queen, strongly supported by her son, counselled open warfare. Richard as usual counselled moderation. On 24th June he and Henry received a petition from the barons, transmitted through the good offices of the citizens of London, who were apparently feeling their way between the warring factions.

Henry indeed might have won the Londoners over but for another amazing act of folly. Two days before the receipt of the petition, the Lord Edward with a band of his henchmen, had contrived to get into the vaults of the New Temple on the pretext of inspecting some of his mother's jewels. They then smashed open various caskets and made off with £1,000 sterling, most of which belonged to magnates and merchants.[10] Henry had almost certainly put him up to it to relieve his own financial embarrassment. It was a step calculated to alienate simultaneously the Templars, the magnates and the Londoners. Edward made tracks for Windsor with his loot, accompanied by his foreign mercenaries. This incident was the signal for a fresh outburst of xenophobia. The Londoners threw as many foreigners as they could out of the city and John Mansel – the King's diplomatic adviser – fled abroad,[11] hotly pursued by Henry of Almayne, who, however, was himself captured at Boulogne by a French knight and held to ransom.[12] The Archbishop Boniface of Canterbury also fled with a number of his clergy.

Richard decided that it was urgent to mediate before it was too late, and left London, making his way to his manor at Cippenham. His intelligence reported that Simon de Montfort was heading for the capital. So he sent messengers ahead of him asking the Earl of Leicester to meet him at the bridge over the River Loddon just outside Twyford. Richard duly arrived at the bridge and waited for him in vain. After many hours his messengers returned bringing Simon's refusal to talk: the Earl of Leicester, they said, was swinging his forces south-eastward to avoid the royalists. What he also doubtless wished to avoid was Richard's persuasive tongue: had he met him, Lewes and Evesham might never have been. Simon pressed on, took the castles of Guildford, Reigate, Pevensey and Dover in turn, and sent his agents over to Boulogne to arrange the release of Henry of Almayne.

Richard returned to Berkhamsted, but the unhappy King was still shut up in the Tower. With him was Queen Eleanor, disgusted at her husband's cowardice. The Londoners brought the King the barons' latest terms – acceptance of the Provisions of Oxford, expulsion of the aliens, and the placing of government in the hands of Englishmen. Henry, realizing that with the Cinque Ports in Simon's hands he could not escape, decided to submit; but he reckoned without his wife. Independent, imperious, very conscious (like her sisters) of her royal dignity, she considered it degrading to submit to anyone of lower birth. There was one man in the kingdom worthy of her presence, and that was her own son, the Lord Edward, now at Windsor. The obvious way to him was by river, and with this intention she duly embarked in her barge at the Tower. But when she came to London Bridge the mob was waiting for her; filth, stones and rotten eggs showered down upon the fastidious lady of Provence.[13]

Fortunately for her the Mayor of London arrived, beat off the citizens, and brought her to sanctuary at the Bishop's house at

St. Paul's. Her husband, having heard of her plight, was too big a coward to readmit her to the Tower, for fear that the mob would pursue her there. Eleanor never forgave the Londoners, and more particularly the barons: from now on she was motivated by implacable hatred, and used all her considerable influence to provoke conflict. The Lord Edward, who adored his beautiful mother, was equally furious; and the royalist defeat at Lewes was the direct result of his determination to get even with the Londoners. He tried to outwit the barons at Bristol by a barefaced piece of duplicity,* for despite his valour and undoubted ability, the future Edward I was 'a lion for pride and ferocity, but a leopard for inconstancy and changing, not keeping his word or promise, but seeking to excuse himself with fair speeches'.[14] Simon de Montfort, who had now returned to England, was well aware of his adversary's character and had no intention of being hoodwinked by him twice; two could play at that game. He inveigled Edward out of Windsor Castle and then refused to let him re-enter it – forcing his mercenary garrison to surrender.

Trouble fomented throughout the rest of 1263, and Henry decided to submit his quarrel with the barons to the arbitration of King Louis, who in France was his overlord.[15] The barons agreed; such was Louis's unequalled reputation for justice that they were quite content to leave their fate in his hands, ardent believer though he was in the divine dignity of anointed kingship. Simon de Montfort was chosen at the September Parliament to be one of three spokesmen to present the baronial cause to him.[16] The French Court met the King and Queen of England and the barons' representatives at Boulogne. Queen Marguerite had the greatest liking for her brother in-law[17] and was disgusted at the recent cockney affront to her sister. She put ceaseless pressure on her husband to espouse the royalist cause; but Louis, impartial as ever, refused to

* A clash occurred between Edward's mercenaries and the citizens of Bristol, who threatened to besiege him in the castle. His reaction was to send for Walter de Canteloup, Bishop of Worcester, a strong partisan of Simon's, and promise him that if he were rescued he would at once make peace with the barons. The Bishop trusted him and placated the citizens, but directly he was clear of Bristol Edward broke his promise.

be rushed into a decision.[18] Henry returned to England, leaving Eleanor behind.

The baronial party was full of division and discord, and when the Lord Edward again got possession of Windsor by craft and turned it into his headquarters, there was a noticeable falling off in the ranks of Simon's supporters. Notable among these defectors was Henry of Almayne. He went to Simon de Montfort and announced that he could no longer fight against his father, his uncle and his cousin, but he swore that he would never bear arms against the Earl as long as he lived. This was particularly galling to Simon, who had expended great energy in securing the release of young Henry after his foolish pursuit of John Mansel. His reply was cutting: 'Lord Henry, I grieve not for the loss of your sword, but for the inconstancy which I see in you. I had accepted your person most cordially, for I looked for particular valour from you. Go home, take your arms; I do not fear them.'[19] Henry of Almayne's friendship with his cousin, the Lord Edward, doubtless influenced this change of heart, but it was to prove fatal in his relations with his other cousins, the young Montforts.

King Henry joined Edward at Windsor, while Simon occupied London and later moved out to Kenilworth. The opposing factions were almost exactly matched and tacitly agreed to a winter truce while awaiting the judgement of Louis. Henry, however, broke the truce by attempting to seize Dover Castle on 3rd December.[20] He thought to obtain command of the garrison by parley in Simon's absence, but they remained loyal to their master and refused to admit the King without the authority of their absent castellan, Robert de Grey. Henry, discomfited and not daring to risk a siege of the Key of England, bundled down the hill again to the more hospitable walls of the Priory.[21] He had been so certain of success that he had sent for Eleanor to come and join him, but had to countermand the order at the last minute. The scene of strife now returned to London,[22] but messengers arrived from Louis just before Christmas bidding both sides to keep the peace pending his pronouncement. The Bishops secured an uneasy truce over the feast.[23] Henry and Edward left for France on 27th December, but

Richard stayed behind,[24] as did Simon de Montfort. His horse had thrown him and broken his leg, and while it was healing he sent his eldest son Henry to France in his place. In almost breathless expectation the two parties awaited Louis's judgement.

The famous Mise of Amiens was delivered on 24th January, 1264. By it King Louis found that the Provisions of Oxford were null and void, that the King of England had full right to govern with complete freedom, saving only that those charters and liberties existing before the date of the Provisions – Magna Carta and its successors – were valid.[25] Moreover, the King might employ aliens in offices of state as and when he pleased. The only crumb of consolation for the barons was the bit about charters and liberties in force prior to the Provisions, but it was not enough. Simon and his supporters rejected the Mise of Amiens utterly, and took it as an excuse to renew the Provisions of Oxford. This was the signal for civil war.

Armed conflict began in Wales and the Marches, with the seizure and counter-seizure of some castles, and the capture of Gloucester by Henry de Montfort and his baronial supporters through a variant of the Wooden Horse trick. The castle held out after the city had surrendered, and while Henry was besieging it the Lord Edward came up to catch him in the rear. In the nick of time de Montfort was reinforced and Edward decided to parley; he and Henry of Almayne put a very plausible plea to their cousin, who naïvely trusted them. No sooner had he removed his army to Kenilworth than the two unscrupulous young princes broke the truce, imprisoned the pro-baronial burghers of Gloucester, and seized their chattels. Pleased with the success of his trickery Edward returned to Oxford to join his father,[26] who had come back from France after another abortive attempt to secure the surrender of Dover Castle *en route*. Richard of Cornwall had joined his brother at Windsor and so the two fathers and two sons were together at Oxford at the start of the main hostilities.

At Oxford Henry began with the major psychological error of sending down the University, including the new foundation of John de Balliol, on the pretext that the presence of mercenary soldiers would render the town unsuitable for studious clerks;[27] moreover, the latter had just been engaging in one of their periodical 'town and gown' riots. His real reason was that he feared the students represented a radical and pro-baronial 'fifth column'. Richard of Cornwall made a last attempt at mediation, persuading his brother to send emissaries to Simon de Montfort at Kenilworth; but his long-standing preference for negotiation to fighting underwent a drastic change as a result of the violent events of 31st March, 1264.

On that day a mob of Londoners, tacitly or overtly encouraged by the Justiciar, Hugh le Dispenser, went out to Richard's Thames-side manor at Isleworth on which he had lavished a great deal of money and affection, looted it, burnt it to the ground, and smashed up his newly-constructed fishpond. This was an act of wanton destruction; and when it was followed by the burning of his town house at Westminster, Richard's fury knew no bounds.[28] In his view he had been generous to the Londoners and this was how they requited him. Henceforward he had done with mediation and joined his nephew Edward in vociferous demands that the rebels be taught a lesson.

The first royalist success was at Northampton, which was captured on 15th April, and young Simon de Montfort along with it. He was sent to Windsor as a prisoner.[29] His father was about to march north to recover Northampton when he heard a rumour of a Jewish plot in London. This was an excuse for a wholesale massacre of the Jews, the barons filling their coffers with the resultant loot: Simon himself was not free from suspicion.[30] He then turned his attention to Rochester and forced an entry by sending a lighted fireboat against the bridge over the Medway, destroying its fortifications. His forces then sacked the city and were besieging the great tower-keep of the royalist castle when news came of another suspected plot in London, and de Montfort hastened back to the capital. Henry III meanwhile, by an out-flanking movement which for him was quite brilliant, marched down from the Midlands to Rochester avoiding London, and raised the siege of the castle, in which amongst others Henry of Almayne had been beleaguered.[31] Probably it was the presence of

Edward and Richard in the royalist forces which made Henry III so uncharacteristically resolute on this occasion.[32] From Rochester they marched to Tonbridge, seized the Earl of Gloucester's castle, and left a garrison in it; thence they proceeded to Winchelsea and obtained an oath of fealty from the men of the Cinque Ports – a rather useless exercise since the same men had just sworn a similar oath to Simon.

Henry now turned westwards and reached Lewes on 11th May, where he, Richard and their immediate entourage were lodged in the Cluniac Priory.[33] While still at Winchelsea the King had been appraised that the barons were moving southwards, and – realizing that it was essential that the great castle of Lewes, held by the Earl de Warenne, should not fall into their hands – he assigned quarters in it to the Lord Edward and his doughtiest warriors.[34] The barons meanwhile had encamped at the village of Fletching, some eight miles north of Lewes, in the extensive forest which stretched northwards for a great distance. No less than 15,000 Londoners had joined de Montfort. The stage was set for one of the most famous battles in English history, but up to the very last minute attempts were made to avert it.

The barons sent the Bishop of Chichester to plead their case with Henry, saying that they were the King's loyal subjects and were prepared to pay a considerable sum to make amends. Henry vacillated. Now, if Richard had given him his normal conciliatory advice, Henry might have agreed to parley, and Lewes and Evesham might never have been. But Richard – incensed at the affront to his royal dignity by the unprovoked aggression of the Londoners – had the bit firmly between his teeth and would not hear of compromise; he egged Edward on to convince his father of the need to fight.[35] Nothing daunted, the barons tried again, sending the Bishops of Worcester and London, but Henry denounced them. Edward and Richard went one better, returning an extremely offensive letter of defiance, addressed in the name of all men true to the King 'to Simon de Montfort, Gilbert de Clare and other perfidious traitors in their company'.[36] The crunch had come; this was the signal for the barons to withdraw their homage.

Simon and his captains took Communion in Fletching Church; then, under cover of darkness on the night of the thirteenth to the fourteenth of May, they crept through the forest towards Lewes and overpowered the solitary sleeping sentry who was supposed to warn the royalists of their advent. At the top of the hill above the castle the barons emerged from the woods and Simon deployed his forces. Henry and Guy were to command the wing which would attack downhill west of the Priory where the King lodged; the centre was led by Gilbert de Clare, and on the other wing was the extensive force of Londoners.

The alarm was given by some royalists early astir. Out under the frowning gatehouse of the castle rode the Lord Edward and the Earl de Warenne to oppose the Londoners, which was just what Edward – athirst to revenge their insult to his mother – wanted. King Henry himself rode out of the Priory to confront the Earl of Gloucester; while Richard, Henry of Almayne and Edmund found themselves faced with Henry and Guy de Montfort.

Everything pointed to a royalist victory; they were greatly superior in numbers, but the Lord Edward threw it away. Neglecting to keep the line unbroken he pursued the fleeing Londoners for four miles; the luckless infantry were hewn down, having no chance against the horsemen. Those who turned and ran downhill towards the River Ouse were ensnared in the marshes. The prince's impetuosity gave the barons their chance and they flung their full weight against the centre of the royalist line. King Henry went down, his horse killed under him, and was swiftly made prisoner. His line broke and many of his knights went pounding away towards Pevensey, hoping to save their skins. On the other wing the young Montforts realized at once from the scarlet lion and silver bezants on the opposing banners that they had to deal with the father and son whom they regarded as their personal enemies. At first Richard made considerable inroads among the barons, but then he saw the royalist line waver and his brother's knights turn tail and bolt for the coast. The green and white of the Downs was already littered with the dead and dying. Away to the north-west the sails of a tall windmill cut the skyline, and towards it the King of Germany and his younger son now turned and rode as fast as their horses would carry them.[37] Dismounting hastily they rushed inside, pushing the protesting miller back among his sacks of flour, and barricaded themselves in.

It was evening before the Earl of Gloucester, having the King already secure, rode up at the head of his almost intact forces. They formed a mocking circle round the mill and taunted Richard: 'Come down, you bad miller! Come forth at once, mill-master! You defied us to fight! You called us perfidious traitors and yourself Semper Augustus!'[38] Richard appeared at the small slit which served as a window, and shouted back that he was a foreign monarch who took no part in local skirmishes. Gloucester retorted: 'As for local skirmishes, you have taken part in this one, and your brother too. For aught I care you are Earl of Cornwall; you have parleyed your way out too often. It shall avail you nothing now.' He paused, and the whole mass of knights and men-at-arms, led by Guy and Henry de Montfort, took up the mocking refrain:

> 'Rickard, though thou be ever trickard
> Tricken shalt thou nevermore!'

Realizing the hopelessness of his position, Richard, with Edmund behind him, emerged and handed his sword to Sir John Giffard, one of Gloucester's knights.

CHAPTER THREE

THE PRISONER OF SIMON DE MONTFORT

THE SHOCK of the result of Lewes was great, not least to Simon de Montfort who found two Kings his prisoners and the supreme power of government thrust into his grasp. Though the author of *The Song of Lewes*, a staunch de Montfort partisan, described Henry and Richard as 'transgressors of the laws'[1] this was an over-simplification of the situation, as Simon well knew; he himself was the rebel now in power and had got to hold the reins tightly, whatever his following among the people.

The King became virtually his puppet, issuing patents as Simon wanted them, and being dragged round by his captor from place to place to lend authority to his acts.[2] On Friday, 16th May, two days after the battle, the Lord Edward and Henry of Almayne, who had escaped capture on the field, gave themselves up as hostages for their fathers, pending a decision on the Provisions of Oxford. This did not prevent Simon lodging Richard in the Tower with them as from the twenty-eighth,[3] but he was only kept there a few days before being handed over to the keeping of Hugh le Dispenser to bring him to his own former castle of Wallingford. As a particularly bitter blow to Richard his lands had been sequestrated and placed in the keeping of Guy de Montfort, but, with an eye to the future, Simon had obtained from him during his brief stay in the Tower a promise that, as part of his ransom, he would found an Abbey on his lands; in addition, he was to make a payment of £17,000.

It must have been extremely galling to return as a prisoner to Wallingford Castle, on which he and Sanchia had lavished so much money and energy; but the bitterness was tempered to some degree by the fact that he was in the keeping of his sister Eleanor, Simon de Montfort's wife, who did her very utmost to render his captivity bearable. He was even allowed some measure of freedom in business matters, as is shown by a patent given under his hand at Wallingford on 8th July by which he fixed the wages of some German miners whom he had brought over to assist in working his Dartmoor tin mines.[4] Traces of the activities and improved techniques of these German miners are to be seen on Dartmoor to this day. The Lord Edward and Henry of Almayne were brought down to Wallingford to join him, and there they remained for the rest of the summer. In October the Countess Eleanor left them to go to Dover.

So things might have continued but for the fact that early one foggy November morning the castle awoke to the sounds of a tremendous battle, and found that the garrison – already driven back into the inner ward – were fighting desperately to prevent the attackers gaining the keep, on its lofty mound, in which the royal prisoners were housed. Wallingford Castle stands on the west bank of the Thames, its outer curtain protected by a moat, the ground within rising to the great motte on which the keep stood. The would-be rescuers were a band of dashing but foolhardy young knights, some from the Marches under Warin de Bassingbourn, bent on releasing the Lord Edward; and others from Devon under Robert Walerand bent on releasing Richard and Henry of Almayne. It was an ill-prepared venture of insufficient strength, but the shock of surprise had caught the Montfort garrison unawares.[5] Fortunately for them there were, within the inner ward, some great siege engines which Richard of Cornwall himself had collected when he was master of the castle. To the vociferous demands of Warin de Bassingbourn that they surrender the Lord Edward, the castellan replied that he would indeed send him – but thrown out in a mangonel. Edward realized that the attempted rescue was doomed to failure for lack of numbers, and came to the wall-walk of the keep and shouted to Warin to desist. After fighting most of the day he did so, retreating at top speed to Wales.[6]

When the news reached Simon de Montfort at Dover he was exceedingly angry and turned on his wife. This, he said, was the result of housing her brother in his own castle, where half the retainers were obviously his sympathizers. Though Eleanor assured her husband that she was certain Richard had no foreknowledge of the assault, the Earl was not convinced, and gave orders for the prisoners to be dispatched under close guard to his own strong castle of Kenilworth, where the garrison were Montfort supporters to a man.[7]

The following winter was rendered more pleasant for Richard by presents from his sister Eleanor – on 29th March she sent him from Odiham twenty pounds of nuts at sixpence, five pounds of rice at ninepence, two pounds of pepper at twenty pence, and two pounds of sugar at two shillings. He had already received spices, wine and whalemeat. More wine and grapes now followed, and some clothes for young Edmund. Knowing Richard's love of red, she even saw to it that he had twelve ells of scarlet cloth for his robes at Whitsuntide.

Simon himself came to Kenilworth at Christmas to indulge in festivities approaching royal estate, while the King – 'nothing but the shadow of a name'[8] – had a poor imitation of a Christmas at his manor of Woodstock. Directly after the festivities ended Simon compelled him to send out a summons for a Parliament at Westminster, on 20th January, 1265. Its deliberations were most protracted, extending over three months; during it the King under duress agreed not to proceed against the Earls of Leicester and Gloucester or the citizens of London. The Marcher Earls were to be banished to Ireland for three years. It was a parliament more like our modern one in texture than anything that had gone before, including an assembly of the lesser gentry, knights of the shire and representatives of the boroughs, and this it was which earned Simon the name of 'the father of the House of Commons'.

When it eventually ended Simon released the Lord Edward and Henry of Almayne from their position as hostages; though – as he rightly regarded Edward as a very dangerous liability – the Prince's freedom was only nominal. Henry of Almayne, however, was dispatched on parole to Boulogne to act, as it was hoped, as an acceptable envoy to King Louis. In our modern eyes this may seem a rather extraordinary choice, especially as the Queens Eleanor and Marguerite were both there and would naturally do their utmost to suborn him from any feeling that he might be beholden to the barons. But the latter hoped that, when Louis saw Henry in the flesh, he would accept their contention that the King of England was in agreement with the government they had imposed on him. Very naturally the French King did not so view Henry of Almayne's arrival; nor did the Papal Legate, Charles the Fat, who – having been refused leave to land in England – was fulminating at Boulogne, issuing sentences of excommunication against the barons.

So the fateful summer of 1265 hastened on. Simon de Montfort, the common people's hero, who might have been a satisfactory Protector if he had not succumbed to gross nepotism, alienated the very men on whom he should have been able to rely. Foremost was Gilbert de Clare, Earl of Gloucester. The trouble was exacerbated by Simon refusing to allow a tournament, arranged by his sons, to be held at Dunstable. Gloucester loved tournaments and had intended to go to this one. The young Montforts also grumbled, but their father threatened them that, if they did not obey, 'he would put them in such a place that they would not see sun or moon'.[9] Furious, Gilbert de Clare quarrelled violently with Simon. Another main bone of contention was that – of the prisoners taken at Lewes – one of the principal and richest, Richard of Cornwall, had in fact surrendered at the windmill to one of Gilbert's knights, not Simon's. The Earl of Leicester contemptuously refused Gloucester's request for the banners of his prisoners. Small wonder that Gilbert de Clare and his sympathizers declared that Simon was becoming a dictator, 'arranging the whole kingdom by his own desire'.[10]

Presently Gloucester departed from the Parliament without Simon's leave and returned to the west. In his retinue was Sir John Giffard, the man to whom Richard had surrendered at Lewes, and who was very much in Simon de Montfort's bad books. Many of the barons were seething at the way in which Simon and his sons graspingly used all the opportunities of power. Young Simon had looted left and right, and had given himself over whole-heartedly to the pursuit of a young, beautiful and wealthy widow, Isabella de Fortibus, the Countess of Devon. She owned vast territories in the West Country and the Isle of Wight, and still lives – immortal if not unblemished – in Devonian memories by the Countess Weir which she threw across the River Exe to spite the citizens of Exeter. This weir adversely affected the prosperity of their city for centuries – indeed, until the canal was built at the instance of Sir Francis Drake. Isabella contrived to dodge Simon eventually, but complained that 'he had pursued her from place to place with horse and arms desiring to capture and seditiously abduct her'.[11] Henry de Montfort seized wool brought into the ports;[12] Guy received other people's deer for his parks; Amaury was given a fat and lucrative post as Treasurer of York.

Simon the elder was at Odiham in March with the Countess, his sons, the King, and the Lord Edward who, though not now officially a hostage, was still kept under close guard. From Odiham they broke up, the Countess returning to Dover, Simon dragging his royal prisoners on westwards to Gloucester and then Hereford. Gilbert de Clare was now in open opposition, and had been joined by new recruits almost daily. He and Roger Mortimer together hatched a plan to help the Lord Edward to escape, using as their agent Gilbert's brother Thomas, nominally a Montfort supporter, and the Lord Edward's daily companion. A splendid charger was presented to Edward at Hereford, and on 28th May he succeeded in escaping on it by the simple ruse of trying out the horses of each of his guard in turn, and eventually leaping on to the back of his own – he was not called 'Longshanks' for nothing – and riding off at top speed to Wigmore Castle, which was held by Roger Mortimer.[13] Before long Edward and Gilbert de Clare had ratified an alliance.

The immediate result was the smashing of all the bridges across the Severn by Edward's command, so as to isolate Simon west of the river. The Earl of Leicester from his headquarters at Hereford sent out an urgent appeal for help. On 4th June he issued a patent – as always in the King's name: 'Whereas Edward the King's son, disregarding the King's counsel, has transferred himself to certain Marchers and other enemies and rebels so that he may go to parts beyond the seas, or send others there to bring aliens into the realm to the confusion of the King and the realm, unless his presumption be quickly repressed and the said Edward is making divers mandates in the King's name, pretending that they are agreeable to the King, which God forbid' – this patent is given to the Mayor, bailiffs and good men of Bristol to be of aid and counsel to Simon de Montfort.[14] On 9th June he issued a similar 'mandate to all persons of Surrey and Sussex to be of counsel and aid to Simon de Montfort the younger'.[15] Simon the elder urgently needed his family's help. His wife moved south-eastwards from Odiham to take charge of Dover Castle; and young Simon was summoned from Pevensey but did not hurry himself. Meanwhile the Lord Edward was known to have captured Gloucester and Worcester, and to the best of young Simon's belief he was still at the latter place. So he made a leisurely journey via Winchester (where he massacred the Jews), and Oxford, to Kenilworth where he and his knights relaxed with a magnificent banquet at which his Uncle Richard was present.

Richard had been in regular communication with Germany during his captivity, and had clearly chafed at his inability to carry out his royal functions. Philipp and Werner von Falkenstein, appealing to him for funds, had been told regretfully that he could do nothing because he was held prisoner in England. All over the Rhineland, which he had successfully brought to heel so recently, robber barons' nests were springing up and anarchy stalked the land. '*Die kaiserlose, die schreckliche Zeit*' Schiller called it. It was all desperately frustrating, but the end was at hand.

Kenilworth Castle stands on gently rising ground. In those days it consisted of the massive red sandstone keep, in which Richard was housed, a wide ward with timber buildings, and a single curtain wall. Entrance was through a gatehouse on the southern side known today as Mortimer's Tower, with a drawbridge giving on to a causeway across the wide and shining mere which surrounded the castle on two sides. On the shores of this mere Simon the younger's army was encamped, taking it easy, with the minimum of precautions and sentinels. Suddenly, in the early hours of the morning, the Lord Edward's forces fell upon it. The prince had made a night forced march from Worcester, having been informed by his agents of the presence and slack watch-keeping of Simon's army. The latter was completely surprised and routed; and young Simon himself, rising hurriedly from his bed, only escaped by swimming the mere naked and being hauled up into the safety of the castle. Edward, loaded with prisoners, returned to Worcester.[16]

Simon senior now set out from Hereford with the intention of calling at Kenilworth where he blissfully assumed he would be supplemented by his son's forces. Thence he intended to march on London. So, on the evening of 2nd August, 1265, he came to Evesham where he sought lodging for the weary King whom he was still dragging around with him. And at Evesham Edward came unexpectedly upon him.

The town stands in the elbow of the Avon, where it makes a great curve, and the only way out of the peninsula was up the hill at the north-eastern end or over the single, narrow bridge. Edward kept his forces hidden beyond the river and sent forward a decoy in the shape of some knights bearing baronial banners which he had captured from Simon the younger; the elder Montfort's scouts mistook them, as Edward intended, for the reinforcements from Kenilworth. When the royalists had completely surrounded the town, cutting off the retreat up the steep hill and blocking the passage of the bridge, they threw down the captured banners and appeared in their true colours. A watcher on the Abbey tower gave the alarm, and Earl Simon, surveying the scene and realizing the truth, remarked with typical grim courage: 'Let us commend our souls to God, for our bodies are theirs.'[17]

On the terrible 3rd August the battle *à l'outrance* began; no quarter was given save to poor King Henry, who, wandering in the mêlée, cried out piteously: 'Do not kill me; I am Henry of Winchester, your King!' Across the battlefield heavy and oppressive storm-clouds hung; Robert of Gloucester was terrified of the rolling thunder and immense flashes of lightning. It was a fitting setting for the sombre butchery. Among the frightful carnage of the baronial force, Henry de Montfort was killed, and the Lord Edward wept over his boyhood's friend; while Henry's father, the great Earl of Leicester, fought to the end like a stag at bay until, surrounded, he was cut down and his body disgracefully mutilated before the monks could bear his remains on an improvised stretcher into the Abbey. The passion and the horror unmanned even the victors. 'Such was the murder of Evesham,' wrote Robert of Gloucester, 'for battle it was none.'

CHAPTER FOUR

THE AFTERMATH OF EVESHAM

WHEN THE NEWS of the disaster to the Montfort cause reached Kenilworth the garrison in their fury wanted to kill Richard, and but for Simon the younger would have done so – an almost inexplicable action in view of his subsequent behaviour.[1] Presumably he was less opposed to his uncle than Guy was, and also realized that good treatment of him might pay dividends later. He probably also remembered that Richard had always been his mother's favourite brother, and that he had been instrumental in assisting his father's rise to fortune. Despite his anguish at his father's death[2] he quickly took steps to ensure Richard's safety. Pressure was put upon him by Warin de Bassingbourn, who had arrived at the castle, and by the Bishops of Worcester and Chester, who had both been strong supporters of the baronial cause, to release Richard and young Edmund; and he did so unconditionally on 6th September. Warin had made up for his blunder at Wallingford, and the two Bishops doubtless felt that Richard's gratitude would stand them in good stead now that the royalists had the whip-hand.

In this assumption they were perfectly right; for no sooner had the King of the Romans passed below the gatehouse of Kenilworth Castle and made his way thankfully into the Priory, than he wrote a letter to his sister promising to take all possible steps to protect her and her sons. When the two Bishops and Warin de Bassingbourn witnessed the document, Richard observed to them that he was taking this step out of gratitude for her kindness to him during his long imprisonment. This duty done, he lost no time in heading for Wallingford, and on 9th September he entered his castle once more as master. His *familia* hurried to greet him; and there is no doubt from the warmth of their welcome how popular he was with those who knew him well.

A delegation from the West Country was awaiting him – burgesses of Helston, Truro, Bodmin, and Exeter seeking protection to export tin to Gascony, which he duly granted them. German emissaries were also there, but their report was one of chaos and rebellion. At home things were even worse, and Henry's malicious urge to get his own back bedevilled the Parliament called at Westminster, which Richard attended. Here he met his brother and nephew again after long separation. At this Parliament Henry decreed the complete disinheritment of all those who had supported the baronial cause, while the Londoners, as their allies, were shorn of all their ancient privileges. This was too much for Richard, who objected strongly, and the new Marshal, Roger Bigod, supported him.[3] They had learned by experience, and knew that the movement which the barons had led was no flash in the pan, but a deep-seated expression of feelings genuinely held. They saw that Henry's vicious and sadistic measures could only rub salt into the wounds. Richard was also mindful of his sister's interests, and seeing that Henry could not be deflected from his purpose, he walked out of the Parliament.

Henry continued to wreak vengeance while Richard remained in the background. Fortunately for the Montfort family he was constrained to emerge again because of the arrival of the new Papal Legate, Cardinal Ottobuono, and go down to Canterbury where King Henry was holding Court while awaiting the Legate's arrival. Henry was delighted to see his brother and looked forward to his wise counsel despite himself.

On 30th October Queen Eleanor landed at Dover after her long exile, and the brothers received her with joy. She had certainly done as much as anybody to keep the flame of royalist resistance to the barons alight and had presented her case to King Louis ceaselessly and energetically. The following day the Legate arrived in Canterbury and was ceremonially received by the King.[4] The august company celebrated All Saints' Day there and moved on to London on the second. The city was subdued, many of its sons being imprisoned by the King's command; but surprisingly enough it was Queen Eleanor, the victim of their assault from London Bridge, who joined Richard in begging her husband to release the prisoners.[5] In exile she had become a sadder and a wiser woman and perhaps all the more convincing for that; so the King gave way.

Shortly before these welcome passengers had arrived at Dover the Lord Edward had been busy in another sphere. On 28th October the fiery Prince flung all his forces into an all-out attack upon the Key of England. The Countess of Leicester had little hope of the outcome and, after a brief siege, surrendered the castle. Edward was persuaded by Richard to let her and her two younger sons, Richard and Amaury, take ship for France; and so the onetime Princess Eleanor sailed away from England for ever. Her ship, outward bound, was passed by the Legate's incoming.

There remained the other two Montfort sons, Guy and Simon. The former was at Windsor, as bitter as ever, and trying every ruse to escape, so Edward ordered his transfer to close confinement at Dover. What he overlooked was the presence there of a former warder of the Countess Eleanor's, so it was not altogether surprising when the young Montfort contrived to escape and was ferried over to France in a fishing vessel.

Simon remained at Kenilworth Castle until 23rd November,[6] and then – leaving a strong garrison behind him – joined the rest of the rebels in the Isle of Axholm, whence they harried the countryside. The Lord Edward and Henry of Almayne marched against them at the head of the royalist forces, but met with very little success.

The King meanwhile, accompanied by the Queen, Richard and the Legate, left London on 8th December and made a leisurely progress via Windsor and Dunstable Priory to Northampton, where they spent Christmas.[7] Edward had begun negotiations with Simon, and prevailed upon him to accept a safe-conduct to Northampton, there to submit to the judgement of Richard, the Legate and Philip Basset. Simon thus appeared before the King; but before Henry could vent any spleen upon him Richard stepped in decisively on the young man's behalf. He expressed gratitude to him again for saving his life at Kenilworth, and, despite opposition from Gilbert de Clare, eventually obtained agreement for Simon to return to the obdurate castle and try to procure its surrender, promising thereafter to remain abroad and not to stir up unrest. As a reward for his magnanimity to his uncle 500 marks from his father's earldom should be sent to him.[8]

Simon did his best, but the castellan at Kenilworth refused to surrender the castle to anyone save the Countess, and as she was in France an impasse was reached. The young Montfort returned to London where on Henry's order he was detained; Richard had withdrawn to Wallingford and so was not there to help him. Simon therefore wisely decided to use his own initiative and escaped to France clandestinely early in February.[9]

Kenilworth thus still held out, and Henry resolved to reduce it. The royal forces were ordered to meet in Oxford after Easter. On 18th April however, Henry was not at Oxford but at Cippenham with Richard who was in his element, doing two things which he enjoyed doing magnificently – granting privileges to West Country towns, and fulfilling a vow of piety. In the hall of Cippenham Manor two groups of people awaited him expectantly. The first, all Cornishmen, were the burgesses of Liskeard, anxious to follow in the wake of Launceston and Bodmin; and they duly received the charter for their borough at their overlord's hands. The second group was there to help him fulfil his vow made in the Tower to Simon de Montfort, that as part of his ransom he would found an Abbey on his lands.

He chose the manor of Cippenham for the purpose, and the fields which lay to the west of it and to the north of Dorney. Richard had long held Cippenham from the Abbot of Westminster for an annual rent of ten shillings, and part of the manor which belonged to the Ferrers family had been alienated to him by them. The manors of Burnham and Eton had been transferred to Richard by Thomas de Lascelles, son of Duncan and Cristiana de Lascelles; and though in 1260 the widowed Cristiana had brought an action against him, he had compensated her with some land in Eton, keeping Burnham for himself. Now the value of having the two contiguous manors was apparent, for he was able to grant 'all the land of Moorfurlong, Broken Furlong and the whole meadow of Dillepool, all the wood of La Strete, and one part of our wood of Hartleigh as far as the wood of John de la Penne' for the building of a nunnery for an Abbess and nine canonesses of the Austin rite. The foundation charter was witnessed by no less august a company than 'Henry, the illustrious King of England, our brother, the Lord Edward, eldest son of the same King, our nephew, the Lord Walter of Bath, chancellor, Richard Bishop of Lincoln and Roger Bishop of Coventry and Lichfield; Henry and Edmund, our sons; Philip Basset; William de Huntercombe; William de Windsor, Richard de Oxeye, Philip de Covele and others. Given at Cippenham on the eighteenth of April in the year of Our Lord one thousand twelve hundred and sixty-six, the ninth year of our reign.'[10]

The name Broken Furlong is still known locally, and Huntercombe Manor still stands just north of Burnham Abbey – for after three centuries of ruin following the Reformation the buildings were restored by a private benefactor and now house an Anglican order of nuns, the Sisters of the Precious Blood, who take their name from the sacred relic at the mother house at Hayles. Local legend still says that when the King's Commissioners destroyed Hayles Abbey in 1540 some monks smuggled the phial of the Precious Blood to Burnham and immured it in the walls, no one knows where.

Be that as it may, the Abbey of Burnham wielded considerable influence locally for three centuries, holding the advowson of the neighbouring church of Dorney, and receiving its tithes in the great barn which still stands. The Abbey buildings were grouped round a central quadrangle; and the dorter range (now the Chapel) and part of the frater survive. It is an oasis of peace a stone's throw from the modern motorway, whose travellers pass within a few hundred yards also of the site of Cippenham Manor, and therefore follow almost exactly the route which Richard and Henry took that April day in 1266, when they went to inspect the site where work was to begin.

Richard was in no hurry to leave Cippenham, which was full of pleasant memories for him, but eventually he was constrained to go to Kenilworth.[11] In July the royalist army had completely surrounded the castle, but had got no nearer to bringing about its surrender. Richard and the Legate Ottobuono arrived there on 2nd July hoping to secure an armistice;[12] they spent a fortnight in their camp across the mere, their heralds going back and forth to the castle gate. They would doubtless have succeeded but for the obdurate attitude of King Henry, who refused to grant the garrison any concessions at all for their surrender. Even the Legate was disgusted and wrote to the Pope to complain of Henry's conduct. Richard retired disillusioned to Wallingford.

Henry of Almayne remained behind to help the Legate. He had gained a brilliant victory over the rebels at Chesterfield earlier in the year, and was now doing his best with the Legate to reduce the influence of Roger Mortimer and other uncompromising advisers over the King. Eventually they succeeded; and at the beginning of November the Legate was able to announce a new peace formula, the Dictum of Kenilworth.[13] By its terms all former adherents of Simon de Montfort could recover their estates against monetary payment of the annual yield. In the middle of December the King reluctantly gave his assent, and simultaneously the great castle which had withstood the royalists so long surrendered, its garrison on the verge of starvation.

Not surprisingly, a large number of the disinherited did not trust him, and had withdrawn, like Hereward the Wake before them, into the Isle of Ely, whence they defied the King across the marshes.[14] Henry marched to Cambridge in February at the head of the royalist army but failed to reduce the Isle. While he was yet hesitating, the news came of a totally unexpected attack by Gloucester on the city of London, where the Legate had taken refuge in the Tower. Many of the disinherited escaped from the Isle of Ely to join Gilbert de Clare, and threatened to return to Cambridge and attack the King. Henry again sent despairingly to his brother, who came up to Northamptonshire and took up residence in Barnwell Priory. But Henry would not stay long in the area. He decided, somewhat impetuously, to attack London; and having got some reinforcements from the north of England marched rapidly south from Dunstable to Windsor, swinging east and coming suddenly up to the capital, which, however, kept its gates firmly shut against him.[15] This manœuvre having failed, he withdrew again into Essex, having described an almost complete circle and achieved nothing. He had spent a great deal of money and was therefore ready to borrow from Richard once more.

This gave his brother the chance to seize the initiative and do something which would enable him to leave England in peace and get back to Germany. He volunteered to negotiate with Gloucester, and on 20th April obtained a safe-conduct from his brother to go to London for the purpose. Here he was joined by Henry of Almayne and Philip Basset, and together they battered away for a month of hard bargaining. Eventually, on 15th June, Richard had the satisfaction of sealing the terms of peace between the royalists and Gloucester at Stratford in Essex. The Dictum of Kenilworth was to be fully implemented and a pardon granted to all the followers of Gilbert de Clare, who in return swore never again to take up arms against the King and to pay as great a sum as the Pope might direct as an earnest of his good faith.[16]

He evacuated London, and the King entered on 16th June at the head of the royalist forces.[17] The citizens agreed to pay Richard a thousand marks' compensation for the damage done to the manor of Isleworth. Henry, not quite certain that the coast was yet clear, decided to stay at the Tower when his brother went down to Windsor early in July, to seal the formal settlement and reconciliation between Gloucester and the Lord Edward, who had arrived fresh from mopping up the last pockets of resistance in the Isle of Ely.

In the autumn Richard was at Marlborough Castle for the publication of the Statutes of Marlborough, which were to settle various vexed constitutional questions. They were based largely on the Provisions of Oxford, and so satisfied most of the barons' demands. A long and bloody road had led at last to this goal, which could have been achieved so much earlier. Most of the credit for the ultimate agreement was Richard's, and at Winchester at Christmas he was able to sing something of a '*Nunc dimittis*' to his brother. He had deserted his Continental kingdom for five long years and was longing to return. From that moment on he began his preparations for this, his final visit to Germany.

CHAPTER FIVE

THE PEARL OF WOMANHOOD

RICHARD took stock of the ugly picture of Germany notified to him by his agents and by his many visitors. With the exception of Werner, Archbishop of Mainz, and Ottokar of Bohemia, both of whom stood by him, all the nobles from the Electors downwards had more or less given Richard up for permanently lost. Even the best of them, Werner himself and Philipp von Bolanden-Hohenfels, had seized the opportunity to line their own pockets by clapping on more Rhine tolls. Archbishop Werner had been engaged in a long feud with Ludwig of Bavaria; and before the Battle of Lewes, Richard had tried to mediate between them, appointing the castellan of Nuremberg and the Graf von Katzenelnbogen as assessors. They gave judgement on 15th April, 1264, and in June Werner and Ludwig signed a treaty of friendship, including a vow never to take up arms against Richard. The incident served to keep Werner friendly towards him throughout his long imprisonment in England.

Frederick II's grandson Konradin had now nearly reached man's estate, and several of the Electors were contemplating choosing him in Richard's stead.[1] The Pfalzgraf took the view that Richard was *hors de combat*, and helped himself to what neighbouring imperial territory he could. Farther down the Rhine, the former imperial town of Sinzig 'accidentally' found its way into the possession of the Archbishop of Cologne. Luckily for Richard, the Pope – anglophobe though he was – regarded the return of the Hohenstaufens as a disaster, and wrote to Werner of Mainz that Konradin must be prevented at all costs from obtaining the throne. Richard backed this up by persuading the Legate Ottobuono, whose writ also ran to the three Rhenish archbishoprics, to write to them in similar vein. As a reward for Werner's constancy Richard appointed him viceroy for his territories west of the Rhine. At the same time – the autumn of 1266 – he wrote to Ottokar of Bohemia, seeking his influence to keep the Electors of Brandenburg and Saxony favourable to him, and promising to come to Germany as soon as possible bringing the Legate with him. Ottokar obliged, but helped himself to the castle of Eger by way of commission.

Delegates from Aachen had visited Richard at Wallingford in October, 1266, and obtained a grant of privileges. The following summer, while he was in camp at Stratford in Essex, during his mediation between the King and Gloucester, he authorized the replacement of the weak-minded Henry of Brabant by his brother John. But apart from, and over and above these comparatively minor bits of imperial business, his concern had been to prevent the Pope deciding in favour of Alfonso of Castile. Pope Urban IV had died at the end of 1264 and had been succeeded by another Frenchman, Clement IV, who was, however, more kindly disposed towards Richard – for the simple reason that he had previously been appointed Legate to England but had been prevented by the barons from taking up his post. He had no penchant towards Alfonso, and in May, 1265, made an abortive attempt to get him to withdraw his candidature completely. Clement then postponed judgement in the matter of the imperial coronation until January, 1267, but sent a message to Ottobuono that Richard must send a plenipotentiary to Rome to plead his cause.[2]

Richard dispatched Henry of Almayne, an indication that he now rated his chances quite highly. The Pope, however, procrastinated, using the excuse that no emissary from Alfonso had appeared. In fact he had realized that he could use the quarrel over the imperial crown to his own advantage and, by deciding in favour of neither party, gradually detach the Italian possessions of the Empire from the German. Despite the persistence of Henry of Almayne, the cunning Pontiff remained obdurate and postponed his decision yet again till March, 1268. A further postponement followed. It was clear to Richard that after eleven years' vacillation he was still no nearer his imperial goal, and that if he was to secure the permanence of his German kingship at least, then he must go there at once.

He therefore devoted his attention to last-minute English business. On 9th June he issued a second charter to the Abbess and nuns of Burnham, and a month later, at Wallingford, he granted a charter to another deputation of Cornishmen, this time from the town of Lostwithiel. A few days before he had appointed Laurence de Broc 'to make inquisition concerning the persons who burned the houses of the King of Almayne at Isleworth in the county of Middlesex, broke his park there, felled his trees there, destroyed his coney warren there, broke his stew of Babworth and the bridge of the said manor and took his fish, and carried away the said fish, the timber of the said bridge, the trees of the said park and timber found at Isleworth'.[3]

Early in July the King granted, from his manor of Woodstock, protection to Richard and those going with him to Germany; granted him amercements from the eyre of justices in Cornwall; and granted power to him 'going shortly to Almayne on his affairs that Philip Basset, Robert Walerand and Walter de Merton, whom he has appointed for this in his place before the King, may attorn with whom they will to gain or lose in all pleas and plaints touching the said Richard within the realm until the return of the said Richard'.[4]

Having settled everything with his usual care, Richard embarked from Dover on 4th August, taking with him his younger son Edmund, now eighteen years old. They landed at the Zwin, and on the sixteenth were at Cambrai for the formal granting of the Dukedom of Brabant to its new lord.* His chancellor, Bishop Nicholas of Cambrai, was still one of his most trusted adherents, as was the new Count of Hainault, Baudouin d'Avesnes; but the news from Germany was not good. The Electors were plotting again, contemplating electing the Landgraf von Thüringen. Richard's diplomatic emissaries went back and forth to them and

* This was John, the second son of the late Duke Henry, whose elder brother had been passed over as he was mentally deficient. Cf. J. F. Bappert, *Richard von Cornwall*, 113.

to Rome; and meanwhile he lingered in the north-western corner of the Empire, not proceeding beyond Aachen till he was satisfied he would be well received.

In those October days he came to Falkenburg, the castle of the noble family of that name, crowning a steep and narrow hill-top above the valley of the River Geul, a tributary of the Maas, some twelve miles north-west of Aachen. The castle's site is virtually impregnable, the ground falling away steeply from it on all sides. Entrance was through a gatehouse by the edge of the escarpment, and the principal structure was a great sixteen-sided tower.[5]

The lord of this castle was Dieter or Dirk von Falkenburg, who as we have seen had attended Richard's coronation in Aachen in 1257 and had been prominent in the battles between Konrad von Hochstaden and the burghers of Cologne, invariably taking the part of the latter. With the death of Konrad, however, Dirk's position changed overnight, for the new Archbishop was none other than his own brother, Engelbert von Falkenburg. Dirk promptly changed sides, and in 1263 was captured and imprisoned by the citizens of Cologne, along with his brother, after what he had intended as a surprise attack on the city – this despite the fact that the Archbishop had concluded a peace treaty with it on 25th August of the same year, and Dirk had witnessed the act.[6] After his release he could not steer clear of the Cologne squabbles for long; and just at the time when Richard came to Falkenburg he was preparing another surprise attack on the city, in concert with his brothers-in-law, the Duke of Limburg and the lord of Heinsberg, with the object of releasing the imprisoned Archbishop. Dirk had his agents in the city, and it was arranged that they would tunnel under the walls so that a party of his knights could enter Cologne by stealth. On the night of 14th October, 1268, this plan was put into force, but unfortunately for him the secret had leaked out, and the citizens – led by the great patrician family of Overstolz – were waiting for them. Dirk von Falkenburg was killed, his forces withdrew, and the Archbishop remained in his foetid dungeon in Nideggen Castle.[7]

Richard was at Falkenburg when this disastrous event took

place, being entertained by Dirk's wife, Joanna van Loon, and their daughter Beatrix. There was one son from Dirk von Falkenburg's first marriage – Walram the Ruddy, who was destined to become the most famous of his line. There were four daughters of the second marriage, the second of whom, Beatrix, could not have been much more than fifteen at the time of Richard's arrival; but the fifty-nine-year-old King was completely captivated by her beauty. The annalist of Oseney Abbey describes her as 'the pearl of womanhood'.[8] Now, on her father's death, she was suddenly in danger; it was not wise for dazzling young girls to be left fatherless in castles, and her brother, Walram, was little older than herself. Probably on Richard's advice she decided to seek the protection of her uncle, Philipp von Bolanden–Hohenfels, whose lands lay far away in the Palatinate Highlands between Bingen and Kaiserslautern, south-west of the Rhine.[9]

How she got there is not related, but it is very probable that as Richard's problems became clarified about the same time, she travelled under his protection. In November Pope Clement had strictly enjoined the Electors to put aside any thought of a further election, whereupon Mainz, Trier and the Pfalzgraf – for this time Cologne was in prison – turned again to Richard and informed him that they would be pleased to receive him.[10] On 15th December therefore he set out from Aachen for Cologne, spent Christmas there, and in the New Year made the familiar journey up the Rhine. At Koblenz the Archbishop of Trier came to do homage to him, and at Mainz Archbishop Werner followed suit. It was indeed fortunate for Richard that the Pope had written when he did, for Clement died on 29th March.

On 7th March Richard entered his favourite city of Worms, which lies only a day's ride from Philipp von Bolanden's castle on the Donnersberg. If Beatrix accompanied him he would doubtless have sent her on the last stage of her journey from here, whence her uncle could protect her. Richard now summoned a Diet to meet at Worms on Easter Day, 14th April. There was general hope in the Rhineland that his presence there would lead to a re-establishment of peace: so far the hopes had been realized, and a large number of princes and nobles assembled at his command. There were the Archbishops of Mainz and Trier, the Pfalzgraf, the Bishops of Worms, Speyer and Chur, and most of the lower nobility of the Middle Rhine.[11] It was indeed a remarkable occasion; and considering his long absence, Richard achieved more in this fourth German visit than ever before.

With his usual perspicacy he realized that the prime essential to restore trade on the great river was to get rid of the tolls set up by the princes and barons in his absence. Archbishop Werner had set the example by abolishing his own lucrative tolls the previous year,[12] and so was able to convince the assembly that they ought to do likewise. The Rhenish towns, in whose interests the abolition was, were eager supporters of this proposal; and eventually the Diet brought about a treaty between them and the princes similar to that of the Rhenish League in 1254.[13] All Rhine tolls save the two ancient imperial stations of Boppard and Kaiserswerth were to be abolished completely. Richard, or in his absence Archbishop Werner, would be personally responsible for seeing that these terms were carried out, and if there was any breach of them an army would be fielded against the transgressors. The contemporary chroniclers confirm that this decisive step stimulated Rhine trade greatly and gave merchants and shipmen the security they had not enjoyed for years.[14]

The general goodwill which it encouraged was reflected in the relations between Richard and the princes. From Worms he travelled to Mainz in the company of the two Archbishops and the Bishops who had attended the Diet; and on 8th May a Synod of the Church was held there, with Archbishop Werner presiding. The main object seems to have been to pronounce sentence of excommunication against Duke Albrecht of Brunswick, who had seized some of Werner's castles – a somewhat embarrassing situation for Richard, since Albrecht had married an English princess in 1266. Albrecht's representative was at the Synod; and when sentence was pronounced he appealed to Richard who – wishing neither to fall out with Archbishop Werner nor to offend the Duke, who recognized him as King – adroitly avoided the issue by advising his representative to appeal to the Pope through the Archbishop.

The Synod over, Richard and the two Archbishops moved on to celebrate Whitsun in Frankfurt. While there he was at pains to mediate between Rudolf von Habsburg and the city of Basle, between whom a violent feud was raging. Richard remained a fortnight in Frankfurt, attending to all kinds of minor and routine business before travelling westwards to the city nearest the castle on the Donnersberg.

The Donnersberg is a vast, rambling massif lying between the Rhine valley on the east and Kaiserslautern in the west. The village of Bolanden lies to the east of it, and among its wooded recesses are the scanty remains of Philipp von Bolanden-Hohenfels's castle. Thence Beatrix was to be brought down by her uncle on 15th June to the city of Kaiserslautern, some fifteen miles away, whither Richard had gone direct from Frankfurt. The Stiftkirche of the Premonstratensian Order was the epitome of the new Gothic style, fresh in its gleaming red sandstone, with springing arches and three tall and striking towers. Here on Sunday, 16th June, 'the first after the feast of St. Barnabas the Apostle', the royal wedding was celebrated, to which a vast concourse of princes, bishops and nobles, including the Pfalzgraf and the Bishop of Speyer, had come.[15]

It was after all a unique occasion. The English King of Germany had found himself a German bride; and though the cynics might say he was 'seeking to marry a native of his kingdom so that he might endear himself to his subjects', yet the truth was that he was 'enthralled not by prospects of her dowry but by her incomparable beauty of body; and immediately the innate grace of the new bride so transfixed the heart of the King that he could not bear to be separated from her for one single night, whatever the reason'.[16]

Beatrix's features have, fortunately, been preserved in a stained-glass window formerly in the Fransciscan Church at Oxford, in which she is shown in velvet cap, crown, close-fitting wimple and ermine-trimmed cloak. Even in the somewhat primitive design of thirteenth-century glass it is clear that the craftsman sought to depict an exceptionally beautiful woman.[17]

Richard had reason to feel extremely content with his achievements in Germany during this latest visit, not only because he had procured himself a supremely lovely girl-wife, but because his political activities had borne so much fruit. 'His German Kingdom stood on a firmer footing and had more supporters to show than ever before.'[18] To have stayed much longer would have caused an adverse drain on his treasury; and besides, he was bursting to show Beatrix his possessions in England. They therefore returned towards the Rhine soon after the wedding, and at the beginning of July were at Mainz as guests of Archbishop Werner von Eppstein. *En route* they had stopped at the Landskron by Oppenheim to admire his rapidly rising Katharinenkirche. The local knights were at loggerheads with the townsfolk and Richard summoned their representatives to appear before him at Mainz, where he adjudicated between them. At the same time he granted his protection to the Order of Teutonic Knights of Sachsenhausen.

Before the royal couple's departure, Richard formally transferred to Archbishop Werner the responsibility of enforcing the Provisions made at Worms. The government of the Wetterau, the region north of Frankfurt, was entrusted to his wife's uncle, Philipp von Bolanden-Hohenfels; that of Alsace to the Bishop of Strasbourg; but elsewhere he placed the reins in the hands of the 'ministeriales' – an adroit political manœuvre probably made in the light of experience. The officials were more to be trusted than the greedy nobles, and yet no one could say that the nobility had been completely ignored. Archbishop Werner indeed was so impressed by Richard's achievements that he went whole-heartedly to work to enforce the Provisions of Worms after the King had left for England. Richard and Beatrix now took leave of him and set out again upon the route so familiar to both of them – Oberwesel, Kaub, Boppard, Cologne, Falkenburg – and all the way along her relatives acknowledged her as their Queen. On 3rd August, 1269, the King of the Romans and the 'pearl of womanhood' came into Dover.

CHAPTER SIX

MURDER AT VITERBO

ON LANDING Richard and Beatrix were greeted by many of the magnates. Richard's third wife made a considerable impact on her new country at once by her exceptional beauty, not least upon the Lord Edward, who after he became King still enjoyed giving her presents.[1] She met him fortuitously a couple of days after her arrival, on 6th August at Gravesend. Edward's ship (bound for France where he would discuss arrangements with King Louis for a joint Crusade) was on the point of sailing, when a boat put off with the news of the arrival of the King of the Romans; whereupon three very important passengers went ashore – Edward, Henry of Almayne and Constance de Béarn.[2] Henry had done very well for himself by marrying this dark French beauty at Windsor on 15th May.[3] She was the daughter of Gaston de Béarn and his wife Mathe, the direct descendant of the Countess Perronelle of Bigorre, and destined ultimately to become heiress to the rich Pyrenean county.

During Richard's absence in Germany, Edward and Henry had virtually run the country, due to the indifferent health of Henry III. They were very attached to each other and had much in common, both being handsome and dashing young men, ready to face danger and equally ready to break their word in the interests of expediency. Henry's career in the eight years prior to Evesham was, as we have seen, full of vacillation; and though for a while in 1260–63 he had been very friendly with Henry de Montfort, he was otherwise disliked by his Montfort cousins. He does not seem to have taken Earl Simon's contemptuous dismissal of him particularly to heart, for – as in most things – he treated the matter lightly. He charged through life with the same aplomb with which he is depicted on his seal,[4] where he is seen galloping along in full armour, vizor closed, broadsword raised, his surcoat and the horse's trappings bearing the familiar lion and bezants of Cornwall – a typical example of the medieval equestrian seal.

As he was still in France at the time of Evesham he had taken no personal part in the battle but, hearing the news, had returned to England in haste, only to be taken ill soon after his arrival. Queen Marguerite of France, who was very fond of him, wrote to King Henry suggesting that his convalescence would be more rapid if he were sent back to her to nurse.[5] However, his health and his fortunes steadily improved. In the summer of 1269 King Louis invited him to return to France;[6] and here he was at Gravesend with the Lord Edward on their way back to Paris.

After mutual greetings the young men and Constance continued to Dover *en route* for Boulogne, while Richard and Beatrix completed their journey to London, where a festive welcome awaited them.[7] On 24th August they joined King Henry and his summer court at Winchester, where for the third time the King met and admired a beautiful sister-in-law. Their arrival in England was most opportune, for years of careful planning by the King and his architects were now approaching fruition in the completion of the rebuilding of Westminster Abbey Church for which Henry had paid from his own resources. The date fixed for the consecration was naturally St. Edward the Confessor's Day, 13th October, and Henry wanted as many of the royal family as possible to be present. In due course on the appointed day Henry and Richard, watched by Eleanor and Beatrix and a vast gathering of nobles, walked in ceremonial procession, bearing on their shoulders the bones of the Confessor to the shrine specially built to receive them at the east end of the great Church.[8]

The young German bride would have cause to remember this, one of the most important occasions of the century. Westminster Abbey indeed is Henry III's most outstanding monument, far outweighing the memories of years of misguided government. High in the nave the craftsmen had carved many of the arms of members of the royal house, and there to this day are the symbols of many who took part in the ceremony of 13th October. They read like a chart of Richard's life – Henry III's arms, his own, those of Sanchia and Raymond Bérenger, and opposite them the fleur-de-lis of Louis IX.[9]

After the ceremony Richard and his bride left London for a tour of their estates. They were at Wallingford for Christmas and until the end of January, while in the late spring they went down to Cornwall and did some very good business there. Richard had had his eyes for a long time on two of the castles of his vassals, and now he had the chance to buy them outright to add to his existing royal strongholds of Launceston and Tintagel. One was the castle of Trematon, whose shell-keep crowns one of the steep hill-tops above the River Lynher, and this the Baron de Valletort now sold to him; while farther west the beautiful widowed heiress Isolda de Cardinan, former wife of Thomas de Tracy, made over to her overlord her lovely castle of Restormel overlooking the Fowey valley. Richard and Beatrix enjoyed themselves designing living quarters to be built inside the circular shell-keep to replace the timber structures in the bailey; the result was to be as cunning and symmetrical a piece of building as any castle could offer, but they were not themselves to see the fruits of their labours.

Trouble was brewing back in London. The Lord Edward had been too familiar with the wife of the fiery Earl of Gloucester;[10] hence the latter refused to attend the Parliament summoned at Westminster for the end of April, and once again Richard was chosen as arbitrator.[11] It could not have been very palatable to adjudicate between his relatives, but Richard did it with determination, announcing his decision on 27th May.[12] Gloucester was to follow Edward on Crusade as soon as possible. If he assisted him in the Holy Land, he would receive a payment of 8,000 marks, but if he did not, it would be 2,000 only. But should he meanwhile cause any disturbance at home, the Bishops would lay an Interdict on his land, redeemable only by a payment of 20,000 marks to be used as Richard should direct. This was drastic enough to keep even Gloucester quiet.

He and Edward were reconciled at Reading on 18th July, where

Richard repeated the formal award;[13] and on 2nd August Edward embarked at Dover for his Crusade. A fortnight later Henry of Almayne and Constance de Béarn sailed for Gascony, and the cousins joined forces at Aigues-Mortes in September, preparatory to sailing for Tunis where they had intended to join Louis.

The saintly King had been a sick man before he started from France, so weak that his faithful seneschal Joinville had had to carry him in his arms;[14] had his advisers not pressed him to persevere with his project, his life might have been prolonged. As it was he had got as far as Tunis when he died on St. Bartholomew's Eve.[15] The news reached Edward and Henry while they were still *en route* to join him, but at the invitation of his son, the new King Philip III, they continued their voyage to Tunis.

But the fire had gone out of the Crusade, and they recrossed the Mediterranean to winter by invitation at the Court of Charles of Anjou, King of Sicily, and his wife Beatrice of Provence, aunt of the two young princes. On 6th February an urgent message reached Edward, telling him to renounce his Crusade and return to England because of the illness of his father: Richard of Cornwall had already been appointed Regent. Edward was most loath to give up his project; his father had been ill before and he rightly assumed that this time would not prove fatal either. Instead he sent off Henry of Almayne on a multiple errand. He was to go first to Viterbo, in central Italy, where he was to act as English Ambassador to the College of Cardinals, still arguing over a successor to Pope Clement who had died two years before.[16] Then he was to proceed to Gascony to arrange for the government of the province, and finally to return to England to assist Richard.[17]

Philip III of France was also going to Viterbo *en route* for Paris and his coronation, bearing with him the bones of his father for interment at Saint-Denis; the august company was completed by Charles of Anjou, who was determined to put pressure on the Cardinals to come to a decision. They all arrived at Viterbo on 9th March, where to Henry's mortified surprise he was welcomed mockingly by Guy and Simon de Montfort and Guy's father-in-law, the 'Red' Count Aldebrandini, so called from the colour of his hair.

Guy and Simon had sought their fortunes in Italy in 1268. Assisted by their cousin Philip* they rose to fame, Guy particularly distinguishing himself at the battle of Alba and earning the trust and approbation of Charles of Anjou, who appointed him his viceroy of Florence and Tuscany. He married the 'Red' Count's daughter Margherita and thus allied himself with one of the chief families of the province. Though Guy was younger than Simon he always led where his elder followed. Spiteful and unforgiving, he ignored the fact that they owed their lives to Richard's mediation after Evesham, preferring to regard Henry of Almayne's tergiversations as the direct cause of their father's death. For the four days that their cousin was in the city Guy played on Simon's filial affection and fanned his anger.

Constance was uneasy about their presence as masters of Viterbo, but Henry nonchalantly made light of her fears. They took up their lodging on the Piazza San Lorenzo, the central square of the city. A stone's-throw away on the north side was the Papal Palace where the Cardinals still haggled; on the western side was the church from which the square took its name.

On the morning of Friday the thirteenth Henry rose early and went alone across the square to hear Mass and pray for a just decision of the Sacred College.[18] Mass over, he knelt for a while longer before the High Altar. The congregation had left, but a couple of deacons were still moving about. Suddenly he was aroused by the sound of mailed feet in the nave, and a loud voice – terrible to hear and shaking with passion – cried out: 'Henry, you traitor, murderer of our father, you shall not escape us! Remember Evesham!'[19]

Henry, still on his knees, turned, and Guy de Montfort, closely followed by Simon and the Count Aldebrandini, fell upon him with drawn broadswords. They slashed at him furiously. The deacons bravely hurried to help him and one was struck down while the other, badly wounded, fled to the vestry. One mighty stroke split Henry's skull while another smote the hand with which he was clutching the altar, trying to rise, and left three of the fingers adhering to it. Then the three murderers turned and fled.

* Philip de Montfort came from a different branch of this powerful family.

CHAPTER SEVEN

BRIEF TWILIGHT

RICHARD AND BEATRIX were at Isleworth when the disastrous news of Henry's murder reached England. Messengers came thick and fast, expressing the horror and indignation of all Europe; and then promises of help and support came from Philip of France and Charles of Sicily, who both felt – albeit needlessly – some measure of responsibility for what had happened. It was Beatrix who made most of the arrangements for the return of Henry's remains; masses were to be said for his soul in many churches. Richard was for the time being too shattered to make these arrangements himself, but he did send an urgent message to his younger son Edmund to return from his Crusade lest a similar fate befall him.[1]

On 15th May the disconsolate widow, Constance de Béarn, accompanying the bones of Henry of Almayne, reached London, where his father and King Henry received them. His heart, in a golden vase inscribed: 'To my father my heart, pierced by a dagger' was interred beside the remains of Edward the Confessor in his shrine in Westminster Abbey. Then Richard and Beatrix set out on the long and gloomy journey down to Hayles.

The cortège halted at Wallingford, where messengers from Cologne arrived to speak urgently with Richard, seeking his support against the Archbishop Engelbert von Falkenburg. He had been recently released from a cage above the gatehouse of Nideggen Castle, in which the Graf von Jülich had incarcerated him as an object of public derision;[2] and the citizens were fearful of further inroads by the Archbishop on their cherished freedom. Richard, however, was too consumed by personal grief to pay much attention. So it was Beatrix who contrived to see them and to arrange for Richard to sign the charter – thus being faced with the conflict of loyalties typical for the medieval woman, asking her husband to take action against her uncle.

They proceeded on their way to Hayles, and the following day Henry's bones were interred before the High Altar close to Sanchia's tomb.[3] With him were buried Richard's hopes of a dynasty in Germany, for he never seems to have contemplated Edmund succeeding him. It was Edmund, however, who was to bring to Hayles its great relic, and place it in a shrine close to where his mother and half-brother lay.

Returning from Hayles, Richard had to plunge rapidly into politics again. Henry III had been taken ill, and Richard presided over the June Parliament in London in his absence. He took the opportunity of being in the capital to obtain a grant of land of the late wife of Walter de Huntercombe, one of his tenants at Cippenham, 'in part satisfaction of the thousand pounds which the King owes him',[4] and a grant to the dean and chapter of Salisbury of three thousand marks 'which they are to pay to the King's brother, Richard, King of Almayne at terms to be fixed between them, a new loan of three thousand marks which the said Richard has now made to the King'.[5]

At the June Parliament also came news of the great financial needs of the Lord Edward in the Holy Land 'on which account Richard, King of Almayne, the King's brother, has on the King's prayers, advanced to the said Edward the remaining two thousand marks; grant to the said Richard, for his courtesy, that he and his executors and assigns shall hold the Jews of England from Michaelmas, 1271, to Michaelmas following, that is for one whole year, so that the said Jews shall pay to him the two thousand marks as follows: at Michaelmas, 1271, 666 marks 8s. 10½d., at the feast of the Resurrection of Our Lord the like sum, at Michaelmas following 666 marks 8s. 11d. and in the case of default the said Jews shall pay to him 500 marks in the name of a penalty'.[6]

His business acumen never deserted him, but a fresh tragedy was at hand. When his nephew, the Lord Edward, had gone on Crusade he had left his little son John in Richard's care; but on

1st August, 1271, the boy died in the Palace of Westminster at the age of five.[7] He was, of course, in the direct line of succession to the throne: John II might have been a very different King from Edward II. His death plunged the whole royal family into the deepest gloom and came as a profound shock to Richard. A week later the child was buried in Westminster Abbey. A month after that Richard was already ill, and withdrew to Knaresborough Castle in Yorkshire, formerly held by Henry of Almayne. On 20th October the King committed to him 'the castle of Rockingham and the forests between the bridges of Oxford and Stamford to have as Henry de Alemannia his son had them in his lifetime'.[8]

Richard was probably on his way south at the time, for he had a castle at Oakham, and near-by Rockingham would commend itself to him. By the beginning of November he was back at Berkhamsted, where he transacted his last German business; but his strength was fast ebbing, as his young wife could see. On the night of 11th December the doctors bled him in the hopes of prolonging his life. Instead, he suffered a stroke which paralysed his right side and robbed him of all power of speech.[9]

A sad Christmas passed with Beatrix and Edmund at his bedside, the latter having renounced his Crusade in answer to his stepmother's plea. There was a slight rally in February, for Richard issued a patent on the eighteenth, at the instance of the Bishop of Metz, granting the new bishop of Verdun his regalia and authority over the secular courts of his diocese.[10] But it was only a flicker and early on the morning of Saturday, 2nd April, after he had received the last Sacraments, the great spirit of the King of the Romans fled its earthly tenement.

Thus, at the age of sixty-three, died Richard of Cornwall, sometime Crusader and sometime Regent of England. Alone of his compatriots before or since he had endeavoured to rule the vast and amorphous realm of Germany; and though for many centuries it was fashionable to regard him as a failure, as little more than the shadow of a king, modern German scholarship is slowly discovering the true value of this 'great and good man'. The septcentenary of the death of Konrad von Hochstaden has thrown more light than ever on the connection with Cologne and the importance to the Rhineland of the choice of an English king. English scholarship too will perhaps soon come to realize that Richard was no minor historical figure, and to evaluate him as the greatest single force in keeping the English kingdom intact throughout the long and troubled reign of Henry III. There are indeed signs that this evaluation is also making headway. Two modern English writers have described him as 'considered to be one of the ablest princes of his time',[11] and as 'a true knight not unworthy of the uncle whose name he bore'.[12]

Richard in fact sacrificed his own position on the Continent in the interests of his native land, though from the first he made it clear that his German kingdom was his own affair, not that of his ineffective brother.[13] The strength of much of his administration lay in this very ability to keep things separate, for in Germany he ruled with the aid of Germans, in England with Englishmen, in Cornwall with Cornishmen. He never made his brother's mistake of provoking xenophobia by surrounding himself with foreigners.

Never of strong physique, he was centuries ahead of his time in preferring the art of mediation and diplomacy to the art of war. His financial acumen enabled him to preserve an independence which made him beholden to no man, and thus an ideal arbiter. Despite his general aversion to conflict he could, when the need arose, take a swift decision and back it up with positive and daring action, as at Taillebourg. He had a flair for summing up a situation and dealing with it calmly and prudently. He was seldom roused to the heights of Angevin anger which bedevilled his father and brother, and only when unprovoked aggression against his property took place was he inclined to harbour lasting resentment.

From the age of twenty-two he was sustained by the advice, borne forward by the pressure, and enthralled by the beauty of his three remarkable wives. He enjoyed good living, colour, beauty in architecture, fine clothes. He was indeed a very human and likeable man, greatly loved and admired by his family and his *familia*. The finer and more artistic virtues were his, including a deep religious sense, but he also revelled in feminine beauty. Throughout his life an admirer of women, of him in particular can be said in Goethe's famous phrase:

'The eternal feminine is our Lodestar.'[14]

THE PERAMBULATION OF THE BOUNDARIES OF THE FOREST OF DARTMOOR

Haec est Perambulatio facta et ordinata per commune consilium Ricardi Comitis Cornubiae et Pictaviae et militum et liberorum tenentium in comitatu Devon per preceptum domini Regis Henrici filii Johannis anno coronationis dicti Henrici vicesimo quarto in vigilia sancti Jacobi apostoli per sacramentum militum subscriptorum, scilicet, Willielmi de la Brewer, Guidonis de Bretevyle, Willielmi de Wydeworthy, Hugonis de Bollay, Ricardi Gyffard, Odonis de Treverbyn, Henrici filii Henrici, Willielmi Trenchard, Philippi Parrer, Nicholai de Heamton, Willielmi de Moreleghe, et Duranti filii Botour, qui incipiunt perambulationen ad hogam de Cossdonne et inde linealiter usque ad parvam hogam quae vocatur parva Hundetorre, et inde linealiter usque ad Thurlestone, et inde linealiter usque ad Wotesbrokeslakesfote quae cadit in Tyng, et inde linealiter usque ad Heighestone, et inde linealiter usque ad Langestone, et inde linealiter usque per mediam turbariam de Alberysheved, et sic in longum Wallebroke et inde linealiter usque ad Furnum regis et inde linealiter usque ad Wallebrokeshede et sic in longum Wallebroke usque cadit in Dertam, et sic per Dertam usque ad aliam Dertam, et sic per aliam Dertam ascendendo usque Okebrokysfote et sic ascendendo Okebroke usque ad la Dryeworke, et ita ascendendo usque ad la Dryfeld ford, et sic inde linealiter usque ad Battyshull et inde linealiter usque ad caput de Wester Wellabroke et sic per Wester Wellbroke usque ad cadit in Avenam, et inde linealiter usque ad Ester Whyteburghe et inde linealiter usque ad la Redelake quae cadit in Erme et inde linealiter usque ad Grymgrove et inde linealiter usque ad Elysburghe et sic linealiter usque ad crucem Sywardi et inde usque ad Ysfother et sic per aliam Ysfother et inde per mediam Mystor usque ad Mewyburghe et inde usque ad Lullingsfote et inde usque ad Rakernesbrokysfote, et sic ad caput ejusdem aque et deinde usque ad la Westsolle et inde linealiter usque ad Ernestorre et inde linealiter usque ad vadum proximum in orientali parte capellae Sancti Michaelis de Halgestoke et inde linealiter usque ad predictam hogam de Cossdonne in orientali parte.

NOTE: These boundaries have remained the basis for the division between Forest and Commons for seven centuries, although slightly amended by the Jurors of 1609 and again by modern usage. Many of the names are easily recognizable in modern Dartmoor nomenclature. Of the more obscure, the following are the modern equivalents: Thurlestone – Watern Tor (the thirlstone is the name given the southernmost rock which appears 'drilled'); Furnum regis – King's Oven, on Water Hill above the Warren House Inn; Okebroke – the Wo Brook; Battyshull – the cairn on Ryder's Hill; Elysburghe – Eylesbarrow; Ysfother – Hessary; aliam Ysfother – North Hessary, now famous for its television mast; Lullingsfote – Lynch Tor; Rakernesbrokysfote – Rattlebrook Foot; Ernestorre – (the mountain of eagles) – Yes Tor.

APPENDIX TWO

FOUNDATION CHARTER OF BURNHAM ABBEY

Rex archiepiscopis, etc. Salutem. Ricardus Dei gratia Romanorum rex, semper Augustus, omnibus Christi fidelibus, tam presentibus quam futuris, ad quos praesens scriptum pervenerit, salutem in Domino sempiternam. Noverit universitas vestra nos, pro nobis et haeredibus nostris, dedisse, concessisse, et hac presenti carta nostra confirmasse Deo, et beatae Mariae et monasterio de Burnham, quod fundavi fecimus, ac monialibus ibidem Deo servientibus, et earum successoribus, in liberam puram et perpetuam elemosinam . . .

Concessimus etiam pro nobis et haeredibus nostris, dictis monialibus, et earum successoribus, totam terram de Morforlong et Brockforlong cum toto prato de Dillepol, quae fuerunt de manerio nostro de Cippeham, tempore istius donationis nostrae, et totum boscum quem emimus de Johanne de eeverngee, qui vocatur la Strete, et unam partem bosci nostri de Hartlegh, sicut fossata proportant, de bosco de la Strete, usque ad boscum Johannis de la Penne . . .

Histis testibus; Henrico illustri rege Angliae, fratre nostro, domino Edwardo ejusdem regis primogenito, nepote nostro; dominis W. Bathon, cancellario Angliae; R. Lincoln et R. Coventram et Lichfelder, episcopis; Henrico et Edmundo filiis nostris, Philippo Basset, Willielmo de Huntercombe, Willielmo de Wyndlesore, Richardo de Oxeye, Philippo de Covele et aliis. Dat' apud Cippeham decimo octavo die Aprilis, indictione nona, anno Domini millesimo ducentesimo sexagesimo sexto, regni vero nostri anno nono.

Concessimus etiam pro nobis, et haeredibus nostris, eisdem monialibus et successoribus suis toto terrano cum pertinentis, quae fuit Johannis de Boveneye.

ARMS, EFFIGIES AND RELICS OF RICHARD AND HIS FAMILY

ARMS

Richard of Cornwall. Argent, a lion rampant gules couronné or within a a border sable bezanty.
To be found at St. Albans Abbey (the crossing), south side of nave in Westminster Abbey, Hayles Church (heraldic tiles).
Imperial arms – the German eagle to be found in stained glass in Exeter Cathedral and in heraldic tiles in Hayles Church.

Isabella Marshal (Marshal arms). Party per pale, *or* and *vert*; a lion rampant gules, armed and langued azure.
To be found in Temple Church on effigy of William Marshal the Younger.
(As Lady de Clare). Or, three chevrons, gules.
To be found in numerous places, e.g. Clare College, Cambridge, Hayles Church (heraldic tiles).

Sanchia de Provence. Or, four pales, gules.
To be found in Hayles Church (heraldic tiles), Church of St. Jean de Malte, Aix-en-Provence, south side of nave, Westminster Abbey (arms of Raymond Bérenger).

Beatrix von Falkenburg. Or, a lion rampant gules.
To be found at Valkenburg Castle, Holland, the gatehouse.

TOMBS AND EFFIGIES

Site of tomb, Richard and Sanchia. Hayles Abbey, Glos. Tablet on the site of the North Quire aisle marks the location.

Site of tomb, Isabella. Beaulieu Abbey, Hants. Tablet 'Hic jacet Ysabella' marks spot on site of North Quire aisle. Leaden coffin shaped to her figure found in 1862. Former grave-slab with trace of effigy moved to Lay Refectory (now the museum). Traces of inscription reading HIC JACET YSABELLA PRIMA UXOR RICARDI REGIS ROMANORUM.

Site of tomb, Henry of Almayne. Hayles Abbey, Glos. Before the High Altar, of which the base remains. Henry's bones seen as recently as 1899 during excavations.

Roof Boss, Richard. In Beaulieu Parish Church, formerly the refectory. Coloured Roof boss believed to represent Richard in imperial Crown.

Roof Bosses, Saint Louis and Marguerite de Provence. Saint Germain-en-Laye, the castle chapel.

EFFIGIES

William Marshal the elder. The Temple Church, London.

William Marshal the younger. The Temple Church, London.

King John. Worcester Cathedral.

Isabella of Angoulême. Fontevrault Abbey, Maine-et-Loire.

Raymond Bérenger (statue). Church of Saint Jean de Malte, Aix-en-Provence.

Béatrice de Savoie (statue). Church of Saint Jean de Malte, Aix-en-Provence.

Henry III. Westminster Abbey.

Eleanor of Aquitaine. Fontevrault Abbey.

Henry II. Fontevrault Abbey.

Richard Cœur-de-Lion. Fontevrault Abbey.

Richard of Cornwall (statue). Front of Rathaus, Aachen.

Blanche de Castille. Abbey of Saint-Denis.

CASTLES ASSOCIATED WITH RICHARD AND HIS FAMILY

ENGLAND

Wallingford, Berks. Scanty remains of keep; earthworks.

Berkhamsted, Herts. Scanty remains of chapel and keep amid extensive earthworks of motte-and-bailey castle.

Eye, Suffolk. Some remains of keep.

Launceston, Cornwall. Impressive remains of double cylindrical keep, walls and gatehouse.

Restormel, Cornwall. Well-preserved shell-keep with domestic buildings within.

Trematon, Cornwall. Well-preserved shell-keep on mound, extensive curtain walls.

Corfe, Dorset. Extensive ruins of keep, inner and outer gatehouses and curtain walls.

Lydford, Devon. Square tower-keep.

Knaresborough, Yorks. Considerable remains of keep.

Winchester, Hants. Great Hall only remains.

Kenilworth, Warwicks. Extensive remains of keep, gatehouse (Mortimer's Tower), curtain walls, site of mere.

FRANCE

La Réole, Gironde. Extensive remains of the castle. ('Chateau des Quatre Soeurs', so called from its four corner towers.)

Tarascon, Bouches-du-Rhône. Excellently preserved remains of the castle of the Counts of Provence, the lower part of which is of thirteenth-century date, the upper rebuilt.

Beaucaire, Gard. Extensive remains of cylindrical donjon and walls.

Taillebourge, Charente-Maritime. Scanty remains of castle.

Loudun, Vienne. Striking white keep of the castle.

Vendôme, Loire-et-Cher. Considerable remains of castle.

HOLLAND

Valkenburg, Limburg. Extensive remains of keep, hall, gatehouse and walls of castle on imposing site above the town.

GERMANY

Andernach. Castle, part of town walls.

Boppard. Castle of Electors of Trier, town walls.

Donnersberg. Scanty remains of castle of Philipp von Bolanden.

Kaub. Extensive remains of Burg Gutenfels on hill above.

Oppenheim. Scanty ruins of Landskron Castle on hill above.

Sinzig. Remains of imperial castle and town walls.

ECCLESIASTICAL BUILDINGS ASSOCIATED WITH RICHARD

ENGLAND

Hayles Abbey, Glos. Ruins of cloisters, base of High Altar, site of tombs.

Beaulieu Abbey, Hants. Site of nave, Quire, site of High Altar and tomb of Isabella, grave slab of Isabella, roof bosses in former refectory, now the Parish Church. Heart coffin.

Burnham Abbey, Bucks. Refectory and dorter range. Tithe barn.

Hayles Church, Glos. Twelfth century. Contains heraldic tiles.

Fawley, Bucks. Rebuilt Parish Church, scene of first marriage.

Beckley, Oxon. Skew chancel added in Richard's time to cruciform church.

FRANCE

Saint Denis (Seine). Abbey, Ossuary of Saint Louis and Marguerite de Provence. Effigy of Blanche de Castille.

Fontevrault (Maine-et-Loire). Abbey. Effigies of Henry II, Eleanor of Aquitaine, Richard Cœur-de-Lion and Isabella of Angoulême.

Saint-Gilles (Gard). Benedictine Abbey, scene of Richard's pilgrimage in 1240.

Paris. Sainte Chapelle, Ile de la Cité. Built by Saint Louis, visited by Richard (1250) and Sanchia (1254).

GERMANY

Aachen. Cathedral, Octagonal Hochmünster containing King's Chair, marble, in which Richard received homage of nobles. Treasury containing his sceptre and other coronation regalia, and chest (Wappentruhe) worked by a smith of Limoges.

Cologne. Cathedral. Effigy of Konrad von Hochstaden.

Heisterbach. Ambulatory and apse of Cistercian Abbey granted charter by Richard.

Kaiserslautern. Three-towered red sandstone Stiftkirche, built *c.* 1250 shortly before Richard's marriage there to Beatrix.

Oppenheim. Katharinenkirche, built partly to Richard's design, and foundation stone laid by him in 1262.

Worms. Romanesque Cathedral.

GENEALOGICAL TREE OF RICHARD OF CORNWALL

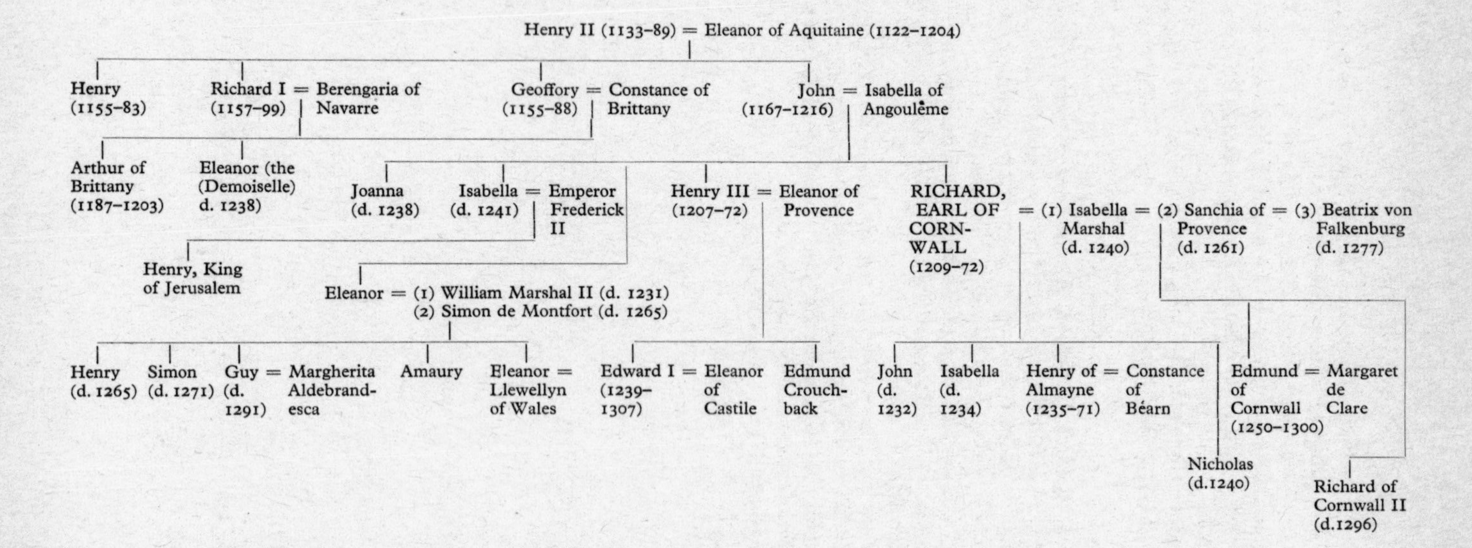

Q*

GENEALOGICAL TREE OF SANCHIA OF PROVENCE

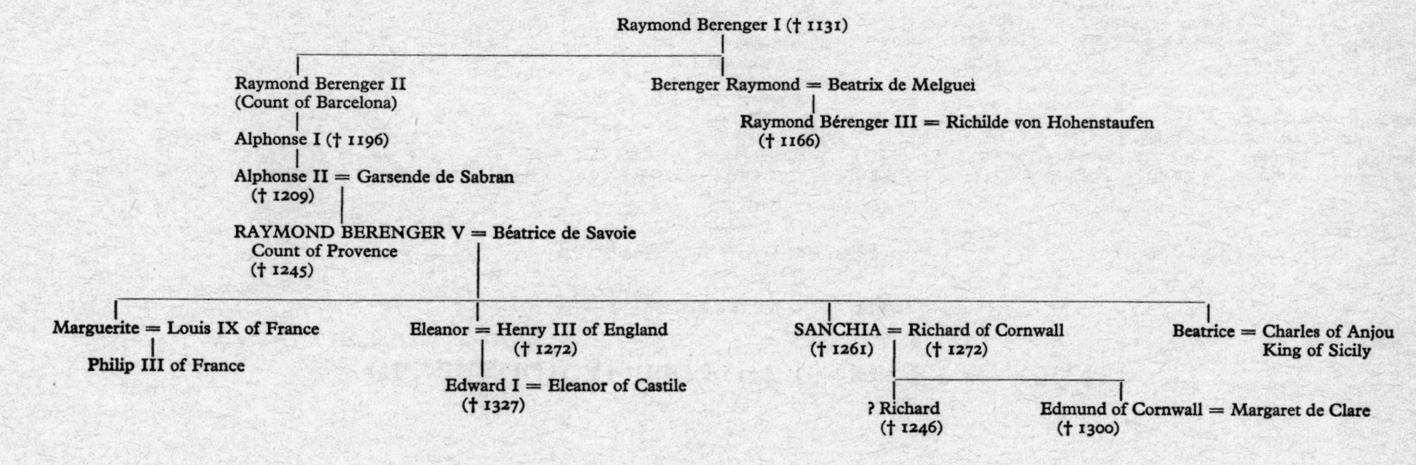

GENEALOGICAL TREE OF ISABELLA MARSHAL

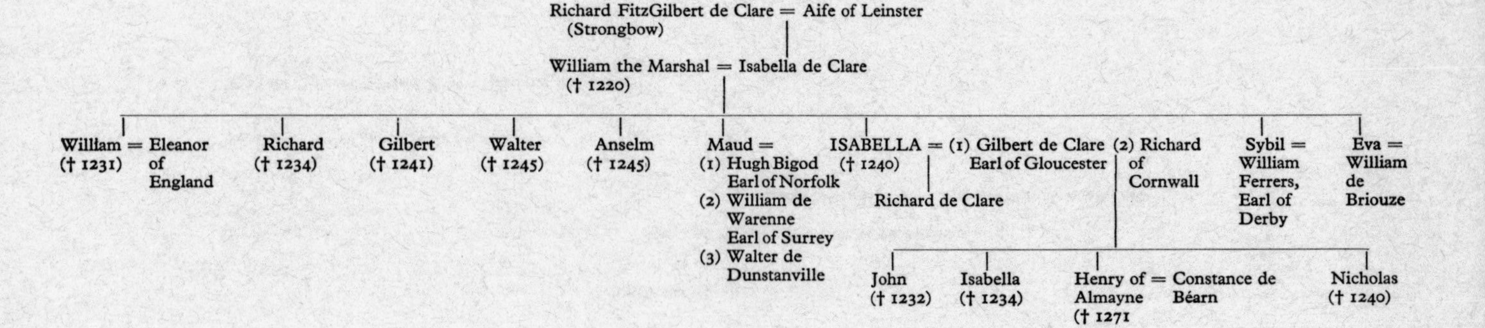

GENEALOGICAL TREE OF BEATRIX VON FALKENBURG

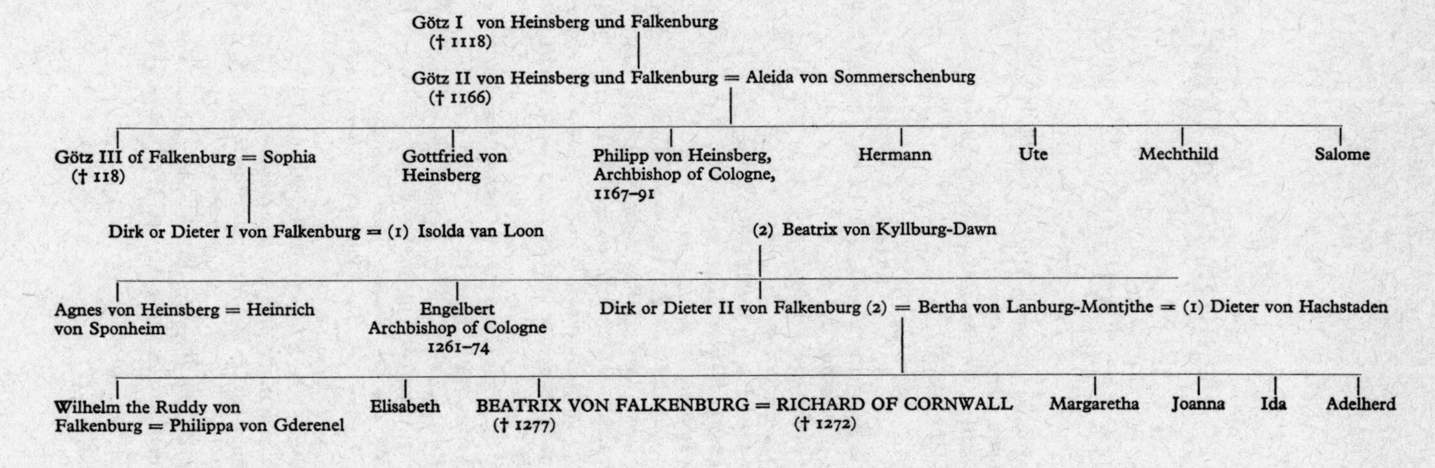

BIBLIOGRAPHY

ENGLISH SOURCES

MANUSCRIPT

PARIS, Matthew, *Chronica Majora*, Corpus Christi College, Cambridge, Manuscript No. 16

PARIS, Matthew, *Chronica Majora*, Corpus Christi College, Cambridge, Manuscript No. 26

PRINTED WORKS

ANNALES MONASTICI, 5 vols., ed. H. R. Luard (Rolls Series, London, 1864–69), *including:*
Annales monasterii de Bermundeseia in Vol. II
Annales monasterii de Burton in Vol. I
Annales prioratus de Dunstaplia in Vol. III
Annales monasterii de Margam in Vol. I
Annales monasterii de Oseneia in Vol. IV
Annales monasterii de Theokesberia in Vol. I
Annales monasterii de Waverleia in Vol. II
Annales monasterii de Winton in Vol. II
Chronicon vulgo dictum Chronicon Thomae Wykes in Vol. IV

'Annales monasterii de Hales', in *Monumenta Germaniae Historica XXVIII*

BADDELEY, St. Clair, *Richard of Cornwall and Henry of Almayne, 1209–1272* (Arrowsmith, Bristol)

BAYLEY, Prof. C. W., 'The diplomatic preliminaries of the double election in Germany' in *English Historical Review* lxii, pp. 457, et seq.

BLAAUW, W. H., *The Barons' War* (London, 1871)

BRACTON, Henry de, *De Legibus et Consuetudinibus Angliae*, ed. T. Twiss (Rolls Series, 1878–83)

BRAUN, Hugh, *The English Castle* (Batsford, 1935)

BROWN, R. Allen, *English Castles* (Batsford, 1954)

BRYANT, Sir Arthur, *The Makers of the Realm* (Reprint Society, London, 1955)

BRYCE, Lord, *The Holy Roman Empire* (Macmillan, 1913)

Calendar of Charter Rolls, Henry III (London, Public Record Office)

Bibliography

Calendar of Liberate Rolls, Henry III (London and Hereford, 1916)

Calendar of Patent Rolls, Henry III (London, 1906)

Cambridge Mediaeval History, esp. Vol. VI, *The Victory of the Papacy* (C.U.P., 1929–57)

CHAYTOR, H., *Savaric de Mauléon* (C.U.P., 1939)

COGGESHALL, Ralph de, *Chronicon Anglicanum*, ed. J. Stevenson (Rolls Series, London, 1875)

COLLIN, Bertha, *The Riddle of a Thirteenth-century sword-belt* (The Heraldry Society, 1955)

COULTON, G. G., *The Mediaeval Panorama* (C.U.P., 1945)

Curia Regis Rolls, Henry III (London, H.M.S.O., 1957)

DAVIS, H. W. C., *England under the Normans and Angevins* (Methuen, 1905)

DENHOLM-YOUNG, N., *Richard of Cornwall* (Blackwell, 1947)

DENHOLM-YOUNG, N., 'Thomas Wykes and his Chronicle' in *English Historical Review*, lxi, pp. 157–9

DENHOLM-YOUNG, N., *Seignorial Administration in England* (C.U.P., 1937)

DUDGALE, W., *Monasticon Anglicanum* (ed. Caley, Ellis & Bandinel, 1817–30)

DUGGAN, W., *Devil's Brood: The Angevin Family* (Faber & Faber, 1957)

FISHER, H. A. L., *A History of Europe* (Fortuna, 1960)

FOWLER, J. K., '*A History of Beaulieu Abbey*' (The Car Illustrated, 1909)

GALBRAITH, V. H., *Roger Wendover and Matthew Paris* (Glasgow, 1944)

GERVASE OF CANTERBURY, *Historical Works* (Rolls Series, 1880)

HEENAN, M. G., *see* Humphrey-Smith

HEER, Friedrich, *The Mediaeval World* (Weidenfeld and Nicholson, 1961)

HENDERSON, A. E., *Beaulieu Abbey and Hayles Abbey* (S.P.C.K., 1952)

HOSKINS, W. G., *Devon* (Collins, 1954)

HUMPHREY-SMITH, C. R., and Heenan, M. G., 'The Royal Heraldry of England' in *The Coat of Arms*, January, 1962, pp. 18, et seq. (The Heraldry Society)

JACOB, E. F., *Studies in the Period of Baronial Reform* (Oxford Studies in Social and Legal History, VIII, 1925)

KANTOROWICZ, E., *Frederick II* (London, 1931)

KINGSFORD, C. L., *The Song of Lewes* (Oxford, Clarendon Press, 1890)

LABARGE, Margaret, *Simon de Montfort* (Eyre & Spottiswoode, 1962)

LEWIS, F. R., 'Beatrix von Falkenburg, third wife of Richard, Earl of Cornwall and King of the Romans' in *English Historical Review*, lii, 1937, pp. 279, et seq.

MASSÉ, H. L. L. J., *The Abbey Church of Tewkesbury with some account of the Priory Church of Deerhurst* (Bell, 1906)

MAXWELL-LYTE, Sir H. (ed.), *The Book of Fees* (Public Record Office)

MELROSE CHRONICLE, Introduction by A. O. and M. O. Anderson (London, 1936)

NATIONAL TRUST, *Hailes Abbey*

NORGATE, Kate, *The Minority of Henry III* (London, 1912)

NORRIS, Herbert, *Costume and Fashion*, Vol. II (Dent, 1927)

OMAN, Sir Charles, *Castles* (Great Western Railway, 1926)

PAINTER, Sidney, *William Marshal* (John Hopkins Press, Baltimore, 1933)

PAINTER, Sidney, *Studies in the History of the English Feudal Barony* (Baltimore, 1943)

PARIS, Matthew, *Chronica Majora* (3 vols., 1216–39, 1240–47, 1248–59; ed. H. Luard, Rolls Series, London, 1876)

PARIS, Matthew, *Additamenta* (Vol. VI, ed. H. R. Luard, Rolls Series, 1882)

PARIS, Matthew, *Historia Anglorum* (ed. Sir F. Madden, Rolls Series)

PEERS, Sir Charles, *Berkhamsted Castle* (H.M.S.O., 1948, M.O.W. series)

POOLE, A. L., *Obligations of society in the 12th and 13th centuries* (O.U.P., 1946)

POOLE, A. L., 'The Interregnum in Germany', Chapter II in Vol. VI, *The Victory of the Papacy*, *Cambridge Mediaeval History* (C.U.P., 1929–57)

POWICKE, Sir F. M., *King Henry III and the Lord Edward* (C.U.P., 1947)

RADFORD, C. A. Ralegh, *Launceston Castle* (H.M.S.O., 1960, M.O.W. series)

RADFORD, C. A. Ralegh, *Lydford Castle* (H.M.S.O., 1960, M.O.W. series)

RADFORD, C. A. Ralegh, *Restormel Castle* (H.M.S.O., 1935, M.O.W. series)

RADFORD, C. A. Ralegh, *Tintagel Castle* (H.M.S.O., 1939, M.O.W. series)

RISHANGER, William, *Chronica et Annales* (ed. H. T. Riley, Rolls Series, 1885)

RISHANGER, William, *Chronicon de duobus bellis apud Lewes et Evesham*, 1263–67 (ed. J. O. Halliwell, Camden Society, 1840)

ROBERT OF GLOUCESTER, *Chronicles* (ed. W. A. Wright, Rolls Series, 1887)

ROWE, Rev. Samuel, *A Perambulation of Dartmoor* (Plymouth, 1848)

RUHLMANN, G., 'Western Europe in the Thirteenth Century', in *Larousse Encyclopaedia of Ancient & Mediaeval History* (Paul Hamlyn, London, 1963)

RUNCIMAN, Steven, *A History of the Crusades* (C.U.P., 1954)

RYMER, T., *Foedera, conventiones et cujuscunque generis Acta Publica* (ed. T. Hardy, London, 1876)

SOUTHERN, Prof. R. W., *The Making of the Middle Ages* (Hutchinson, 1953)

TOUT, T. F., 'Richard of Cornwall' in *Dictionary of National Biography*, Vol. xlviii, 1876

THROOP, P. A., *Criticism of the Crusade; a study of Public Opinion and Crusade Propaganda* (N.V. Swets en Zeitlingen, Amsterdam, 1940)

TREHARNE, R. F., *The Baronial Plan of Reform* (Manchester, 1932)

VAUGHAN, Prof. R., *Matthew Paris* (C.U.P., 1958)

VICTORIA COUNTY HISTORIES (especially *Bucks* and *Hants*)

WARREN, W. L., *King John* (Eyre and Spottiswoode, 1962)

WENDOVER, Roger, *Flores Historiarum* (Bohn, London, 1849)

WOOD, S., *English Monasteries and their Patrons in the 13th century* (O.U.P., 1955)

WRIGHT, Thomas, *The Political Songs of England from the reign of John to that of Edward II* (Camden Society, 1839)

WYKES, Thomas, *Chronicon vulgo dictum Chronicon Thomae Wykes* (in Vol. IV, *Annales monastici*, ed. H. R. Luard, Rolls Series, 1864–9)

CONTINENTAL SOURCES

BAPPERT, J. F., *Richard von Cornwall seit seiner Wahl zum deutschen König* (Hanstein, Bonn, 1905)

BÉMONT, Charles, *Simon de Montfort, comte de Leicester* (Paris, 1884)

BENOIT, Fernand, *Receuil des actes des Comtes de Provence* (Picard, 1952)

BERNARD, Cyprien, 'Notice historique et littéraire sur les filles de Raymond Bérenger' in Vol. XV, *Annales des Basses-Alpes*, pp. 112–22 and 170–79

BÖHMER–FINCKER–WINCKELMANN, *Regesten des Kaiserreichs*, 1198–1273

BOUTARIC, E., 'Marguerite de Provence, son caractère, son rôle politique' in *Revue des questions historiques*, Vol. 3 (Palme, Paris, 1921)

BOUTARIC, E., *Saint Louis et Alphonse de Poitiers* (Paris, 1870)

BRESSLAU, H., *Geschichte der Monumenta Germaniae Historica* (Hanover, 1921)

BRUCHHAUSER, K., *Heimatbuch der Stadt Sinzig* (Steffgen, Koblenz-Lützel, 1953)

BUSQUET, Raoul, *Histoire de Provence* (Imprimerie Nationale de Monaco, 1954)

CARDAUNS, H., *Konrad von Hochstaden* (Regesten der Kölner Erzbischöfe, 1238–61, Commissions Verlag, Köln, 1880)

CHAMPOLLION-FIGEAC, M., *Lettres des rois, reines et autres personnages, des Cours de France et d'Angleterre*, Vol. (Paris, 1839)

CLEMENS, Paul, *Die Kunstdenkmäler der Rheinprovinz* (Schwann, 1940)

D'OUËT D'ARCQ, L., *Collection des sceaux* (Paris, 1863–70)

EBHARDT, Prof. Bodo, 'Burg Gutenfels' in *Deutsche Burgen*, Vol. I

ENJOUBERT, H., *Les quatre soeurs qui furent reines* (Boivin, Paris)

FARAL, Edmond, *La vie quotidienne au temps de Saint Louis* (Hachette, 1938)

FÖRSTER, Otto H., *Cologne Cathedral* (Staufen Verlag, Köln, 1948)

GAVRILOVITCH, M., *Etude sur le traité de Paris, 1259* (Paris, 1899)

GEBAUER, Christian, *Leben und denkwürdige Thaten Herrn Richards von Kornwallis* (Leipzig, 1744)

GEBELIN, François, *La Sainte Chapelle et la Conciergerie* (Laurens, 1946)

GRILLPARZER, G., 'König Ottokars Glück und Ende' in *Grillparzers Sämtliche Werke* (Deutsches Verlagshaus Bon & Co., ed. Stefan Hoch, Berlin and Leipzig) (Reprinted 1937)

GROUSSET, René, *Histoire des Croisades et du royaume franc de Jérusalem* (Librairie Plon, Paris, 1934–36)

GROUSSET, René, *L'Epopée des Croisades* (Librairie Plon, Paris, 1939)

GÜTTSCHES, A., *Konrad von Hochstaden, Erzbischof von Köln* (Archiv der Stadt Köln, 1961)

HALPHEN, Louis, *Initiation aux etudes d'Histoire du Moyen Age* (Paris Presses Universitaires de France, 1946)

HALPHEN, Louis, *Les classiques de l'histoire de France au Moyen Age* (Paris, 1923, et seq.)

HOLTZMANN, W., *Papsturkunden in England* (Göttingen, 1952)

HUPPERTZ, A., *Der Kölner Dom und seine Kunstschätze* (Greven, 1963)

JOINVILLE, Sieur Jehan de, 'Vie de Saint Louis' in *Historiens et Chroniqueurs du Moyen Age* (Paris, La Pleiade, 1938)

KAMMERER, W., *Geschichtliches Aachen* (Bromberg, Aachen, 1957)

KNIPPING, B., *Regesten der Kölner Erzbischöfe im Mittelalter*, Vols. I and II (Hanstein, Bonn, 1905)

KOCH, Hugo, *Richard von Kornwall, Erster Theil, 1209–1257* (Heitz, Strassburg, 1888)

LACOMBLET, T. J., *Urkundenbuch für die Geschichte des Niederrheins* (Düsseldorf, 1846)

LEMCKE, G., *Beiträge zur Geschichte König Richards von Cornwall* (Ebering, Berlin, 1909)

MAHN, J. B., *L'Ordre cistercien et son gouvernement et origines au milieu du XIIIe siecle* (Paris, 1951)

MEYER, Paul, *Histoire de Guillaume le Marechal, Comte de Striguil et de Pembroke, poème français* (Librairie Renouard, Paris, 1891)

MONNIER, Thyde, *La ferme des quatre reines* (Plon, 1963)

MÜLLER, Otto, *Der Aachener Domschatz* (Langewiesche Verlag, Königstein, 1956)

PERNOUD, Régine, *Les Croisés* (Hachette, 1959)

PERNOUD, Régine, *Un chef d'Etat, Saint Louis de France* (Gabalda, Paris, 1960)

PINDER, Wilhelm, *Der Kölner Dom* (Langewiesche, 1948)

RÖSSLER, Prof. H., *Ein König für Deutschland* (Oldenbourg, München, 1960)

STEPHANY, Erich, *Der Dom zu Aachen* (Kuhlen Verlag, Mönchen-Gladbach, 1958)

STEPHANY, Erich, *Der Dom zu Aachen* (Arend und Ortmann, Aachen, 1960)

TRAUTZ, Fritz, *Die Könige von England und das Reich* (Heidelberg, 1961)

VAN DE VENNE, J. M., *Geschiedenis van het Kasteel van Valkenburg* (De Stichting 'Kasteel van Valkenburg', Valkenburg, 1951)

VOGTS, Hans, 'Die Bauten der freien Reichstadt Kölns' in *Kölner Almanach*, 1951

WINCKELMANN, *see* Böhmer–Finckel–Winckelmann

NOTES

PART ONE

Chapter One — pp. 11–18

1. *Ann. Wav.*, 261; Warren, *King John*, 3
2. Coggeshall, *Chronicon Anglicanum*, 103
3. Davis, *England under the Normans and Angevins*, 357; Warren, 170
4. Wendover, *Flores Historiarum*, II, 48–9; Bryant, *Makers of the Realm*, 293
5. Wendover, II, 62; *Ann. Wav.*, 268; Coggeshall, 165
6. Paris, *Historia Anglorum*, II, 146–8
7. Paris, *Chronica Majora*, II, 535
8. Wendover, III, 101
9. Coggeshall, 167
10. ibid, 168
11. Wendover, II, 99–100
12. *Ann. Wav.*, 281
13. Paris, op. cit., IV, 601
14. Bryant, 314

Chapter Two — pp. 19–24

1. Powicke, *King Henry III and the Lord Edward*, 3; Paris, *Chron. Maj.* II, 1–2
2. Powicke, 3, et seq.; Bryant, 314
3. Bryant, 316
4. Warren, 230
5. Bryant, 317
6. Painter, *William Marshal*, 281
7. Bryant, 319
8. Paris, *Chron. Maj.*, C.C.C.C. MS. No. 16, f. 147b
9. Meyer, *Histoire de Guillaume le Maréchal*, v. 14392
   Isabella's grave-slab in Beaulieu Abbey, showing the outline of her now-vanished effigy, indicates that she must have been 5 feet 9 or 10 inches tall. Her skeleton, discovered in 1862 in a leaden coffin beneath the nave, still showed traces of her flaxen hair. The inscription on the slab reads: HIC JACET YSABELLA PRIMA UXOR RICARDI REGIS ROMANORUM, and was therefore evidently carved long after her death.

CHAPTER THREE pp. 25–33

1. Powicke, 46
2. ibid., 47
3. Paris. Chron. Maj., III, 59; Coggeshall, 188
4. ibid., III, 58
5. Warren, 192
6. Paris, op. cit., II, 661
7. ibid., 92–3
8. ibid.
9. ibid.
10. ibid.
11. Wendover, IV, 26
12. Paris, op. cit., III, 113
13. ibid., 101–2
14. ibid., 116
15. Powicke, 175
16. Paris, op. cit., III, 123
17 *Ann. Wav.*, 303; *Ann. Dunst.*, 104

CHAPTER FOUR pp. 34–44

1. Paris, *Chron. Maj.*, III, 123–4
2. ibid., 124
3. ibid.
4. ibid.
5. ibid., 124–5
6. ibid., 157
7. ibid., 165
8. ibid., 190
9. ibid., 191
10. *Calendar of Liberate* Rolls, I, 179
11. ibid.
12. ibid., 173
13. Paris, op. cit., 195
14. *Ann. Theok.*, 76
15. Paris, *op. cit.*, 199
16. *Ann. Theok.*, 77
17. Paris, op. cit., 198
18. Labarge, *Simon de Montfort*, 31
19. ibid.
20. Wykes, *Chronicon vulgo*, 72. 'Admirandae pulchritudinis mulier'
21. *Ann. Theok.*, 78. This makes it clear that William Marshal caught his fatal illness at the wedding.
22. ibid.; *Ann. Marg.*, 38
23. Paris, op. cit., III, 201

Chapter Five — pp. 45–56

1. *Ann. Theok.*, 81
2. Paris, *Chron. Maj.*, III, 246
3. C.L.R., 190
4. Paris, op. cit., 246; *Ann. Theok.*, 90
5. *Ann. Theok.*, 92
6. *Ann. Theok.*, 89; *Ann. Dunst.*, 130
7. Powicke, 136
8. *Ann. Theok*, 93
9. Norris, *Costume & Fashion*, 145
10. Busquet, *Histoire de Provence*, 163
11. Norris, op. cit., 145
12. Paris, op. cit., 334
13. Calendar of Patent Rolls, 97
14. Paris, op. cit., 334
15. C.P.R., 66
16. C.P.R., 299
17. *Ann. Theok.*, 78

Chapter Six — pp 57–60

1. Paris, *Chron. Maj.* C.C.C.C. MS. No. 16, f. 121
2. ibid., 123 b
3. Labarge, 54; Paris, *Chron. Maj.*, III, 566–7
4. Denholm-Young, *Richard of Cornwall*, 168
5. Rowe, *Perambulation of Dartmoor*, 266
6. Paris, op. cit., IV, I
7. Rowe, 266; Hoskins, *Devon*, 447
8. Rowe, 266
9. Paris, *Chron. Maj.*, C.C.C.C. MS. No. 16, f. 131b
10. *Ann. Theok.*, 106
11. C.L.R., 448

PART TWO

Chapter One — pp. 63–71

1. Paris, *Chron. Maj.*, IV, II
2. Labarge, 56
3. Joinville, *Vie de Saint Louis*, 404; Boutaric, *Marguerite de Provence*, 417
4. Boutaric, op. cit., 457
5. Joinville, CXXIV
6. Joinville; Pernoud, *Les Croisés* and *Saint Louis*
7. Norris, *Costume & Fashion*, 159 (cf. *Roman de la Rose*)
8. Paris, op. cit., IV, 44

9. Busquet, 157
10. Paris, op. cit., IV, 45
11. ibid.
12. Pernoud, *Croisés*, 271

CHAPTER TWO pp. 72–83

1. Grousset, *Histoire des Croisades*, III, 396
2. Paris, *Chron. Maj.*, IV, 139
3. Grousset, op. cit., 393
4. ibid., 272
5. Paris, op. cit., IV, 326
6. Grousset, op. cit., 379. The opportunity certainly existed. The Sultan Malik Al-Kamil of Egypt, with whom Frederick had made his treaty, had died a year before its expiry, and his kingdom had been split up between sons, brothers and nephews; his son Al Adil became Sultan of Egypt, his brother Al-Salih Ismail King of Damascus, while his nephew Al-Nasir Dawud was King of Transjordan. It was this Nasir who made the treaty with Richard of Cornwall. Another son, Al Salib Aiyub, was King of Jazira; but shortly before the advent of the French, Al Nasir Dawud captured him, with the intention of coming to an agreement with him to depose Al Adil and give him the Sultanate of Egypt.
7. ibid., 377
8. Grousset, op. cit., 395
9. Grousset, op. cit., 385
10. Paris, op. cit., IV, 62
11. ibid., 71
12. Paris, *Chron. Maj.*, C.C.C.C. MS. No. 16, f. 138
13. ibid., f. 148
14. Paris, *Chron. Maj.*, IV, 144
15. ibid., 141–3
16. Grousset, op. cit., 399
17. ibid.
18. Runciman, *A History of the Crusades*, III, 219
19. Paris, op. cit., IV, 169

CHAPTER THREE pp. 84–93

1. Paris, *Chron. Maj.*, IV, 144–8, 166–7. The mahout, labelled 'magister bestiae', is ringing a bell, presumably to warn onlookers of the elephant's approach. For those unfamiliar with elephants, Paris obligingly labels the trunk 'promoscida'.
2. Wykes, 114–16. 'Coronata est cum eo serenissima conjux sua Sanchia, cujus inestimabilis pulchritudo solemnitatem ipsam non mediocriter illustravit'.
3. Powicke, 196; Labarge, 68

4. Paris, op. cit., IV, 180
5. ibid.
6. Powicke, 172
7. Joinville, Ch. XXI
8. Powicke, 188
9. Labarge, 60; Powicke, 188
10. Powicke, 190
11. Koch, *Richard von Cornwall*, 62
12. ibid.
13. Paris, op. cit., IV, 207
14. Joinville, Ch. XXI
15. Paris, op. cit., IV, 209
16. Joinville, Ch. XXI
17. Paris, op. cit., IV, 207
18. ibid., 211
19. ibid.
20. ibid.
21. ibid., 212
22. Joinville, Ch. XXIII
23. C.P.R., 35; Paris, op. cit., IV, 190; and 228 for the de Ros incident. He was unjustly disseized of his property by Henry.
24. Paris, op. cit., IV, 252
25. ibid.

CHAPTER FOUR pp. 94–99

1. C.P.R., 329
2. Paris, *Chron. Maj.*, IV, 190
3. Norris, *Costume & Fashion*, 163
4. Paris, op. cit., IV, 252
5. Boutaric, *Marguerite de Provence*, 421
6. Paris, op. cit., IV, 261
7. *Ann. Theok.*, 132
8. C.P.R., 414
9. Paris, op. cit., 263
10. C.P.R., 408
11. ibid., 437
12. ibid., 414

CHAPTER FIVE pp. 100–111

1. Paris, *Chron. Maj.*, m IV, 283
2. ibid., 303–7. Ultimately Beatrice was to marry Charles of Anjou, King of Sicily, and so not only had the largest portion of her father's estate but also became a Queen like the other three.
3. Busquet, 164

4. ibid.
5. Paris, op. cit., IV, 406
6. ibid., 415
7. Pernoud, *Saint Louis*
8. C.P.R., 434
9. Paris, op. cit., IV, 437
10. ibid., 491
11. ibid. The heiress of the Marshals became Joan, wife of Warin de Munchesney. Their daughter Joan married William de Valence, one of the Lusignan half-brothers of Henry III.
12. ibid., 562
13. ibid., 568
14. Koch, 81
15. *Ann. Dunst.*, 175
16. C.P.R., 511
17. ibid., 508
18. Koch, 83
19. C.P.R., 504
20. Paris, op. cit., VI, 135; Koch, 78
21. Paris, op. cit., IV, 635
22. ibid., V, 73; Koch, 79
23. Paris, op. cit., IV, 631–2; Koch, 75
24. Paris, op. cit., 645
25. ibid., 646
26. ibid., 635
27. *Cambridge Mediaeval History*, VI, 106
28. Grousset, *Epopée des Croisades*, 248; Pernoud, *Croisés*, 249
29. Bryce, *The Holy Roman Empire*, 289
30. ibid., 203–4
31. *Cam. Med. Hist.*, VI, 164

Chapter Six pp. 112–120

1. Paris, *Chron. Maj.* V, 25
2. ibid., 35
3. ibid., 94
4. ibid., 97
5. ibid., 110
6. ibid.
7. C.P.R., 62
8. Paris, op. cit., 127–8; Koch, 88
9. Paris, op. cit., 239
10. ibid., 214
11. C.P.R., 101
12. Paris, op. cit., V, 262–3
13. Vaughan, *Matthew Paris*, 135–6
14. Paris, op. cit., V, 457

15. Koch, 91–2
16. Paris, op. cit., V, 383; C.P.R., 200
17. C.P.R., 208

Chapter Seven pp. 121–128

1. C.P.R., 363
2. ibid., 364
3. ibid., 368
4. ibid., 373
5. *Cam. Med. Hist.*, VI, 173
6. Paris, op. cit., V, 467
7. Norris, 158
8. Paris, op. cit., V, 467
9. ibid., 476
10. Powicke, 240
11. Paris, op. cit., IV, 91
12. ibid.
13. ibid., V, 484
14. Powicke, 240
15. Boutaric, '*Marguerite de Provence*', 424
16. *Cam. Med. Hist.*, VI, 173
17. Paris, op. cit., V, 513
18. C.P.R., 461
19. Paris, op. cit., V, 513

Chapter Eight pp. 129–138

1. Fisher, *History of Europe*, 210
2. Vogts, *Die Bauten der freien Reichstadt Köln*
3. Knipping, *Regesten der Kölner Erzbischöfe*, 28
4. Koch, 114
5. Lemcke, *Richard von Cornwall*, II; C.P.R., 463
6. Koch, 110
7. ibid., 114
8. ibid., 120
9. *Ann. Burt.*, 392
10. C.P.R., 591
11. Paris, *Chron. Maj.*, IV, 601
12. ibid., 602
13. ibid., 626
14. ibid., 603
15. ibid.
16. Bayley, 'The diplomatic preliminaries of the double election in Germany' in *Eng. Hist. Rev.*, lxii, 457, et seq.
17. Bappert, *Richard von Cornwall*, 2

18. Trautz, *Die Könige von England und das Reich*, 113
19. Paris, op. cit., IV, 626
20. C.P.R., 554
21. ibid.
22. Matt. Par. *Addita.*, 366
23. ibid.
24. ibid., 369
25. Wykes, op. cit., 114–6

CHAPTER NINE pp. 139–145.

1. Wykes, 117
2. Robert of Gloucester, *Chronicles*, XXVIII, 667
3. Bappert, 7
4. Lemcke, 37
5. Lemcke, 38
6. Rymer, *Foedera*, I, 358
7. Lemcke, 40
8. Bappert, 15
9. ibid., 16
10. Paris, *Chron. Maj.*, IV, 653.
11. Bappert, 19

CHAPTER TEN pp. 146–154.

1. Lemcke, 35
2. Paris, *Chron. Maj.*, IV, 674
3. ibid., 683
4. Cardauns, *Konrad von Hochstaden*, 98
5. Paris, op. cit., IV, 694
6. ibid., 673–4
7. Bappert, 29
8. Wykes, 118
9. Powicke, 386
10. Denholm-Young, *Richard of Cornwall*, 98
11. *Cam. Med. Hist.*, VI, 277, et seq.
12. Paris, *Addita.*, 397–400
13. *Ann. Burt.*, 444; Paris, *Chron. Maj.*, 497
14. ibid., V., 732
15. Bappert, 33. The previous quotation is also from the same page
16. Cardauns, 49
17. *Ann. Burt.*, 461; Paris, op. cit., V, 720
18. Paris, op. cit., 733
19. Bappert, 37
20. Paris, op. cit., 738

CHAPTER ELEVEN pp. 155–162.

1. Powicke, 399
2. Bappert, 39
3. Wendover, 428
4. C.P.R., Hy III, 1258–66, 57
5. *Ann. Wint.*, 98
6. *Ann. Osen.*, 125
7. Bappert, 64
8. C.P.R., 79
9. ibid.
10. Cardauns, 104
11. Güttsches, *Konrad von Hochstaden*, 13
12. Bappert, 36
13. ibid., 48
14. ibid., 49
15. Wendover, 457
16. ibid.
17. *Ann. Lond.*, 55

CHAPTER TWELVE pp. 163–168.

1. Bappert, 53; Wendover, 461
2. Rishanger, *Chronica et Annales*, 7
3. ibid., 8
4. Wendover, 464
5. Rishanger, op. cit., 8; Wykes, 125
6. Bappert, 58
7. C.P.R., 193
8. Bappert, 60
9. *Ann. Osen.*, 128
10. C.P.R., 195

PART THREE

CHAPTER ONE pp. 171–174.

1. Bappert, 61
2. Wykes, 131
3. Bappert, 64
4. ibid., 65
5. ibid., 68
6. Wykes, 130

CHAPTER TWO pp.175–184.

1. *Ann. Osen.*, 131
2. *Gervase of Canterbury*, 216

3. Labarge, 207
4. *Ann. Burt.*, 500
5. *Ann. Dunst.*, 220
6. Wykes, 133
7. *Ann. Dunst.*, 222
8. Wykes, 134
9. *Ann. Wigorn.*, 449
10. *Ann. Dunst.*, 222
11. Labarge, 211
12. *Ann. Dunst.*, 223
13. *Ann. Dunst.*, 223–4
14. Kingsford, *The Song of Lewes*, 431
15. C.P.R., 275
16. ibid., 276
17. Boutaric, *Marguerite de Provence*, 429
18. *Ann. Dunst.*, 25
19. Rishanger, *De Bellis*, 17
20. Bappert, 77
21. Wykes, 137
22. ibid., 138
23. ibid.
24. Rishanger, *Chron. et Ann.*, 17
25. Wykes, 139
26. *Ann. Dunst.*, 227
27. C.P.R., 307
28. Wykes, 140
29. *Ann. Dunst.*, 230
30. Wykes, 141
31. Wendover, 491
32. Labarge, 232
33. *Ann. Wigorn.*, 451
34. Rishanger, *Chron. et Ann.*, 22
35. ibid.
36. Rymer, 440
37. Wright, *Political Songs*, 69
38. *Melrose Chronicle*, 128

CHAPTER THREE pp. 185–192

1. Kingsford, 387
2. C.P.R., 318
3. Rishanger, *Chron. et Ann*, 27
4. Bappert, 90
5. Rishanger, *De Bellis*, 40
6. Wendover, 503
7. *Ann. Dunst.*, 235
8. Rishanger, *Chron. et Ann.*, 29

9. ibid., 32
10. ibid.
11. *Victoria County Histories*, Hampshire, IV, 158–9
12. Wykes, 158–9
13. ibid., 113–14; *Ann. Wav.*, 362; Rishanger. *Chron. et Ann.*, 33–4
14. C.P.R., 429
15. ibid., 430
16. Wykes, 169–171
17. Rishanger, *De Bellis*, 45

CHAPTER FOUR pp. 193–200

1. Rishanger, *De Bellis*, 42
2. Wykes, 175
3. Bappert, 96
4. Wykes, 179
5. *Ann. Wav.*, 367
6. ibid., 368
7. *Ann. Dunst.*, 240
8. *Ann. Wav.*, 368
9. *Ann. Dunst.*, 240
10. Dugdale, *Monasticon Anglicanum*, VI, 545–6. Foundation Charter, Burnham.
11. Wykes, 191
12. *Ann. Wav.*, 371
13. Wykes, 194
14. ibid., 196
15. *Ann. Osen.*, 199
16. C.P.R., 70 ff.
17. Rishanger, *Chron. et Ann.*, 57

CHAPTER FIVE pp. 201–208

1. Bappert, 107
2. ibid., III
3. C.P.R., 285
4. C.P.R., 243–4
5. Van de Venne, 17, et seq. The town of Valkenburg, dominated by the picturesque ruins of the castle, is today one of the favourite resorts in the Dutch province of Limburg.
6. Van de Venne, 74 ff.
7. Lewis, 'Beatrix von Falkenburg', in *Eng. Hist. Rev.*, lii, 1939, 279, et seq.
8. *Ann. Osen.*, 223–4; 'gemma mulierum'
9. Van de Venne, 76. The complexities of the noble families of Germany and Holland are not easy to unravel. Johanna van Loon was Dirk's second wife; the first was Beatrix von Limburg-Montjoie, daughter

of Walram Longshanks and Isabella de Bar, who in turn was the widow of Dietrich von Hochstaden, brother of Archbishop Konrad. Beatrix's paternal grandmother – Beatrix von Kyllburg-Daun – who had married Dirk I von Falkenburg, was the widow of Philipp II of Bolanden-Hohenfels.

It is not surprising that many of the English chroniclers of the time mistakenly assumed that Beatrix was a von Falkenstein and not a von Falkenburg. It was wrongly assumed, because Isabella de Bar, her maternal grandmother, was the widow of Dietrich von Hochstaden, that the girl was Archbishop Konrad's niece. In fact she was the niece of his successor, Archbishop Engelbert von Falkenburg, and Konrad's great-niece.

Another cause of error is the close connection of Richard with the von Falkensteins. Philipp and Werner von Falkenstein were, as we have seen, two of his chief officers in Germany, but their family was of lower station than the von Falkenburgs – 'ministeriales', or imperial officials, as distinct from the old aristocracy – although succeeding generations were to make the name von Falkenstein one of the most famous in the Rhineland. They had castles in the Kronberg hills near Frankfurt, near Vianden in present-day Luxembourg, and in the Eifel hills west of the Rhine. Moreover, most confusingly, one of the two castles on the Donnersberg was also known as Falkenstein. See also the genealogical table of Beatrix.

10. Bappert, 115
11. Wykes, 222
12. Bappert, 116
13. Wykes, 222
14. ibid.
15. Bappert, 118
16. Wykes, 223
17. See illustration, p. 128. The inscription reads: 'BEATRICE DE FALKENBURG REGINA ALEMANNIAE'
18. Bappert, 119

CHAPTER SIX pp. 209–213

1. Lewis, *E.H.R.*, lii
2. Bappert, 120
3. *Ann. Osen.*, 222
4. C. R. Humphrey Smith and M. Heenan, 'The Royal Heraldry of England' in *The Coat of Arms*, January, 1962
5. Boutaric, *Marguerite de Provence*, 442
6. Bappert, 120
7. *Ann. Osen.*, 224
8. Wykes, 226
9. *The Coat of Arms*, July, 1962, pp. 90–95
10. Bappert, 121

11 Wykes, 9 22
12. ibid., 228
13. ibid., 133; Bappert, 122
14. Joinville, CXLIV
15. ibid., CXLVI
16. Labarge, 268; Denholm-Young, *Richard of Cornwall*, 150; Bappert, 128
17. Wykes, 239–40
18 Rishanger, *Chron. et Ann.*, 67. Rishanger gives the place of the murder as the Church of San Lorenzo, which is the most likely in view of the layout of the city of Viterbo; Denholm-Young gives it as the Church of St. Blaise and Baddeley as that of San Sylvestro.
19. Wykes, 241

CHAPTER SEVEN pp. 214–218

1. Wykes, 244
2. Van de Venne, 76
3. *Ann. Osen.*, 242
4. C.P.R., 533
5. ibid., 543
6. ibid., 545
7. Wykes, 246
8. C.P.R., 581
9. Wykes, 247
10. Bappert, 128
11. Runciman, III, 218
12. Duggan, *Devil's Brood*, 266
13. Trautz, 409 ff.
14. Goethe, '*Faust*', *Part II*, 'Das ewig Weibliche führt uns hinan'

INDEX

Aachen, Germany, 73, 110, 135, 137 ff., 147, 166, 171, 202
Abbeville, France, 156
Acre, Palestine, 72, 73, 74, 77, 78, 82
Aigues-Mortes, France, 68, 70
Aiyub, Salih, Sultan of Jazira, 77, 79
Aix-en-Provence, France, 50, 69, 86, 101
Albi, France, 29, 101
Albigensian Crusade, 29, 50, 119
Alexander, King of Scotland, 25, 102, 163
Alexander, Pope, IV, 126, 146, 155, 166
Albrecht of Brunswick, 206
Aldebrandini family, 212 ff.
Alfonso of Castile, 4, 127, 133, 134, 146, 147 ff., 159, 161, 202
Alphonse II of Provence, 50
Alphonse de Poitiers, 87
Almayne, *see* Henry of: King of,
Amiens, Mise of, 180
Alsace, 144, 145
Amadeus of Savoy, 51
Andernach, Germany, 141
Are, Burg, Germany, 129
Arles, France, 68, 69, 70, 82
Arnold von Isenburg, Archbp. of Trier, 133, 139, 140, 141, 143, 160
Arlotus, Papal Nuncio, 146, 147, 149
Arthur of Brittany, 13, 15
Ascalon, Palestine, 75, 77, 78, 108
Aubigny, Philip d', 25, 27, 28
Austria, 133
Auvergne, 30
Avesnes, Jean d', Count of Hainault, 127, 133, 147, 171
Axholm, Isle of, Lincolnshire, 195
Aymer de Valence, Bishop of Winchester, 150
Babenburg, Kunigunde von, 172
Balliol, John de, 180
Bar, Henri, Comte de, 75, 77
Barcelona, 50
Barnwell Priory, 198
Basle, 173
Bassingbourn, Warin de, 186, 193
Baudouin II, Emperor of Byzantium, 68
Béarn, Constance de, 209, 212, 214
  Gaston de, 117, 209
Béatrice de Provence, youngest daughter of Raymond Bérenger, 85, 123, 126
Béatrice de Savoie, Countess of Provence, 49, 52, 95, 99, 100, 123
Beatrix von Falkenburg, 6, 205, 208, 210
  great beauty, 6, 205, 207
    marries Richard of Cornwall, 207
  attends consecration of new Westminster, 210, 214
Beaucaire, France, 69, 100, 101
Beaulieu Abbey, Hants., 27, 60, 72, 104, 105
Beauvais Cathedral, 130
Beckley, Oxon, 44, 48, 163
Bedford, 26
Berkhamsted Castle, Herts., 54, 58, 59, 96, 112, 163, 166, 216
Berne, Switzerland, 145
Bigod, Hugh, Earl of Norfolk, 141, 157
  Roger, 194
Bigorre, France, 41
Bingen, Germany, 143, 144
Biscay, Bay of, 30
Blackheath, 32

Index

Blakemore Forcet, 120
Blanche de Castille, Queen-Mother of France, 30, 32, 39, 52, 64, 75, 112, 113
Bodmin, Cornwall, 94, 194
Bolanden-Hohenfels, Philip von, 143, 152, 166, 171, 174, 201, 205, 207, 208
Bonn, Germany, 141
Bonquer, William, 131, 132, 133
Boppard, Germany, 142 ff., 152, 160, 208
Boniface of Savoy, Archbp. of Canterbury, 143, 144
Bordeaux, France, 27, 39, 120
Bouillon, Geoffrey de, 72
Boulogne, France, 21, 36, 175, 177, 178, 188, 210
Bouvines, France, 16, 135
Boston, Lincs., 130
Brandenburg, Markgraf von, 133
Breauté, Fawkes de, 26
Brest, Brittany, 111
Brewer, William, 59
Brienne, Gautier de, Count of Jaffa, 75, 78, 79
  Jean de, King of Jerusalem, 73
Brindisi, Holy, 63
Briouze, Matilda de, 13
Bristol Castle, 39, 178
Brittany, 15, 36, 38 ff., 88
Broc, Laurence de, 203
Bromholm Priory, Norfolk, 88
Burgh, Hubert de, 21, 26, 32, 34, 37, 39, 45, 47, 48
  defended Dover Castle, 21
  appointed Justiciar, 26
  made Earl of Kent, 32
  quarrels with Henry III, 37, 45
  imprisoned at Devizes, 45, 47
  escaped from Devizes, 48
  Meggotta de, 53
  Raymond de, 30
Burnham Abbey, Bucks, 2, 196 ff., 203
Busquet, Raoul, writer, 69
Byzantium, 68, 70

Cairo, Egypt, 77, 79, 80
Camargues, France, 71
Canterbury, Kent, 19, 21, 32, 52, 86, 153, 158, 162, 194
Capet, House of, 16
Cardinan, Andrew de, 94
Caversham, Oxon, 22, 36, 43
Champagne, *see* Thibaut
Charente, river, France, 88
Charles of Anjou, King of Sicily, 101, 212, 214
Charles the Fat, Papal legate, 188
Chilham Castle, Kent, 21
Chur, Switzerland, 206
Cippenham Manor, Bucks, 43, 171, 196, 197, 215
Clare, Amicia de, Countess of Devon, 58
  Gilbert de, Earl of Gloucester (the elder), 23, 36, 39, 40, 60
  Gilbert de, Earl of Gloucester (the younger) 175, 182, 188, 196, 198, 211
  Richard de, Earl of Gloucester, 53, 132, 150, 154, 155, 156, 158, 175, 187
Clement IV, Pope, 202, 205
Colemere, John de, 38
Cologne, 2, 3, 130, 133, 135, 140, 143, 144, 147, 153, 159, 204, 205, 208, 214, 217
Cologne Cathedral, 2, 3, 112, 129, 130, 134, 140
Cordoba, Spain, 147
Corfe Castle, Dorset, 13, 14, 16, 17, 25, 26, 27
Cornwall, 27, 33, 34, 44, 59, 60, 93, 102, 156, 210, 217
Cosdon Hill, Dartmoor, Devon, 59
Cranborne, Dorset, 40
Cremona, Italy, 84
Crockern Tor, Dartmoor, Devon, 58
Crown of Thorns, The, 68, 125
Crusade, 63 ff.
  description of embarkation, 71
Curçay, France, 32
Curragh, The, Ireland, 48

Damascus, Syria, 74, 75
Damietta, Egypt, 65, 68, 112
Damme, Belgium, 14, 15
Dartmoor, Devon, 1, 57, 186
Dartmouth, Devon, 16, 121
David, Tower of, Jerusalem, 75
David of Wales, 102

Index

Devizes, Wilts, 17, 45
Devon, 26, 40, 44, 58, 121, 156, 186, 189
Devon, Earl of *see* Redvers, Baldwin de; Countess of *see* Clare, Amicia de and Fortibes, Isabella de
Dispenser, Hugh le, 181, 185
Dominican Order, 176
'Domstift', Cologne, 160
Donnersberg, Germany, 152, 205, 207
Dordrecht, Holland, 137
Dorney, Bucks, 2, 196
Dorset, 40
Douarnenez, Brittany, 40
Dover, Kent, 14, 21, 32, 51, 52, 93, 96, 103, 153, 155, 157, 158, 162, 164, 175, 177, 179, 187, 194
Dunstable, Beds., 188, 195, 199
Dunwich, Suffolk, 121, 122
Durham, 14
Düsseldorf, Germany, 145

Edmund of Cornwall, 112, 136, 183, 187
Edmund Crouchback, 3, 57, 101, 117, 126, 127
Edmund Rich (Saint), Archbp. of Canterbury, 52, 53, 55, 109, 112
Edward, the Lord, 3, 6, 7, 57, 101, 117, 119, 126, 127, 133, 150, 156, 159, 164, 174, 177 ff., 185, 186, 195, 197, 208, 211, 215
Egypt, Sultan of, 73, 74, 80, 101, 113
Ela, Countess of Salisbury, 29
Eleanor of Aquitaine, Queen of England, 30, 40, 52, 64, 123
Eleanor, Demoiselle of Brittany, 15, 25, 38
Eleanor of Castile, wife of the Lord Edward, 127
Eleanor, sister of Henry III and Richard of England, 26, 43, 54, 55, 99, 116, 164, 180
  married William Marshal the younger, 26
  married Simon de Montfort, 54, 55
Eleanor of Provence, Queen of England, 3, 49, 50, 52, 57, 67, 85, 86, 95, 101, 102, 104, 119, 121, 126, 149, 164, 177, 188, 194, 195
  married Henry III, 52
  gave birth to Edward, 57
  attacked by London mob, 164, 177
Ely, Isle of, Cambs., 198
Engelbert von Falkenburg, Archbp. of Cologne, 166, 171, 172, 204, 214
Eton, Bucks., 196
Eustace the Monk, 21, 22
Evesham, Worcs., 177, 191 ff.
Ewell (Temple), Kent, 14
Exeter, Devon, 58, 156, 189, 194
Eye, Suffolk, 44

Fair Rosamund, 15
Falkenburg, Beatrix von *see* Beatrix
  Dieter or Dirk von, 139, 204
  Englebert von *see* Engelbert
Falkenstein, Philip von, 132, 138, 143, 152
Fawley, Bucks., 43
Fitzjohn, Richard, 21, 22
Flanders, 14, 16
Fleet Street, London, 22
Fletching, Sussex, 182, 183
Fontenay, France, 88
Fontevrault, France, 95, 123
Fortibus, Isabella de, Countess of Devon, 189
Frankfurt, Germany, 133, 144, 172
Frederick II, Emperor, 7, 16, 37, 49, 51, 69, 71, 72, 80, 84, 101, 110, 111, 129, 143
Frethorn, John, 94
Friedburg, Germany, 144
Friesland, Holland and Germany, 131

Gaza, Palestine, 72
Galilee, Palestine, 77
Gannock, Wales, 102
Garsende de Sabran, Countess of Provence, 50
Gascony, 24, 25 ff., 34, 92, 97, 117, 122, 149

Geoffrey, Brother, Keeper of the King's wardrobe, 54, 60
Gelnhausen, Germany, 144
Gerhard, Archbishop of Mainz, 132, 133, 137, 139, 142, 144, 159
Gerhard, Meister, architect of Cologne Cathedral, 130, 160
Ghent, Belgium, 171
Geul, river, Holland, 204
Ghibellines, 116, 146, 161
Gifford, Sir John, 184, 188
Gironde, river, France, 28, 34, 88, 92
Gloucester, 19, 20, 25, 46, 176, 180, 189
Goethe, Johann Wolfgang von, writer, 218
Gilbert Marshal, 23, 53, 92, 104
Granusturm, Aachen, Germany, 172
Gravesend, 158, 208
Gregory IX, Pope, 7, 49, 52, 85, 108
Gregory of Montelengo, Patriarch of Aquilegia, 147
Grillparzer, Franz von, writer, 1
Grosmont Castle, Monmouthshire, 53
Grousset, René, writer, 72, 74
Gualo, Papal legate, 19, 20
Guelphs, 177
Guildford, Surrey, 177

Hainault, Belgium, 127, 135
Harwich, Essex, 121
Haughley, Suffolk, 52
Haverill, Henry de, 94
Haye, Nicola de la, 21
Hayes Abbey, Glos, 27, 105, 115, 167, 215
Heinrich von Vinstingan, Archbp. of Trier, 160, 172
Heinrich Raspe, Landgrave of Thuringia, 110
Heinrich, Bishop of Strasbourg, 144, 152
Heinrich von Mullenark, Archbp. of Cologne, 129
Heisterbach Abbey, Germany, 141
Helston, Cornwall, 194
Henry of Bath, 114
Henry de Siptune, Prior of Tewkesbury, 60
Henry II, King of England, 11, 15, 34, 64, 123
Henry III, King of England, 3, 4, 5, 17, 18, 19, 24, 25 ff., 35, 38 ff., 57, 89 ff., 96, 101, 103, 104, 115, 117, 118, 119, 123, 149, 151, 153, 164, 174, 175, 179, 183, 191, 197, 210
  first coronation, 19, 24
  second coronation, 25 ff.
  campaign in Brittany, 38 ff.
  at dedication of Beaulieu, 104
  at dedication of Hayles, 115
  seeks crown of Sicily for his son, 117
  quarrels with Simon de Montfort, 57, 117, 118
  confirms Magna Carta, 119
  visits Paris and meets Louis IX, 123
  called 'wax heart', 149
  afraid of thunderstorm, 151
  takes refuge in the Tower, 164
  discredits Simon before Louis IX, 174
  rebuffs Gilbert de Clare, 175
  submits to judgment of Louis, 179
  taken prisoner at Lewes, 183
  pleads for life at Evesham, 191
  attends foundation of Burnham, 197
  attends consecration of new Westminster Abbey, 210
Henry of Almayne, 6, 52, 136, 139, 144, 151, 171, 177, 179, 180, 181, 183, 185, 186, 195, 198, 202, 209
  page in Richard's household, 6, 53
  knighted at Aachen, 6, 139
  deserts Simon de Montfort, 179, 180
  murdered by Guy and Simon de Montfort, 213 ff.
  buried at Hayles, 216
Hereford, 104, 189
Hohenstaufen, House of, 3, 73, 110, 123, 126, 130, 131, 161, 201, 209

Index

Holy Roman Empire, 2, 36, 49, 127
Honorius, Pope, 73
Hospitallers, Order of, 73, 76, 78, 101
Hugo, Duke of Burgundy, 75, 76, 77, 79, 82, 83
Huntercombe, William de, 197, 215
Huy, Belgium, 147

Ile de France, 34
Innocent IV, Pope, 101, 114, 123
Interdict, Papal, 11, 13
Ipswich, Suffolk, 121
Isabella of Angoulême, Queen of England, 11, 12, 14, 39, 86, 92, 95
Isabella de Brienne, first wife of Emperor Frederick II, 110
Isabella, baby daughter of Richard and Isabella, 47
Isabella of Hainault, 66
Isabella, sister of Henry III and Richard, married Emperor Frederick II, 51, 84
Isabella Marshal, 6, 23, 42, 46, 75, 50, 51, 59, 104, 152, 167
  great beauty, 6, 23
  married Gilbert de Clare 23
    married Richard of Cornwall, 42 ff.
  saves Richard Marshal, 46 ff.
  death from jaundice, 59 ff.
Isleworth, Middlesex, 181, 203
Isobel of Scotland, Princess, 16, 25

Jerusalem, Kingdom of, 4, 73, 77, 80, 90, 101
Jews, 127, 181, 215
Jezebel, nickname of Isabella of Angoulême, 11, 12, 95
Johann, Bishop of Lübeck, 145, 147, 148, 166
Joan, daughter of John and Isabella of Angoulême, 15, 28
Joan, daughter of William Marshal, 23
John, King, 11 ff., 40, 41, 60
John, baby son of Richard and Isabella, 45, 46, 47
Joinville, Sieur Jehan de (writer), 65, 71, 90
Jordan, river, 77
Jülich, Counts of, 139, 142, 143, 214

Kaiserslautern, Germany, 152, 207
Kaiserswerth, Germany, 145, 147
Katzenelnbogen (Count), Graf von 162, 201, 216
Kenilworth Castle, 99, 179, 181, 187, 193, 196, 198
Kent, 21
Kilkenny, Ireland, 13
King's Lynn, 121
Knaresborough, Yorks, 152
Koblenz, Germany, 139, 140, 142, 148, 160, 169, 205
Konrad IV, 101, 110, 114, 123
Konrad von Hochstaden, Archbp. of Cologne, 2, 3, 110, 128, 129, 132 ff., 143, 147, 152, 160, 162, 166, 204, 217
Konradin, 123, 126, 159, 171, 172, 201
Krak of the Desert, 75, 79

Lackland, nickname for John, 11
Landskron Castle, Germany, 145, 173
Langon, France, 28
Lauguedoc, France, 70
Launceston, Cornwall, 1, 34, 156, 211
Leinster, Ireland, 13, 14, 20, 48
Lewes, Sussex, 6, 56, 177, 182 ff.
Lincoln, 21, 45
Lincoln, Fair of, 21
Linz-am-Rhein, Germany, 140
Liskeard, Cornwall, 196
Llantilio Castle, Monmouthshire, 53
Llewellyn of Wales, 12, 26, 175
Loddon, river, 177
Loire, river, 39
London Bridge, 32, 96, 177
Longespée, *see* William Longespée
Lombardy, 63, 114, 146, 148
Loon, Johanna van, 205
Lorelei Rock, 143
Lostwithiel, Cornwall, 203

Louis VIII, King of France, 15, 16, 17, 20, 22, 29, 30, 34, 41
Louis IX, King of France (Saint Louis), 5, 7, 36, 49, 50, 52, 64, 82, 85, 87 ff., 109, 112, 124 ff., 141, 148, 152, 155, 165, 179, 188, 212
Lusignan, France, 12
Lyd, river, 58
Lydford, Devon, 1, 57, 94
Lyons, France, 68, 112, 125

Mainz, Germany, 142, 159, 162, 205, 206, 208
Maison Dieu, Dover, 32, 36
Mansel, John, 132, 164, 176
Marche, Hugo de la, the elder, 11 12, 15, 28
  the younger, 26, 86, 87, 89 ff., 95
Manfred, bastard son of Frederick II, 114, 123
Margaret of Scotland, 16, 25, 26
Marguerite de Provence, Queen of France, 3, 50, 52, 64, 85, 95, 123, 126, 178, 188 (character 65 ff)
Marlborough Castle, Wilts., 12, 36, 107, 199
Marlow, Bucks, 46, 49
Marseilles, France, 63
Marshal, Anselm, 23, 104
  Gilbert, 23, 53, 92, 104
  Eva, 23
  Isabella, 6, 23, 42, 46, 50, 51, 59, 106, 152, 167, *see also under* Isabella
  Maud, 23
  Richard, 23, 45, 48, 53, 56
  Sybil, 22
  Walter, 104
  William the elder, 7, 12, 14, 17, 18, 19 ff., 25, 42
  William the younger, 22, 26, 36, 43, 44, 54
Matilda, Empress, 16
Malik al-Kamil, 74
Martin, Master, 103, 108
Mauley, Peter de, 17, 25, 26, 27
Melusine, 11
Mechthild, Gräfin von Sayn, 154
Mere, Wilts, 120, 156
Metz, France, 217
Mirebeau, 40
Montaperto, Italy, 161
Montfort l'Amaury, France, 41, 57
Montfort, Amaury de, Constable of France, 41, 75, 76, 77, 79
  Guy de, 6, 97, 104, 153, 183, 185, 212, 213 ff.
    page in Richard of Cornwall's household, 6, 106
    stopped Richard at St. Omer, 153
    opposed Richard at Lewes, 183
    in charge of Richard's lands, 185
    murdered Henry of Almayne, 6, 213 ff.
  Henry de, 3, 73, 110, 123, 126, 130, 131, 164, 201, 209
  Simon de ('The Crusader'), 29, 41
  Simon de, the elder, Earl of Leicester, 6, 27, 34, 41, 54, 55, 57, 63, 82, 83, 91, 97, 114, 149, 150, 151, 153, 155, 156, 164, 165, 174, 177 ff., 185 ff., 193, 209
    seeks Earldom of Leicester, 6, 14
    co-godfather to the Lord Edward 6, 57
    marries Princess Eleanor, 27, 54
    quarrels with Henry III, 57, 117, 118
    goes on crusade with Richard, 6, 63, 82, 83
    produces Provisions of Oxford, 150
    meets Henry after thunderstorm, 151
    victor of Lewes, 185 ff.
    killed at Evesham, 193
Montfort, Simon the younger, 6, 97, 104, 153, 169, 183, 189, 193, 196, 212
  page in Richard's household, 6, 104
  stops Richard at St. Omer, 153
  opposed Richard at Lewes, 183
  pursued Countess of Devon, 189
  saves Richard at Kenilworth, 193

tries to procure settlement at Kenilworth, 196
murders Henry of Almayne, 212
Mortimer, Roger, 189
Murten, Switzerland, 145

Nantes, France, 15, 39
Nasir, Al Dawud, King of Transjordan, 75, 77, 79
Neuss, Germany, 130, 145
Newark, Notts, 17
Newlyn, Cornwall, 94
Nicholas de Cambrai, Bishop, 133, 143, 203
Nideggen Castle, Germany, 204, 214
Norfolk, 51, 88
Normandy, 12, 13, 16, 20, 24, 36, 131
Northampton, 181, 195
Nottingham, 70
Nuremberg, 144, 201
Nussa, Thierry de, 63

Oakham, Rutland, 216
Oberwesel, Germany, 143, 152, 208
Odiham Castle, Hants., 17, 99, 187, 189, 190
Odo, Archbishop of Rouen, 158
Okehampton, Devon, 58, 59, 94
Okement, river West, 58
Oppenheim, Germany, 149, 162, 177, 208
Oriflamme, the, 5, 89
Oseney Abbey, Oxon, 5, 163
Otto IV, Emperor, 16, 110, 135
Ottobuono, Legate, 194, 198, 201
Ottokar of Bohemia, 131, 132, 133, 171, 172, 201
Ouse, river, 183
Oxford, 1, 3, 150, 180, 207

Pandulf, Papal Legate, 14, 25, 26
Paris, 3, 63, 68
Pembroke, 23, 26, 45
Peninnis Head, Scilly Isles, 93
Pennepié, Gautier de, 80
Penros (Perros-Guirec), Brittany, 40
Perambulation of Dartmoor, 1240, 57, 219
Peter des Roches, Bishop of Winchester, 14, 16, 19, 25, 36, 47, 80
Peter of Savoy, 167
Pevensey, Sussex, 177
Philip Augustus, King of France, 12, 13, 15, 16, 20, 36
Pierre d'Aigueblanche, Bishop of Hereford, 92, 95
Pierre de Sangines, 75
Pierre Mauclerc, Count of Brittany, 38, 76, 78, 91
Pierrepoint, William, 29, 30
Plymouth, Devon, 40, 121
Plympton Castle, Devon, 58
Pfalzgraf, the (Count Palatine), 126, 132, 133, 143, 169, 172, 190, 201, 205, 207
Philip Basset, 199
Philip III, King of France, 212, 214
Pfalzgrafenstein (Castle), Germany, 140, 142
Poitiers, France, 40, 87
Poitou, France, 11, 12, 14, 24, 30, 32, 39, 87, 92, 131
Pomfret, Peter of, 13, 14
Pontoise, France, 64
Pons, France, 89
Pons, Reginald de, 88
Pontigny, France, 109
Portchester Castle, Hants, 37, 38
Porth Enys, Scilly Isles, 93
Portsmouth, Hants, 37, 38, 120, 121
Powicke, Sir Maurice, writer, 2
Provence, 49, 59, 138
Provisions of Oxford, 1258, 3, 150, 157, 164, 167, 174, 177, 185
Prague, Bohemia, 132
Punchardon, Sir Richard de, 46

Radnor, Wales, 46
Rançon, Geoffrey de, 89, 90
Ranulf, Earl of Chester, 20, 38, 39, 41, 42
Raymond Bérenger V, Count of Provence, 3, 49, 50, 52, 67, 69, 70, 86, 95, 100, 123, 211
Raymond, Count of Toulouse, 29, 69, 70, 86, 92
Reading, Berks., 36, 47, 49, 63, 211
Redon, Brittany, 40

Index

Redvers, Baldwin de, Earl of Devon, 58, 72, 94
Régine Pernoud, writer, 65, 66
Restormel Castle, Cornwall, 1, 34, 94
Rhineland, the, 1, 4, 15, 129, 159, 205
Richard, Coeur de Lion, King of England, 11, 73, 123, 142
Re-coinage, 106 ff.
Rayner of Brussels, 107
Rheineck Castle, Germany, 142
RICHARD OF CORNWALL
love of magnificence, 5
rumoured murdered as child, 12
to Poitou with King John, 15, 16
at Corfe Castle, 25 ff.
at Henry III's coronation, 25
in Gascony, 25 ff.
Earl of Cornwall, 27, 33
dispute over Tamerton, 34
intercedes for Simon, 42
granted Beckley and Eye, 44
marries Isabella Marshal, 42 ff.
anger at marriage of Eleanor, 54
co-godfather to the Lord Edward, 57
hears of Isabella's death, 60
goes on Crusade, 63 ff.
robbed at Vienne, 68
meets Sanchia, 70
makes treaty with Nasir, 79
goes to Poitou with Henry III, 88 ff.
in danger at sea, 92
vows to found Abbey at Hayles, 93
marries Sanchia, 96
at Hayles for foundation, 105
visits the Pope at Lyons, 112
at Hayles for dedication, 115
interviewed by Matthew Paris, 115
refuses crown of Sicily, 116
protects Simon against Henry III, 117
co-Regent with Queen Eleanor, 119
sole Regent of England, 122
elected King of the Romans, 133
reasons for his election, 134 ff.
leaves for Germany, 136
coronation at Aachen, 137 ff.
sends corn ships to England, 149
stopped by Guy de Montfort, 153
second visit to Germany, 160
lands at Dover impoverished, 162
third visit to Germany, 173
goes to Zürich with Rudolf von Habsburg, 173
awaits Simon at Twyford, 177
makes last attempt at mediation, 181
refuses to parley any further, 182
mocked by Simon's men-at-arms, 184
captured in the windmill at Lewes, 184
imprisoned at Wallingford, 185
attempted release, 186
released from Kenilworth, 193
kindness to de Montfort family, 193 ff.
founds Burnham Abbey, 196 ff.
attempts mediation at Kenilworth, 198
reconciles Edward and Gloucester, 199
last visit to Germany, 203 ff.
marries Beatrix von Falkenburg, 210
shock at news of Henry of Almayne's death, 214
death, 216
character, 216 ff.
Robert Grossetête, Bishop of London, 108, 115
Robert of Gloucester, 191, 192
Rochester, 181, 182
Roche-au-Moine, La, 15
Rochelle, La, 28, 89
Roese of Dover, 21
Rogate, Walter de, 156
Roger of Acaster, 17, 25
Rome, 3, 156, 165
Roque, La, 71
Ros, William de, 92
Rosamund Clifford (Fair Rosamund), 15
Rudolf von Habsburg, 173, 207
Runnymede, 17
Rye, 21

St. Albans Abbey, 5, 27, 63, 134, 163

Index

Saint-Gilles, France, 70
St. James de Beuvron, 41, 42
St. Jean de Malte, church of, 50
St. Germain en Laye, 124
San Lorenzo, church, Viterbo, Italy, 34
St. Malo, Brittany, 38, 40
St. Mathieu, Brittany, 88
Saint Pathus, Guillaume de, 65
St. Valery, honour of, Oxon, 48
Sanchia of Provence, 3, 85, 92, 95, 105, 112, 120, 123, 128, 137, 138, 140, 143, 153, 158, 167, 168
  great beauty, 6, 138
  writes to prior, 137
  coronation, 138
  buried at Hayles, 167, 168
Sandwich, Kent, 22, 121
Saracen dancers, 84
  Savaric de Mauléon, 29
Sainte Chapelle, 125, 176
Schiller, Friedrich von, writer, 1, 4
Schönberg, 143
Scilly Isles, 93
Sens, 50, 68
Sicily, Kingdom of, 3, 113, 116, 123, 126, 131
Siegburg, 147
Siward, Richard, 48, 164
Skenfrith Castle, Monmouthshire, 53
Soissons, Raoul de, 75, 76
Somerset, 26, 40
Southampton, 38, 121
Speyer, 141, 149, 162, 206, 207
Stamford, Lincs., 36
Stephen of Agnani, 37
Stephen Langton, Archbp. of Canterbury, 14, 17, 19, 22, 25, 26, 27, 32, 36
Stolzenfels, Germany, 142
Striguil (or Chepstow), Monmouth, 14, 23, 47, 53
Sutton Valence, 119
Suzanne, 81

Taillebourg, France, 5, 89 ff., 156, 217
Tamar, river, 58
Tamerton, Manor, Devon, 34, 37, 55
Tarascon, Provence, 50, 69, 82
Teignmouth, Devon, 121
Templars, Knights, 14, 48, 73, 76, 78, 142
Temple Ewell, Kent, 14
Temple, the, London, 22, 176
Tewkesbury Abbey, Glos., 23, 40, 42, 60
Tewkesbury, Abbot Peter of, 23, 40, 43
Teutonic knights, 76
Thibaut de Champagne, 4, 64, 74 ff., 78
Thomas of Savoy, 51, 147
Tonbridge, 152
Topsham, 121
Trematon Castle, Cornwall, 34, 211
Trier, 133, 148, 174, 205
Trip to Jerusalem, 70
Tunis, 212
Twenge, Robert de, 71
Twyford, Berks, 177

Urban IV, Pope, 166
Ushant, 92
Usk, Castle, Mon., 47

Valletort, Baron de, 34, 211
Valenciennes, France, 16
Vaughan, Dr. Richard, writer, 5
Vendée, France, 88
Vendôme, France, 32, 64
Vianden, Luxembourg, 129
Vianden, Mathilde von, 129
Vienne, France, 68 ff.
Villeneuve, Romeo de, 50
Viterbo, Italy, 6, 212 ff.

Walerand, Robert, 132, 186
Wallingford Castle, Berks., 5, 44, 53, 54, 58, 97, 98, 100, 105, 106, 115, 133, 156, 163, 164, 185, 193, 202, 203
Walram the German, 34
Walter de Canteloup, Bp. of Worcester, 141, 167
Walter von Geroldseck, Bp. of Strasbourg, 161
Wareham, Dorset, 14
Weissenburg, Alsace, 145
Wells, Somerset, 19

Wellstream, 17, 19
Werner von Eppstein, Archbp. of Mainz, 160, 171, 172, 174, 201, 206, 208
Westminster Abbey, 12, 24, 25, 27, 32, 52, 54, 96, 113, 118, 210, 216
Westminster Hall, 27, 33, 34, 118
Wetzlar, Arnold von, 143, 149, 166
Wetzlar, 144
Weymouth, Dorset, 121
Wight, Isle of, 184
Wigmore Castle, Herts., 189
William the Lion, King of Scotland, 17
William Longespée, Earl of Salisbury, 15, 16, 27, 28
William of Holland, 111, 112, 131
William Raleigh, Bp. of Winchester, 104
Winchcombe, Glos., 105
Winchelsea, Sussex, 21, 122, 168, 182
Winchester Cathedral, Hants. 11
Winchester Castle, Hants, 14, 58, 150, 165, 200
Windsor Castle, Berks., 13, 17, 43, 122, 177, 178, 181, 195, 198
Wissant, France, 93
Wistlegray, Simon, 38
Wolvesey Castle, Winchester, Hants., 150
Woodstock, Oxon., 46, 47, 56, 114, 187, 203
Worcester, 17, 20
Worms, Germany, 141, 156, 162, 205, 206, 208
Wulstan, St., 17

Yarmouth, Great, Norfolk, 121, 122, 136
Yes Tor, Dartmoor, Devon, 59

Zürich, Switzerland, 173, 174
Zwin, river, Belgium, 171, 203